BATTLE EXHORTATION

Studies in Rhetoric/Communication
Thomas W. Benson, Series Editor

BATTLE Exhortation

THE RHETORIC OF COMBAT LEADERSHIP

Keith Yellin

THE UNIVERSITY OF SOUTH CAROLINA PRESS

Cloth edition published by the University of South Carolina Press, 2008
Paperback edition published in Columbia, South Carolina,
by the University of South Carolina Press, 2011

www.sc.edu/uscpress

Manufactured in the United States of America

20 19 18 17 16 15 14 13 12 11   10 9 8 7 6 5 4 3 2 1

The Library of Congress has cataloged the cloth edition as follows:
Yellin, Keith, 1964–
    Battle exhortation : the rhetoric of combat leadership / Keith Yellin.
        p. cm. — (Studies in rhetoric/communication)
    Includes bibliographical references and index.
    ISBN 978-1-57003-735-1 (cloth : alk. paper)
    1. Command of troops—Handbooks, manuals, etc. 2. Morale—Quotations, maxims,
etc. 3. Leadership—Handbooks, manuals, etc. 4. Oratory—Handbooks, manuals, etc.
5. Exhortation (Rhetoric) 6. Combat—Psychological aspects—History. 7. Speeches,
addresses, etc. I. Title.
    UB210.Y45 2008
    355.3'3041—dc22

                                                                    2007048829

Grateful acknowledgement is made to the following publishers for permission to publish
    previously copyrighted material:
Excerpts from *With the Old Breed* by E. B. Sledge, copyright © 1981 by E. B. Sledge. Used
    by permission of Presidio Press, an imprint of The Ballantine Publishing Group, a
    division of Random House, Inc.
Excerpts from 1:39–41, 2:19–21, 2:25–27 of *Julius Caesar: Seven Commentaries on the
    Gallic War* (1998), translated by Carolyn Hammond. By permission of Oxford University Press.

ISBN: 978-1-61117-054-2 (pbk)

To Nicholas Tavuchis

That moment had come of moral vacillation which decides the fate of battles. Would these disorderly crowds of soldiers hear the voice of their commander, or, looking back at him, run on further?

Leo Tolstoy, *War and Peace*

Yet volumes are devoted to armament; pages to inspiration.

George S. Patton Jr., "Success in War"

CONTENTS

SERIES EDITOR'S PREFACE

In *Battle Exhortation: The Rhetoric of Combat Leadership*, Keith Yellin considers the history and the generic features of speech addressed by commanders to troops about to go into battle. Yellin, a former United States Marine Corps captain with a Ph.D. in communication from the University of Iowa, brings together an unusual range of learning and experience, which he puts to excellent use in this analysis of a mode of address that has gone largely without notice in rhetorical histories or officer training but is nearly universal in military campaigns, often with decisive effects.

Yellin's account considers the battle exhortation over the course of two millennia in Western experience. He takes us to historical accounts of actual battles as well as to literary and cinematic representations that, he argues, have shaped the genre and our expectations. He has a keen eye for the enduring topics of battle exhortation, for their development over time, and for the actual circumstances of battle experiences that shape exhortation and response. Yellin's account is rich in extended case studies, in which detailed military history at the tactical level is combined with astute and nuanced critical analysis of the texts, sights, and sounds of the discourse of military leaders at every rank.

Yellin's re-creation of how Spartan rhetoric made sense to fifth-century B.C.E. foot soldiers calling to each other as they marched into battle to the sound of flutes is vivid, immediate, and convincing. The Spartan case is accompanied by similarly detailed accounts of exhortations from the Bible, the *Iliad*, Shakespeare's *Henry V*, George C. Scott portraying General George S. Patton, Tim O'Brien in Vietnam, Julius Caesar at the head of Roman legions, Teddy Roosevelt on San Juan Hill, Colonel Robert Gould Shaw at Fort Wagner, Dwight D. Eisenhower on D-Day, and many others. In all these cases, Yellin is alert to the symbolic structures that contribute to military outcomes, to the intense skepticism of men and women about to risk their lives toward anything that smacks of empty verbal display, to the tensions that must be held in balance when violence becomes an arm of policy, and to the cultural and tactical differences that require leaders to adapt to circumstances while staying in touch with enduring principles under conditions of stress and danger.

This balanced and crisply argued book will be interesting and useful to students of both rhetoric and military leadership.

THOMAS W. BENSON

ACKNOWLEDGMENTS

In some endeavors fidelity is the expectation. To stand faithfully beside another may be difficult, but it is one's obligation, one's duty. This project by contrast has taught me more about generosity. To give generously of one's resources when there is neither obligation nor personal advantage is beyond expectation. Only as the beneficiary of such generosity have I been able to produce this book.

While many have contributed in important ways, I am particularly grateful to extended family Harry Nave and Marc Stern; professors Nicholas Tavuchis and Donovan Ochs; Marines Thomas Draude and Darin Morris; Benjamin Abramowitz, U.S. Army Infantry; and Linda Fogle and Karen Rood at the University of South Carolina Press.

For her understanding I am especially indebted to my wife, Kristal.

Introduction

A familiar practice is so pervasive, in civilian and military life alike, that we take it for granted. Troops about to go into harm's way expect to hear from their commander. Athletes about to begin or resume play expect to be addressed by their coach. Employees anxious about their own or their employer's future expect to be told what the future holds. Political enthusiasts expect their candidate or incumbent to rally them. The faithful expect to be encouraged by their clergyman. Commanders, coaches, business leaders, politicians, and preachers expect to be heard. Likewise, when we enjoy literature, history, television, or cinema, we often encounter someone encouraging a group to rise above adversity, pull together, and succeed. While this phenomenon has been noticed by others, it has not received the careful attention it deserves. Exactly what is the nature of such discourse? How does it speak to us? Why its broad appeal? This work is an attempt to answer such questions, focusing on what I regard to be their primary context—the military battlefield. Civilian leaders may "pick their battles" and "rally the troops," but real, close combat is the source of such metaphors.

There are a number of likely reasons why this type of speech has not been sufficiently studied. First, we have not had a good name for it. In antiquity the familiar general's speech came to be known as a *harangue* or *exhortation*. But there are problems with these terms today. *Harangue* sounds dated and stiff, if not haughty. Rather than encouraging a group, it connotes vehement critical speech, a tirade. *Exhortation* is better, earnestly pleading or mildly rebuking others to some conduct, but unqualified, the term has religious resonances. It also has four syllables, seemingly too many for a culture that prefers one or two. Perhaps that is why today we tend to think in terms of the *pep talk*. Pep invigorates and stimulates, as in pep rallies, pepper, and pep pills. And yet this expression has its own shortcoming: though succinct, there is something too playful about it. Pep talks are intended to arouse us, particularly in the context of sporting events. In more sober settings, however, where the stakes are particularly high, a pep talk can be received with disdain. So lacking a stable, generally accepted name, this genre of speech has escaped comprehensive definition. I shall refer to it as *battle exhortation*. Still at its core exhortation, the phrase preserves a spirit of giving direction with great intensity. Qualified by battle, it implies conflict, not conversion, and typically on a scale larger than two antagonists. As for the term's many syllables, a variety of shorter verbs remain available when commanders exhort, encourage, or rally their troops.

Another reason this speech has eluded concerted study has to do with its ephemeral nature. The closer to the battle, the more immediate the discourse, the more elusive it becomes. Renditions in ancient chronicles are sometimes dismissed as inaccurate. More contemporary versions still tend to be those of high-ranking officers because of the generative and preservative resources of their headquarters. Generals and their aides also have lower mortality rates, improving the opportunity for memoirs. Yet even in upper military echelons, battle exhortation can be difficult to find. Douglas MacArthur is a case in point. He is perhaps the United States's most famous warrior, and the one most noted for his eloquence, but MacArthur's memorialized addresses are to the West Point cadets, the Congress, Filipinos, and the press. His exhortations as a junior officer are unrecorded, and his remoteness as commanding general earned him the nickname "Dugout Doug." MacArthur, it would seem, directed his communiqués to the home front more than to his front line.[1]

The battle exhortation of senior officers can also be elusive because of the evolution of warfare. While technologies have made recording discourse easier, they have at the same time led to the dispersion of troops, radio silence, and hair-trigger employment, all diminishing opportunities for exhortation. Opposing forces no longer embattle within sight of one another, within earshot of their general, and within minutes of the clash. Instead they huddle in significantly removed staging areas and ship compartments, awaiting the signal to begin their long-range assaults. And yet, upon closer examination, battle exhortation proves so pervasive on the battlefield and within our culture that it is not nearly as fleeting as it first appears.

A third reason for the lack of attention may be that the disciplines that should take most interest in battle exhortation regard it as unworthy. Students of speech communication, for instance, tend to avoid military discourse today. A progenitor of the current tradition, I. A. Richards, deliberately avoids "the combative impulse," preferring the study of rhetoric to focus on "misunderstanding and its remedies."[2] But in avoiding martial venues, speech scholars overlook a significant body of communicative practice. Millions of persons are serving under arms. What are they saying? What are they hearing? In battle exhortation (which addresses but one recurrent military situation) scholars would encounter rhetoric at its limits. At stake are life and limb. Impediments can include paralyzing fatigue and fear, significant differences between commander and troops, and the din of battle. Age-old appeals, such as favorable omens, plunder, or execution for cowardice, are no longer available. Soldiers do not expose themselves for frivolous reasons. They must be motivated by a greater good, or some great evil. Studying articulated reasons can tell us more about ourselves.

Similarly, the military shows little interest in battle exhortation, often regarding talk as cheap. A Marine commandant epitomizes this frame of mind when he writes: "The indispensable condition of Marine Corps leadership is action and attitude, not words." True, troops have little patience for bombast, but it is also true that they often prefer one officer over another because of the way officers address them. The commandant's thinking also underestimates how words complement and contextualize action. For instance, when the Theban general Pelopidas was surprised and outnumbered by Spartans at Tegyra, a scout grimly reporting, "We have fallen into our enemies' hands," the fate of the Sacred Band hinged in no small part on what Pelopidas said next. At that critical instant, his reply—"No, they have fallen into ours"—reframed the situation and galvanized his men. So too during the Battle of the Bulge when General George S. Patton Jr. openly put his arm around a numb division commander and asked, "How is my little fighting son of a bitch today?"[3] Tactical genius or finely honed training count for little if leaders cannot connect with their soldiers at the moment of truth. Instances abound where troops failed to pull the trigger or pulled the trigger without discretion, because commanders were no longer in charge of their men.

This leads to the most probable reason for the neglect of battle exhortation—a simple lack of awareness. Any number of assumptions may be at work here, which can be expressed as follows:

Firepower and logistics win conflicts, not talk.
Bold, authentic speech is the sum and substance of battle exhortation.
Properly trained and cared-for troops do not need it.
Sound doctrine, selection, training, and equipment necessarily produce effective combat communicators.

The problem is that all of these assumptions are flawed. History demonstrates that force of will regularly, ultimately, trumps force of arms. And what so crucially influences force of will, if not the right word at the right time? Moreover, empirical study demonstrates that officers can seriously misjudge which incentives best keep their troops fighting when the going is tough.[4] Indeed, battle exhortation is a sophisticated type of speech, drawing from a variety of topics, managing tensions, varying by rank and conflict, and often making the difference. In his book *The Mask of Command* John Keegan makes two striking claims about the genre. As to its relative importance, "Among the imperatives of command, that of speaking with all the arts of the actor and orator to the soldiers under his orders stands with the first." As to its study, "For all the importance of prescription"—Keegan's term for battle exhortation—"military literature is curiously deficient in discussion of how it should be done."[5]

I trace my interest here to two personal experiences. As an officer of Marines, I embraced the warrior ethos with its stress on discipline, enthusiasm, and fraternity. I relished the seriousness of the mission and its responsibility. At the same time, given my interest in speech communication, I found the absence of public speaking in the training regimen surprising. Other than learning the importance of a strong resolute "command voice," and being coached upon joining the fleet to speak to enlisted men "in their terms," I cannot remember being taught how to be articulate in combat. Senior enlisted men and other officers I spoke with recounted their own lack of training in this regard. Naturally the need to be levelheaded and poised was emphasized, but learning what to say and how to say it was left to experience. In short, no other aspect of military leadership is treated so casually—and we reap bitter fruit. In the words of one disabled veteran, "We were over there, all these young guys, doing our jobs, but we really didn't know why we were there."[6]

Similarly, when I was doing graduate work, I delighted in the study of argument and persuasion. I relished having an academic lineage that included Aristotle, Richard Whately, and Richard Weaver. But I found rhetoricians' study of war discourse limited to examinations of civilian texts (such as presidential addresses) or material chronicled long ago. Historians were doing more but showed less interest in contemporary application. The gap between combat and rhetorical studies has not always been this dramatic. Quintilian, first-century Rome's Imperial Chair of Rhetoric, explained that "the art of war will provide a parallel" to the art of rhetoric; elsewhere he referred to "the weapons of oratory." Conversely, archetypal warrior Julius Caesar filled his war commentaries with battle exhortation, terming the harangue a "military custom."[7] And yet my review of the literature confirms Keegan's impression that study on how commanders should address their troops has always been limited.

This book integrates rhetoric and combat in pursuit of two primary objectives: to understand battle exhortation (an intellectual goal) and to offer insight for improving it (a practical, especially military goal). As a result, this work addresses two general audiences: academics and military professionals.

Interdisciplinary work can be exciting when it bridges typically unconnected communities and offers new vantage points. But it is also risky because of the hazard of combining disparate technical vocabularies, producing a hodge-podge of jargon. To craft a text accessible to as wide an audience as possible, I have often substituted common terms for more specialized ones, for example, *pressing need* for the rhetorical term *exigence* and *intercom* for the Navy term *1MC*. At the same time I have sought to avoid colorless language. The title of chapter 4, "Evolutions," for instance, probably connotes different things to different groups. For scholars the connotation may be of progressive change, simultaneously, given the plural. Military professionals and military historians are more likely to think of multiple but distinct activities, such as conducting a forced march or changing formation. Chapter 4 accommodates both senses.

At the highest level this study of combat motivation is organized by four facets of rhetoric identified by Lloyd Bitzer. In a "rhetorical situation," Bitzer suggests, someone is apt to speak up with the intent to influence others be-cause (1) there is a pressing need to do so, and (2) the audience might resolve that need. All the while there are constraints to audience reception and re-sponse: (3) influences that originate more personally from the speaker, and (4) those that are more environmental but still require the speaker's atten-tion.[8] Each chapter observes exhorters addressing necessity, their audiences, and personal and environmental constraints, but the relative focus shifts. Specifically:

Chapter 1, "Bracing for Combat," establishes battle exhortation as a distinct genre of discourse, largely through the timeless need that calls for it. After alluding to a handful of examples, I review the pertinent literature, then identify boundaries, dimensions, and directions of the discourse. Here I draw especially from the plausible circumstances of a Spartan com-mander, the combat memoirs of a Spanish conquistador, and two Ameri-can infantrymen (one from World War II's European theater, one from the Pacific; one an officer, the other an enlisted man).

Chapter 2, "Indoctrination," investigates how we—all of us—are socialized to recognize and anticipate battle exhortation and understand its conven-tions. In other words, the audience of this discourse is much broader than troops on the battlefield. To further identify appeals common to the genre, I refer to exemplars from literature and cinema such as Shakespeare's *Henry V* and George C. Scott's impersonation of Patton. I examine a say-ing from antiquity and a contemporary parody as well.

Chapter 3, "Tensions," considers how issues inherent to battle exhortation—reputation, distance, violence, and love—are particularly subject to the exhorter's personal style, character, and sensitivity. I draw examples from the American Revolution and the Civil War but range as widely as Teddy Roosevelt and Julius Caesar.

Chapter 4, "Evolutions," explores military permutations of the genre. When more mindful of the circumstances of the war, the presence of journalists, the combat arm of the audience, and other factors, one may discern changes in tenor to battle exhortation. I trace variations over the last sixty years among U.S. theater commanders, and across a multifaceted (combined-arms) expeditionary group during a single operation.

In my conclusion, I summarize, identify questions for further study, and speculate about the future of battle exhortation.

A word more about material and method: In each chapter I ground discussion in examples drawn from my general experience. When I developed an interest in this subject twenty years ago, I knew that combatants, real or virtual, often grew irresolute before combat. I knew that one response was to be overcome by one's fear, running or hiding or performing poorly, and the other response was to face the threat and fight reasonably well. I knew that encouraging words could help produce the latter response. Ever since, I have collected battle exhortation wherever I have encountered it—as a student of speech communication and history, as a consumer of Western culture, as a Marine. In this book I group and juxtapose salient examples. Comparing one instance with another, noting similarities and differences between several, I have come to my conclusions more often by analogy than by generalization, invoking "essential (though not exhaustive) correspondences."[9] Human discourse, particularly human discourse seeking to influence the vagaries of war, may not lend itself to conclusive, quantifiable analysis. But we should be able to arrive at probable conclusions and better choices.

Bracing for Combat

Speeches alone do not compel men to fight or fight well. Xenophon rightly observed, "There is no exhortation so noble that it will in a single day make good those who are not good when they hear it. It could not make good bowmen, unless they had previously practiced with care, nor spearmen, nor knights." There are innumerable sources of combat motivation: previous training, the prospect of reward or punishment, the comfort of overwhelming odds, self-defense, even hormones. But situations arise in war in which other combat motivators come up short. "The soldier will forget or discount much that training has taught him as the danger mounts and fear takes hold," S. L. A. Marshall notes. "It is then that the voice of the leader must cut through the fear to remind him of what is required."[1] Consider examples of such speech across considerable time and space:

When Moses prepares the Hebrews for crossing the Jordan and beginning a national existence without him, he issues five dictates for waging war. The first prescribes battle exhortation: "When you are about to go into battle, the priest shall come forward and address the army. He shall say: 'Hear, O Israel, today you are going into battle against your enemies. Do not be fainthearted or afraid; do not be terrified or give way to panic before them. For the LORD your God is the one who goes with you to fight for you against your enemies to give you victory.'"[2]

When Agamemnon, leading Greek at the battle for Troy, ranges through his embattled ranks, he exhorts: "Be men now, dear friends, and take up the heart of courage, and have consideration for each other in the strong encounters, since more come through alive when men consider each other, and there is no glory when they give way, nor warcraft either."[3]

Caesar almost without fail encourages his men before battle. Regarding battle exhortation a custom of war, he lists it among the activities he barely has time for when surprised by an enemy: "Caesar had to see to everything at once. The flag must be unfurled (this was the signal to stand to arms), the trumpet sounded; the soldiers must be recalled from working on the defenses, and all those who had gone some way off in search of material for the earthworks had to be ordered back to camp. He must draw up his battle line, encourage the men, give the signal. There was too little time, the enemy pressed on so fast, to complete these arrangements. . . . Once he had given all the appropriate orders Caesar ran down where luck would take him to speak his encouragement to the men. . . . His speech was long enough only to urge them to remember their long-established record for bravery, and not to lose their nerve but to resist the enemy assault with courage."[4]

When Cortés implores his conquistadores to strike inland for Mexico City, exceeding his orders from Cuba, Bernal Díaz del Castillo recalls: "When the ships had been destroyed, with our full knowledge, one morning after we had heard mass, when all the captains and soldiers were assembled and were talking to Cortés about military matters, he begged us to listen to him, and argued with us as follows: 'We all understood what was the work that lay before us, and that with the help of our Lord Jesus Christ we must conquer in all battles and encounters . . . and must be ready for them as was fitting, for if we were anywhere defeated, which pray God would not happen, we could not raise our heads again, as we were so few in numbers, and we could look for no help or assistance, but that which came from God, for we no longer possessed ships in which to return to Cuba, but must rely on our own good swords and stout hearts'—and he went on to draw many comparisons and relate the heroic deeds of the Romans."[5]

Queen Elizabeth I's most famous address is battle exhortation, encouraging English troops before Spain's expected invasion. Mounted sidesaddle, wearing a breastplate, holding a truncheon, she exhorts at Tilbury: "My loving people, [my entourage and I] have been persuaded by some that are careful of our safety, to take heed how we commit ourself to armed multitudes for fear of treachery; but I assure you, I do not desire to live to distrust my faithful and loving people. Let tyrants fear. I have always so behaved my self, that under God, I have placed my chiefest strength and safeguard in the loyal hearts and goodwill of all my subjects, and therefore I am come amongst you, as you see, at this time, not for my recreation and disport, but being resolved in the midst and heat of the battle, to live or die amongst you all, to lay down for my God, and for my kingdom, and for my people, my honour, and my blood, even in the dust. I know I have the body but of a weak and feeble woman, but I have the heart and stomach of a king, and of a King of England too, and think foul scorn that . . . any Prince of Europe should dare to invade the borders of my realm. . . . I myself will take up arms, I myself will be your general, judge and rewarder of every one of your virtues in the field."[6]

Young Hawk, a seventeen-year-old Arikara scout attached to Custer's Seventh Cavalry at the Battle of Little Bighorn, remembers of that day: "Before the attack began, the older men spoke to the younger men, as is the custom of our tribe. Stabbed [one of the elders] said, 'Young men, keep up your courage. Don't behave like you are children. Today will be a hard battle.' He said these things because he saw many of us were young and inexperienced. He wished to prepare us for our first real fight."[7]

The commander of the First Marine Division, Major General James Mattis, offers considerable encouragement during the United States's second war with Iraq. Immediately prior to invasion, he exhorts his men: "For decades, Saddam Hussein has tortured, imprisoned, raped, and murdered the Iraqi people; invaded neighboring countries without provocation; and threatened the world with weapons of mass destruction. The time has come to end his reign of terror. On your young shoulders rest the hopes of mankind. When I give you the word, together we will cross the Line of Departure, close with those forces that choose to fight, and destroy them." When stubborn resistance in Iraq requires the Marines to return, Mattis explains: "We are going back into the brawl. We will be relieving the magnificent Soldiers fighting under the 82nd Airborne Division, whose hard won successes in the Sunni Triangle have opened opportunities for us to exploit. For the last year, the 82nd Airborne has been operating against the heart of the enemy's resistance. It's appropriate that we relieve them. . . . Our country is counting on us even as our enemies watch and calculate, hoping that America does not have warriors strong enough to withstand discomfort and danger. You, my fine young men, are going to prove the enemy wrong—dead wrong." Even to the Marines' families, Mattis gives confidence: "We are returning to Iraq. None of us are under any illusions about the challenges that await our troops there. We also know the understandable anxiety that will be felt by our loved ones when we deploy. We are going to stand by one another, all of us, reinforced by our faith and friendship, and together overcome every difficulty. It will not be easy, but most things in life worth doing don't come easily. Our country needs us in the struggle to put Iraq back on its feet. Our enemies are watching, betting their lives and their plans on America not having the courage to continue this fight. Our Sailors and Marines, reinforcing the Army and our many allies' forces already in Iraq, will prove the enemy has made a grave mistake.

As the Division goes back to this combat zone, your loved ones will need your spiritual support so they can focus on their duty."[8]

These examples do not constitute a scientific sample. They address but a tiny fraction of the wars and battle speech in Western history. But they do bear witness that from the dawn of history commanders have complemented other forms of battle preparation with exhortation, perceiving a need in combat beyond training, planning, and supply.

Previous Consideration

To what degree has this phenomenon been studied before? First, we should acknowledge that the need for combat *morale* is well appreciated. Defined by the U.S. Army's basic leadership text as that which "holds the team together and keeps it going in the face of the terrifying and dispiriting things that occur in war," morale is widely recognized as the nebulous, sometimes capricious, terribly important emotional state of a military unit. Typically the higher the morale, the greater the effectiveness of the troops and the likelihood of accomplishing the mission. In *Crusade in Europe*, for instance, General Dwight Eisenhower regarded morale as "the greatest single factor in successful war." Chief of Naval Operations Admiral Ernest King told the 1942 graduating class at Annapolis, "Machines are nothing without men. Men are nothing without morale." Napoleon famously declared, "Morale makes up three quarters of the game; the relative balance of man-power accounts only for the remaining quarter." Some two thousand years prior, rallying the Greek Ten Thousand to begin their fighting withdrawal from Persia, Xenophon reminded: "You are well aware that it is not numbers or strength that bring the victories in war. No, it is when one side goes against the enemy with the gods' gift of stronger morale that their adversaries, as a rule, cannot withstand them."[9]

A particularly sensitive consideration of combat morale is found in the writings of the nineteenth-century French colonel Ardant Du Picq. "In the last analysis," he decided, "success in battle is a matter of morale. In all matters which pertain to an army, organization, discipline, and tactics, the human heart in the supreme moment of battle is the basic factor." Du Picq was among the first to recognize the special challenge that "modern battle" poses to morale. There is something in human nature, he explains, that leads troops to be emboldened by numbers, particularly when they are shoulder to shoulder. The ancients understood this and created their dense formations known as phalanxes, which shoved each other about on relatively small battlefields.

By contrast, modern weaponry, communications, and logistics produce immense battlefields, where "the distances of mutual aid and support have increased" and "death is in the air, invisible and blind, whispering, whistling." Dispersion and chance produce a psychologically isolating affect, and "the more one imagines he is isolated, the more has he need of morale." For these reasons Du Picq concluded, "Combat requires today, in order to give the best results, a moral cohesion, a unity more binding than at any other time."[10] This perspective might strike the uninitiated as unlikely, since modern war can reduce the gore of hand-to-hand combat. Those left alone in a threatening environment understand the point, however. We despair more easily alone.

Curiously, studies on combat morale are typically silent about battle exhortation. Prominent investigations with promising titles such as *Anatomy of Courage; Morale: A Study of Men and Courage; Fighting Spirit;* and *Combat Motivation* do not seriously consider speech as a means for bolstering combat motivation. After World War I the chief of the Morale Branch of the U.S. War Plans Division acknowledged that the commander "must be able to reach and enthuse his men by the spoken word," but his 775-page *Handbook on the Systematic Development of Morale* devotes only 3 pages to the language of military leaders. Likewise, the post–World War II social-science study *American Soldier: Combat and Its Aftermath* contains chapters such as "Combat Motivations among Ground Troops" and "Problems Related to the Control of Fear in Combat" without factoring in speech.[11]

There are hints in this research that verbal encouragement is an important component of combat leadership. For example, in a survey of U.S. infantrymen who saw action in the Mediterranean during World War II, the combat veterans were asked to describe officer leadership practices that gave them confidence in tough or frightening situations. Comments fell into the following categories:

Led by example; did dangerous things himself, displayed personal courage, coolness (31 percent)
Encouraged men, gave pep talks, joked, passed on information (26 percent)
Showed active concern for welfare and safety of men (23 percent)
Showed informal, friendly attitude; worked along with men (5 percent)
Miscellaneous or unclassifiable (15 percent)[12]

Responses here are consistent with other research and experience, underscoring the importance of leadership by example. There is no denying the stimulus of a leader who eschews the safety that rank may afford and shares in the danger of the troops. This is the essence of combat leadership, particularly at the squad and platoon level, and why these leaders learn the call and gesture "Follow me." The practice that receives so much less attention is the second leadership activity identified by the veterans: verbal encouragement.

Du Picq is a case in point. For him the morale required today was realized through minimizing the change of personnel within combat units, practicing "iron discipline," and employing tactics that maximize close-order formation. He appreciated that rifle fire permitted a reduction in the number of infantrymen and that it necessitated they be engaged as skirmishers, "in thin formation, scattered," but he would keep troops in morale- and supervision-preserving column as long as possible. What is it about column, a denser, follow-the-leader formation? For Du Picq it was two things: the soldier imagines "that the more numerous we are who run a dangerous risk, the greater is the chance for each to escape" and, from the commander's perspective, once troops deploy from column to skirmishers, "they no longer belong to you." The extent of Du Picq's documented appreciation for battle exhortation is a single, indirect sentence about animating the troops with passion. In practice he seemed to have thought more of it, cut down in 1870 while directing his regiment from a road under fire—desiring "to put heart into his troops by his attitude." In the moment that Prussian shell exploded over the road and mortally wounded Du Picq, we find him doing two things, almost assuredly. First, by standing amid incoming artillery fire, he was displaying a contempt for danger, a physical example for his men. It is unlikely that the colonel was sharing his attitude in silence, however. An eloquent writer, a successful field commander, Du Picq was almost certainly putting heart into his troops by exhorting them, too.[13] Other studies about morale probably assume battle exhortation as well.

Quite simply, while histories and chronicles record hundreds of battle exhortations, there is little theoretical investigation into the matter. Even the first-century C.E. authority of Roman oratory Quintilian did not probe the matter, though he recognized battle exhortation's frequency and import by asking: "Has not oratory often revived the courage of a panic-stricken army and persuaded the soldier faced by all the perils of war that glory is a fairer thing than life itself?"[14] Study of battle exhortation is sometimes brief, sometimes fuller, but interest tends to be on antiquity, and nowhere is there a book-length investigation.

A review of the surviving literature finds Onasander, a Greek contemporary of Quintilian, to be the first to discuss battle exhortation at any length. We know little more about Onasander than that he wrote a commentary on Plato's *Republic*, which no longer exists, and a military work titled "The

General," which does. In "The General," which enjoyed considerable popularity through the Renaissance, Onasander's sketch of the ideal commander includes the characteristic of "a ready speaker," because "no city at all will put an army in the field without generals, nor choose a general who lacks the ability to make an effective speech." Onasander's rationale: "If a general is drawing up his men before battle, the encouragement of his words makes them despise the danger and covet the honour; and a trumpet-call resounding in the ears does not so effectively awaken the soul to the conflict of battle as a speech that urges to strenuous valour rouses the martial spirit to confront danger."[15]

Conceiving exhortation broadly, Onasander considered the encouraging effect of example and drama alongside speech. In fact, "The general must inspire cheerfulness in the army, more by the strategy of his facial expression than by his words; for many distrust speeches on the ground that they have been concocted especially for the occasion, but believing a confident appearance to be unfeigned they are fully convinced of his fearlessness; and it is an excellent thing to understand these two points, how to say the right word and how to show the right expression."

Pursuing this nonverbal vein further, Onasander explained how skillfully displaying prisoners can embolden the army. Basically the general should kill or hide fearsome-looking prisoners but terrify the weaker ones, then "lead them, weeping and supplicating, before his army, pointing out to his soldiers how base and wretched and worthless they are, and saying that it is against such men that they are to fight."[16] In our first theorist to address battle exhortation at any length, then, we already see its necessity, its limitations, and larger communication practices. (Such flagrant treatment of prisoners, however, is unlawful today.)

The insights of Vegetius and Paleologus are briefer but also relevant. Vegetius, the fourth-century C.E. Roman author of *Epitome of Military Science*, popular and influential into the nineteenth century, proffered maxims that are still commonplace. He coined "Few men are born brave; many become so through training and force of discipline," as well as "He, therefore, who aspires to peace should prepare for war." While Vegetius' agenda was to provide a roadmap for restoring Roman military virtue through proper selection, drill, and discipline, he did briefly recognize a role for battle exhortation. Developing his rule of thumb that "Troops are not to be led into battle unless confident of success," he recommended gauging their self-confidence by observing them closely. When more confidence was necessary, it could be added through battle exhortation: "An army gains courage and fighting spirit from advice and encouragement from their general, especially if they are given such an account of the coming battle as leads them to believe they will easily win a victory. Then is the time to point out to them the cowardice and mistakes of their opponents, and remind them of any occasion on which they have been beaten by us in the past. Also say anything by which the soldiers' minds may be provoked to hatred of their adversaries by arousing anger and indignation."[17] What is particularly worth noting in this brief commentary is that battle exhortation may employ a wide variety of subject matter. Vegetius would, in his words, "say anything" that might incite the troops to a combat lather. This interest in employing *any* topic to get troops performing proves a common theme.

Most of Theodore Paleologus's fourteenth-century treatise on war and government is lost, but this active son and knight of one of Byzantium's reigning dynasties characterized important aspects of battle exhortation, namely, its variability in length and the rank of the speaker: "It is certainly appropriate for the lord or the governor of the people, when he draws up his forces and they take up arms, to inspect them and to talk to them and give speeches to them, short ones, according to the time available, but they should be grand and of substance, to encourage them and to make them bold, and to place them in order to make a good defense against the enemy, and to seize a glorious victory. . . . Moreover, if there are common folk in the infantry, the commander should put some knights with them, to command them and encourage them during the battle."[18] Paleologus's insights are evident from the examples of battle exhortation at the beginning of this chapter. There Agamemnon and Caesar exhort amid the fight and are brief. Cortés and Elizabeth speak prior to the fight and so speak longer. In both settings, however, the discourse is substantive. Agamemnon appeals to his troops' sense of manhood, fraternity, and glory. Caesar cautions his men not to squander a long-established record for bravery. Cortés compares his conquistadores to Caesar's legions. Elizabeth loves her troops, despises the invaders, burns with the heart and stomach of a king. From these cases it does appear that troops require reasons "of substance" to hazard life and limb. At the same time Paleologus recommended that battle exhortation not be reserved to the lord or governor. Lower-ranking officers ("knights") should have a role in exhortation as well, even if—or especially because—they operate among the troops in the middle of the fight. Whether their discourse need be as grand, Paleologus did not say, but we shall address that issue in time.

Although best known today for *The Prince* and *The Discourses*, Niccolò Machiavelli wrote about applying speech to warfare in his 1521 *The Art of War*. Written as a fictive dialogue, but primarily a monologue of an invented papal captain, this treatise is clear about the need for rhetorical skill before troops. "It is necessary that a general should be an orator as well as a soldier," Machiavelli's captain emphasizes, "for if he does not know how to address himself to the whole army, he will sometimes find it no easy task to mold it to his purposes." Allowing for compulsion by other means, the captain points to Alexander, then fleets through potential discursive appeals: "Read the life of Alexander the Great, and you will see how often he was obliged to harangue his troops; otherwise he never could have led them—rich and full of spoil as they were—through the deserts of India and Arabia where they underwent every sort of hardship and fatigue. Many things may prove the ruin of an army, if the general does not frequently harangue his men; for by so doing he may dispel their fears, inflame their courage, confirm their reso-lution, point out the snares laid for them, promise them rewards, inform them of danger and of the way to escape it; he may rebuke, entreat, threaten, praise, reproach, or fill them with hopes, and avail himself of all other arts that can either excite or allay the passions and the appetites of mankind."[19] This account delineates what classical rhetoricians would call "topics" (*topoi*) or commonplaces, the typical places to find something to say about a matter. In combat, for instance, troops may be goaded into action by appealing to their sense of courage, one common concern for men under arms. Or, on the contrary, they may be encouraged by discourse that diminishes the threat, requiring little courage at all. The combat leader must discern which of the two topics suits the temperament of his troops and the realities of the tactical situation, or whether another topic better applies. The more one studies bat-tle exhortation, the more evident the scope of this repertoire becomes.[20]

As Paleologus would have *knights* reiterate and model these messages, so Machiavelli would put "a corporal over every ten soldiers in all armies; this corporal should be a man of more spirit and courage—at least of greater authority—than the rest in order to inspire them by both his words and his example; he should continually exhort them to hold their ranks firm and conduct themselves like men." Broadening Onasander, Machiavelli stipulates, "Therefore, if any prince or republic would make their armies respectable, they should accustom their generals to harangue the men and the men to listen to their generals."[21] How is it that armies accustomed to battle exhorta-tion are made respectable? It seems, based on Machiavelli's analysis of Alexan-der, that through battle exhortation troops rise above hardship, fear, and excess. Unaddressed, such stresses turn armies into rabbles.

Raimondo Montecuccoli, the seventeenth-century Italian-born Prussian general, provides one of the lengthiest investigations into battle exhortation.

It is contained within his tactics treatise, *Concerning Battle,* written relatively early in his eventful career. Formations were Montecuccoli's primary interest in *Concerning Battle,* because experience and study had taught him that most casualties occur during flight, not stand-up combat. Correctly selecting and executing formations had two advantages in Montecuccoli's mind. They disrupt enemy formations, so "being disorganized and panic-stricken, he lacks the courage to defend himself"; and they embolden one's own army, which "does not become self-assured merely by virtue of bravery but also by having well-ordered alignments."[22]

For all of this attention to formations and the high morale that they inspire, Montecuccoli did devote one of his five chapters to other confidence-generating measures, and exhortation is its centerpiece. Here we receive a definition and some historical context: "The exhortation is when the general speaks publicly to his soldiers in order to urge them to demonstrate [virtue] and to infuse them with courage. Thus, full of ardor, they plunge into the struggle, the image of their leader still reflected in their eyes and the sound of his voice still ringing in their ears. As far as the Ancients are concerned, one reads that certain great captains never gave battle without first haranguing their soldiers." We receive, for the first time, an indication that exhortation may be interactive: "After such speeches it is customary for the second-ranking person in the army to reply in the name of the others, declaring that everyone will fight valorously and do his duty. This form of approbation is like the practice of the Ancients, all of whom cried out simultaneously, raising their right hands and shaking the arms of their neighbors. For nowadays, when the senior officers have finished with their utterances, the multitude replies by clamoring 'yea' in unison. The chief individuals among the troops also add a few words of agreement or good will." Montecuccoli also made allowances for hurried situations and large audiences, recognizing that "sometimes the captain speaks without forming a circle, simply riding between the alignments and talking briefly to the soldiers before whom he is passing."[23]

As to the topics of battle exhortation, Montecuccoli considered them in some detail. "Captains can incite soldiers to fight well," he begins, "by indicating the necessity of the battle, which deprives the men of all hope of saving themselves except through victory." Other reasons for fighting that might be articulated:

Our cause is just.
Fight for love of country or captain.
The enemy is disdainful.

Our property or religion is threatened.

"Better to die generously than to languish under tyranny."

Better to risk death "in manly fashion" than to pass away later a shameful coward.

Death ends all suffering.

The soul fares better without the body anyway.

We enjoy some advantage over the enemy.

We have beaten this enemy before.

When previously beaten by this enemy, we were hamstrung in ways that no longer apply.

There are rewards and prizes if we succeed.

Defeat shall result in "all imaginable evils."

It becomes clear that like Vegetius (one of his sources), Montecuccoli was ready to say anything that might get or keep troops functioning. Nowhere is this more evident than in his discussion of omens: "If the troops should be so superstitious as to permit themselves to be influenced by auguries or portents, as soon as something like this happens to take place, the captain must show the reason for the incident, interpret it rationally, or construe it appropriately and to his own advantage." Before we condemn such manipulation, we should remember that Montecuccoli regarded poorly motivated, poorly functioning troops as sheep for slaughter. Persuading, even manipulating, troops to stay in formation and fight—and thereby probably saving their lives—might be regarded the lesser evil.[24]

Montecuccoli's exhorting commander is not a hypocrite, loitering in the rear except for some big speech. His commander must be "everywhere," mindful of the character of his men: "Some individuals he must exhort with hope of reward, others he must impress with fear of punishment. With everybody he must do something." If troops begin to flee, the commander must meet and rally them through "good counsel," proper gestures, and an encouraging tone. While he "must not expose himself to peril heedlessly," should the commander see "his men routed and the army imperiled, he must follow the example of Caesar" and demonstrate his own nerve and skill in combat. Such activity not only bolsters the commander's authenticity. It keeps him visible, leading troops to believe that their own actions might be witnessed by him, so that they will fight more spiritedly. At the same time, Montecuccoli would have us remember the lighthearted side of this business, namely, the value of the timely quip. Pointing to the examples of Hannibal and Leonidas, Montecuccoli suggests that witty banter on the part of the commander cannot help but convince troops that the danger is manageable.[25]

While Montecuccoli regarded both exhortation and prayer as confidence-generating measures, he regarded them at emotional odds with one another. Prayer, whether entreating publicly or privately, celebrating Mass, or singing psalms, is good and useful because troops are braver when reconciled to their Lord or protected by him. Nevertheless, by the time battle is joined, prayer becomes "untimely." Troops should not "have to mumble prayers at the moment they are terrorizing the enemy with their war cries and spurring themselves and their comrades to do battle." Nor should they "have to count off pater nosters on their rosaries when it is time to be pouring bullets into the enemy ranks." Montecuccoli desired "fury" in his formations when they neared the enemy, not introspective calm. "If one must fight," he concluded, "one should beg for divine aid beforehand."[26]

Battle signals—routinized communications during combat itself—are another matter. They serve an immediate coordinating end but, employed shrewdly, may build morale as well. For instance, any musical instrumentation enables formations "to enter the fray in better order," but some instruments "are more suitable than others for arousing pugnacity." Montecuccoli favored trumpets, kettledrums, and tambourines. He noted others' use of pipes, trombones, and flutes. Coordinating formations with proper instrumentation offers real advantage, because "it is quite certain that among all the techniques for producing the effect of improved morale, music holds the principal place."[27]

Countersigns are another type of battle signal that can serve both coordinating and morale-building ends. The response of a soldier or unit when challenged by another trying to distinguish friend from foe, countersigns may be, rather than any brief word or phrase, mottos or names that anticipate a favorable outcome from the fight. "Liberty," for instance, not only serves the purpose of force recognition but reminds troops what they are fighting for. "Good fortune" is generally uplifting. "Apollo" or "Jesus Christ" recognizes divine authority. Montecuccoli sandwiched exhortation between prayer and signals in his consideration of confidence-generating measures. His arrangement seems chronological in that soothing prayer should occur well before battle, while heartening signals may be employed during combat itself. The most appropriate moment for exhortation is in between, immediately prior to combat.[28]

Because Montecuccoli's discussion of morale-building measures includes some nondiscursive means, we should pause to distinguish which are within the purview of this study and which are not. To be considered here, an encouraging battlefield practice must involve "symbolic action." Speech is symbolic in that it uses the symbols of words to represent or construct reality, but symbolic action extends beyond verbalization to nonverbal symbols, too. Mathematics, music, traffic lights, military protocol—all convey meaning through symbol systems. So when Montecuccoli discusses the general's speech, he is discussing the employment of verbal symbols to encourage the troops. When he discusses musical instrumentation, he is addressing a more symbolic means of encouragement, because music conveys meaning without words (although words were used *to train* the troops how to respond to the music). Even when Montecuccoli alludes to the commander's grin, his flamboyant dress, and the display of venerated objects and prisoners, such measures involve "symbolicity," because they shape the situation through symbols. When, however, Montecuccoli starts contending that "a very sure way of making soldiers bold is to give them something to drink," he moves beyond verbal and nonverbal symbolic action into the realm of physiological intoxication. Into that realm this study does not follow.[29]

The next clear recognition of the need for verbal encouragement on the battlefield comes from S. L. A. Marshall, an officer and historian of the U.S. Army, in his well-known *Men against Fire.* Interested in increasing the combat efficiency of infantrymen, Marshall observed during World War II the same dilemma that Du Picq identified in the Franco-Prussian War: Modern weapons make close-order formations obsolete, but it is the near or presumed presence of comrades that psychologically emboldens troops to fight. Whereas Du Picq would keep troops in column as long as possible, Marshall advocates talk, warning: "We do not teach our men from the day they first put on the uniform that speech in combat is as vital as fire in combat." Marshall's primary interest is in basic coordinating communication within smaller fighting units (for example, "Cover me!"). But some examples from his postcombat interviews appreciate broader, deliberate encouragement.

In one case a regimental commander explains how he got his unit across the Elbe so quickly: "When we got to the water's edge, I moved along the line of my men, giving them a love kick in the butt. I kept shouting to them as I moved along: 'Don't waste the opportunity of a lifetime. You're on the way to Berlin. We can get there. You can cross now without a shot being fired. But you've got to move *now.* Don't wait to organize. Get into those boats! Get going!'"

In another case, a platoon sergeant explains how he revived his demoralized platoon under fire in the Pacific: "I asked myself why it was that we felt fear . . . and I realized it was because all of the leaders had quit talking. I knew then that the only way to get confidence back into the platoon was to talk it up, as a man might do in a football game. I continued my own attack on the enemy shelters and spider holes, but there was this difference, that I now began yelling to the others, 'Watch me! This is what you're supposed to do. Get at it. Keep working. Keep your eyes open.' Soon the platoon become collected and began to operate methodically. But I kept talking until the end because I had learned something new. Leaders must talk if they are to lead. Action is not enough. A silent example will never rally men."[30]

These examples as much as any others demonstrate the essential combination of speech and action, or walk and talk, when it comes to generating fighting spirit. The regimental commander does not simply jump into a boat, figuring his urgent example will inspire others to follow. He does not just pass the order down the chain of command, then stand impatiently by. Neither does he only speak to his men, explaining how the tactical situation makes moving quickly imperative. The colonel hastens among his men and shouts to them. He gives them reasons to act, and in so doing offers them a glimpse into the sort of regimental commander he is, one they want to follow. The platoon sergeant's example is still more compelling. He realizes that the absence of talk is the very thing that has unnerved his platoon. Merely attacking enemy fortifications himself, providing a silent example, is insufficient to revive the unit. So he becomes coach as well as player, coaxing fellow soldiers to action through speech.

Philosopher Hannah Arendt helps us understand this tight coupling between speech and action in *The Human Condition*. Without the accompaniment of speech, she explains, action loses its revelatory character and subject, becoming work "not by acting men but performing robots." Speechless action is as incomplete and uncompelling as mere talk—but through action *and* speech one "identifies himself as the actor, announcing what he does, has done, and intends to do."[31] A nonmilitary parallel might be how we respond to professional or Olympic athletes. We are impressed by their physical performance, but it is by hearing them interviewed or learning their biographies that we are truly inspired (or not). Speech offers context for acts, providing meaning and significance.

Marshall's *Men against Fire* is remembered more for its controversial contention that only a quarter of American infantrymen were firing their weapons in combat than for the remedy that "when you prepare to fight, you must prepare to talk." A reason for this may be that for all of his advocacy for "contact and communicating," Marshall failed to include articulateness or anything like it among his list of "characteristics which are required in the minor commander if he is to prove capable of preparing men for and leading them through the shock of combat." In his ideal profile, Marshall delineated more familiar and muted traits: sound administration, military bearing, courage, physical fitness, and respect for others. The irony of Du Picq is that he did not write about exhortation but was mortally wounded doing it. The irony of Marshall is that he praises exhortation until his conclusion.[32]

Several scholars have investigated our subject more recently, but their focus is invariably on the record in epics and chronicles, and their interest often in the reliability or authenticity of the discourse there. Kendrick Pritchett argues that Herodotus, Thucydides, Xenophon, and Polybius describe actual practice, then he identifies the common topics or appeals between them. John Bliese collects and analyzes hundreds of battle orations, not from Greco-Roman sources but from nearly a hundred western European chronicles written between 1000 and 1250 C.E. He too catalogs topics and determines that "seventeen identifiable appeals recur with some frequency." Bliese's work demonstrates that battle exhortation extends beyond the most commonly known histories. It shows that topics can be affected by cultural or temporal factors. For instance, some of his cases involve fighting for Christ or the holy rewards of martyrdom, while this is never the case in Thucydides. At the same time, Bliese's work shows that many fighting appeals do seem constant— honor, justice, and the interest of one's God, to name three. Of course, Bliese concedes, "these are not verbatim reports of speeches; they are the rhetorical products of the historians themselves. But many writers of history in those days had extensive military experience. And at the very least, the enormous numbers of battle speeches show a widespread belief that such exhortations were appropriate, important and effective."[33]

Other contemporary scholars are less certain. Theodore Burgess questions the authenticity of speeches reported in Greco-Roman histories generally. Observing an ornate, even extravagant style to them, he suspects they are largely concocted by ancient historians "in a conscious effort to please" readers and as a means to demonstrate the historian's rhetorical prowess. He finds this posturing most evident in the general's oration before battle—"the most distinctive, fully developed, and persistent single type of speech among historians." Comparing eleven battle exhortations, Burgess concludes, "All speeches of this character follow with varying exactness a well-defined series of [topics] and are artificial in the extreme." His list of "the usual" topics largely coincides with the lists formulated by Bliese, Montecuccoli, and others, which is not surprising, since they share many of the same sources. But whether

Burgess believes exhortation actually takes place on the battlefield, even if it is poorly represented in chronicles, is unclear. On the one hand, he warns that "it does not agree with modern taste to ascribe long speeches to generals in impossible conditions." On the other hand, he concedes that Napoleon's relatively recent prebattle proclamations exude "a style comparable to that ascribed to generals by the ancient Greek historians." Burgess does not reconcile this seemingly odd fact, that battle exhortation in ancient secondary sources strikes his ear as implausible, but more recent and reliable primary sources show Napoleon exhorting his troops this very way.[34]

Elizabeth Keitel and Mogens Herman Hansen also question the reliability of battle exhortation in histories. Keitel cautions us to remember "just how literary and artificial a genre" the general's speech to his troops before battle became. She finds that Homer's *Iliad* powerfully influenced what battle speeches look like in later Greek and Roman chronicles, more powerfully, it seems, than actual words and events. Hansen goes so far as to reject the whole genre as "a literary and rhetorical fiction, not a historical fact." Though he acknowledges that generals often shouted *something* as they traversed their lines, he cites lack of treatment in rhetorical treatises, the challenges of public address on the battlefield, and the careful correspondence of chronicled speeches by opposing generals (as if one commander were rebutting points made by the other) as reasons to dismiss traditional battle exhortation.[35]

Now some skepticism regarding chronicled battle exhortation is healthy. From a situational perspective, we know that lengthy addresses immediately prior to battle could face physical and temporal challenges. From a primary source perspective, we know these speeches are not transcripts. In most cases they were reported by someone other than the battle orator, in many cases not even an eyewitness. Sometimes, as Burgess suggests, it was by a posturing historian. (Plutarch and Polybius found fault with some of their predecessors in this regard.)[36] We also know that the use of speeches to record issues was common historical method during antiquity, expected by oration-accustomed audiences—which did not regard quoted speech with the same reverence we do today. But it is also true that the chroniclers were relatively close to the moment. There was a conventionality to ancient warfare. And because historical narratives have often proven trustworthy, we should be slow to dismiss historical speeches out of hand.[37]

Above all we ought to appreciate the powerful conditioning role of chronicled material, even if a fair amount of it was reported with license. Why does a seasoned colonel of cavalry such as Montecuccoli spend so much time writing about, and presumably practicing, battle exhortation? Because he has studied ancient chronicles and taken their battle exhortations to heart. Whether they are factual or not, he believes them to be so and draws on them as models when he encourages his own troops. He sees contemporaries behaving similarly. How is it that Napoleon delivers proclamations that sound like Caesar's "impossible" speeches? Because Napoleon is imitating Caesar. Just as Homer influenced historians, so these historians influence readers, some of whom are or become combat leaders. Perhaps the crispest example of tale becoming actual speech on the battlefield is Henry V's appeal to his weary, outnumbered troops before Agincourt, asking them to face the threat as a "band of brothers." This beloved expression now permeates our culture and graces not only the titles of books and movies but is indeed uttered with affection between military men. And yet Henry V never said such a thing. The words, originally, are Shakespeare's. (In chapter 2, we look at this conditioning more closely.)

The relevant literature may be summarized this way:

For the sake of effective armies, commanders should be effective speakers.

In its most traditional form, battle exhortation is a commander's address to his troops immediately prior to combat. It is designed to embolden them.

Subordinate leaders and messages should reinforce the commander's determination.

Exhortation may vary in length, given the tactical situation.

In the fuller sense of symbolic action, battle exhortation may employ nondiscursive means such as music and visual aids.

There is place for the wisecrack and grin.

The relationship between word and deed is delicate and crucial, because speech provides context for physical action, and physical action reinforces or cancels speech.

Battle orators have a fairly stable repertoire of rhetorical topics from which to draw. (These are consolidated in the table in chapter 2.) As Keitel puts it, "Only so many arguments would be plausible and compelling when asking men to go into battle."[38]

The constancy and number of these appeals in ancient sources bothers some academic observers, who find them artificial and rehearsed. And yet, these scholars acknowledge that some exhortation occurs.

Defining Exemplar: Mantinea, 418 B.C.E.

To define battle exhortation more clearly still, let us examine a historical description of armies joining battle. It is the start of the Battle of Mantinea in

418 B.C.E., where Mantineans, Argives, and Athenians face Spartans (Spartiates and their allies). Why focus upon a classical Greek battle when some scholars struggle with the realism of battle exhortation reported from the period? For several reasons: First, it would be difficult to offer a definitive account of most any Western practice without starting in Greece. Everything from our conception of politics to our architecture—and especially our conceptions of rhetoric and warfare—originate from Greece. Second, this is a significant Greek land battle, probably the largest of the Peloponnesian War, and Thucydides' commentary is so revealing that it is commonly referenced by scholars of various disciplines. Finally, if some of the exhortations in Thucydides' *History of the Peloponnesian War* seem long-winded, those recorded here do not. Instead Thucydides summarizes "the type of encouragement" each army receives:

> The armies were now on the point of joining battle, and the generals on each side spoke to the troops under their command to encourage them. The Mantineans were told that they were to fight for their country, that it was a question of power or of slavery, of keeping the power which they had won or of relapsing again into the slavery of the past. The Argives were told that the battle was for their old position of supremacy, for the equal share in the Peloponnese which they had once had, to prevent them being deprived of this forever, and at the same time to requite the many wrongs that had been done to them by an enemy and a neighbor. The Athenians were told of the glory they would win if, fighting at the side of so many brave allies, they showed themselves second to none, that to defeat the Spartans in the Peloponnese would make their own power greater and more secure, and that no one would ever again come to invade the territory of Athens. This was the type of encouragement given to the Argives and their allies. The Spartans on their side spoke their words of encouragement to each other man to man, singing their war songs and calling on their comrades, as brave men, to remember what each knew so well, realizing that the long discipline of action is a more effective safeguard than hurried speeches, however well they may be delivered.
>
> After this the two armies met, the Argives and their allies advancing with great violence and fury, while the Spartans came on slowly and to the music of many flute-players in their ranks. This custom of theirs has nothing to do with religion; it is designed to make them keep in step and move forward steadily without breaking ranks, as large armies often do when they are just about to join battle.[39]

There is no doubt that battle exhortation is taking place here and other types of discourse are not, so we begin narrowing our definition by eliminating what does not apply. Calling battle exhortation "war discourse" or "the rhetoric of war" is not sufficiently precise because the assembly debates and messages from envoys, so common in Thucydides' *History,* are absent. As opposing armies close, the time for civilian justifications for war or negotiations to avoid it has passed. Likewise, "military" or "martial discourse" is too wide-ranging a characterization, because military discourse addresses a host of situations. Among officers (and where applicable, their civilian chiefs), there are deliberations or councils of war to determine courses of action. For the masses, there is recruiting discourse that entices potential troops with promises of adventure, glory, and civic reward. There is indoctrinating discourse, which transforms recruits into soldiers. There is sustaining discourse, which preserves the fighting force through hardship, changes in command, and other stresses. And later there is commendation and consolation.[40] But none of these situations resembles the scene Thucydides describes. Even thinking of battle exhortation as "combat discourse" is insufficiently precise, because there is a good deal of discourse directly related to combat that is not involved here. It is in surrounding paragraphs that Thucydides details the coordinating orders of Spartan King Agis and the reports dispatched to approaching reinforcements.

The communication reported above encourages men to fight, not abstractly, not eventually, but imminently. Its focus is that particular. At the same time, we see the multiple dimensions of battle exhortation insofar as it encourages combatants through different means and for different reasons. Mantinean, Argive, and Athenian troops are addressed by their commanders and variously so. In response, and almost certainly to further encourage themselves, these troops advance with fury. By contrast, the Spartans are not addressed by their commanders but address one another—and sing. They are reassured by one another's voices, their pipes, and almost certainly by the sound of their collective, measured step. Thus the source of battle exhortation is neither limited to commanders nor the spoken word.

Because battle exhortation encourages men to believe something (that fighting is their best course of action) and to behave accordingly, *it is essentially rhetorical discourse.* Rhetorical discourse aims to persuade an audience to belief and action through good reasons. Its most basic form is argumentative: Believe/do this; here is why. The allied generals through their grand speeches and the Spartans through their talking, singing, and piping are all seeking to present good reasons for troops to stay, advance, and fight. Ideally "good reasons" are good in that they are moral, but at a minimum they are good enough, representing sufficient grounds for the audience to be persuaded. It is also important to remember that by "discourse" we more broadly mean symbolic action, as discussed in relation to Montecuccoli.

Battle exhortation may include elements from other major genera of communication. For instance, it is not scientific discourse with the fundamental end of instruction, but there might be some instruction to it. It is not poetic with the fundamental end of pleasure, imperative with the fundamental end of direction, or cant with the fundamental end of obscuration, yet there can be some pleasure, some order-giving, some obscuration to it. The important point is that being rhetorical discourse, with the fundamental end of persuasion and the fundamental means of good reasons, battle exhortation involves certain essentials while scientific and the rest involve others. Specifically, there will be (1) a pressing need that prompts the discourse from someone; (2) an audience that can resolve the need if persuaded; and constraints (3) personal and (4) environmental that influence or complicate the exhorter's task. Alert to such rhetorical sensitivities, we continue our investigation.[41]

Thucydides' continuing account of the Battle of Mantinea may be summarized this way: As the adversaries closed, each began inadvertently to outflank the other to the right. To protect his left, King Agis ordered his leftmost regiments to extend their line and other regiments to preserve the link between left wing and main body. Because he ordered the maneuver at the last minute, however, there was some confusion, and the left wing found itself separated from the main body upon contact with the enemy. This wing fared poorly but was eventually rescued by the rest of the Spartan army. Sparta carried the day.[42]

Supplementing Thucydides' account with other classical reports of infantry combat, and with modern scholarship,[43] let us formulate the plausible circumstances of a regimental commander who is part of Sparta's troubled left. His rhetorical situation and choices will be useful for the remainder of this chapter.

Our commander leads the Brasidans, troops in the center of Sparta's three-regiment left wing. The Brasidans earned their name and freedom a few years earlier after participating in a bold, well-executed campaign by the Spartan general Brasidas. They are not fully franchised citizens of Sparta, as their regimental commander is, but landed freemen. On cue the commander steps off, and his nearly six hundred men follow suit at quick time, the normal rate of march.

Initially the situation is well in hand. Although the enemy five hundred paces to the front is aggressive, our commander knows that many things encourage his men to march toward the fight, carefully maintaining their formation. They are accustomed to Spartan military tactics and success, tested in combat, and proud of their special identity as Brasidans. Shortly before, they witnessed the morning's sacrifices, heard the priest's prayer, and celebrated a good omen. There is the regimental commander's own confident striding before them (and even breakfast wine still coursing through their veins). But what encourages the Brasidans most—indeed, what encourages the commander most—are the sounds of a Spartan phalanx girded for and grinding toward war: its songs, pipes, collective rhythmic step, and, during pauses between songs, familiar voices. Such structured, man-made sounds convey unit cohesion and synchronization, keys to success in pitched battle.

Suddenly, however, the situation changes. A herald hastens to the commander, recites a dispatch, then hastens on to the regiment further left. At once the commander shouts the preparatory command to move obliquely left, and his word passes down the chain of command. Trumpets sound, indicating that the Spartan left wing will move as one. Although Spartans regularly rehearsed the maneuver, it is not typical three hundred paces before a storming enemy. As the singing subsides, so as not to interfere with the coming command of execution, there is an abrupt change in Brasidan confidence. No sooner do trumpets signal and commanders shout the command of execution than reason for the change is plain. Pivoting on its collective right foot and continuing to advance obliquely left, the regiment has exposed its right side, for its members carry their shields on their left arms, which now face away from the enemy. Weapon-bearing right arms, in addition to being bare, are less able to thrust forward with momentum because they are already forward. So though their pipes continue to play and their feet continue to tread, unnerving questions begin to creep into Brasidan minds:

When will the order come to face the enemy squarely again?
Are regiments to the right maintaining our link to the main body?
Is the original source of the command, King Agis, fit for command?

Just days before, Agis had nearly stumbled into battle. Months earlier he had accepted a bogus armistice and prematurely left the field. Perceiving such doubt behind him, our regimental commander feels his own heart sink, for doubt has no place in a phalanx two hundred paces from the enemy. Unless his unit is psychologically steeled, it will collapse upon impact with the opposing phalanx. This is the crisis as the foe lurches forward into double time, tridents on their embossed shields starting to serrate like teeth.

Consistent with the specified number of oblique paces, signal trumpets sound in quick succession, enabling the commander to redress his most immediate tactical problem: He commands the regiment to march straight forward again. Although he suspects, based on the number of trumpets he has heard, that the left wing has lost contact with the Spartan main body, he takes comfort knowing that every forward stride now helps his regiment dress its lines and regain momentum. Still, there is need to stiffen his troops, for they have not resumed their high-spirited banter.

If there was more time or quiet, the commander might fashion some clever remark, imitating heroic Leonidas, but a situation this urgent requires something else. With scarcely one hundred paces remaining, in time and sonority with the regiment's pipes, the commander begins a familiar war song still unsung this day: "Come, O boys of Brasidas, rich in manhood and savage valor, thrust forward your shield with your left hand, shaking your spear with courage and not sparing your life. For it is not the ancestral custom of Sparta."[44]

Answering this verse as trained and practiced, Brasidans stamp on their next left step, and the first three ranks snap down their thrusting spears from the carry to the ready. Often such menacing precision is all the warfare needed, astounding more amateur armies into terror and flight. Today, however, the on-guard movement does not intimidate the fast-approaching enemy. These Mantineans, after all, are defending their homes.

The Spartan war cry quickly follows, started by the officers of the regiment, then taken up heartily by the ranks. Part appeal for divine protection, part regulation of mood and movement, part intimidation for the enemy, the cry combines with stamping left feet and adjusts the regiment's march from a normal gait to one where left feet stomp forward and right feet shuffle up behind. This stamp/shuffle/singing produces a relentless forward motion, resembling a song-dance both encouraged and encouraging since youth.[45] As a result, shields rise a bit and stiffen. Spears are jostled, loosening weapon hands for action. The next several paces are covered more firmly, even as the dust grows thicker and equipment heavier. The regiment's center of gravity shifts from waists to almost six hundred left-leaning shoulders. Continuing their rhythmic stamping and chanting, the Brasidans grow numb to danger. Parched throats, fatiguing shield-bearing arms, King Agis's dubious competence—all recede from consciousness.

On impact, the running, hollering Mantineans directly before the Brasidans are demolished. These first ranks of the enemy are underfoot before individual sounds and movements begin returning to Brasidan senses. But the accomplishment is short-lived. So numerous are the Mantineans that they envelop the unmoored left wing of the Spartan army. Because the wing's leftmost regiment seems to have hurriedly withdrawn and the rightmost disintegrates, the Brasidans suddenly face encirclement and the prospect of annihilation.

Our commander, grimacing from a freak wound to his left foot, commands his regiment to shift from forward-facing ranks, eight deep, to a defensive square. Looking about, though, he recognizes that his unit is losing cohesion. His men—the audience that must respond to this new need—are discarding thrusting-spears for short swords and facing whichever direction presents the most immediate danger. Pipers, unarmed and unshielded, are slaughtered while trying to find a helpful melody. Terrified Brasidan eyes, beneath increasingly battered helmets, look anxiously about for their officers. What tools of command and encouragement remain available to the commander? His signal trumpeter is missing. The regimental pipes have effectively been silenced. There is no reviving a war song or war cry. Officers are shouting directions with little effect and falling. Even the reassuring, synchronized tread of Brasidan feet is gone, replaced by the din of a free-for-all. In time, the shrinking regiment is driven rearward.

Our commander determines that he can only place hope in the sound of his voice. Many of his men will not be able to hear him or hear him well, but those who catch a word or two will know their regimental commander still lives, commands, and calls to them. If those men are encouraged, their revived spirit might revive others. So the commander begins speaking, not an address, in which the Spartan is unskilled, but by expertly reciting Tyrtaeus, Sparta's preeminent war poet, a source of battle exhortation for more than two hundred years: "I would neither call a man to mind nor put him in my tale . . . though all fame were his save warlike strength; for a man is not good in war if he has not endured the sight of bloody slaughter and stood nigh and reached forth to strike the foe. This is the noblest virtue . . . a common good this both for the city and all her people, when a man standeth firm in the forefront without ceasing, and making heart and soul to abide, forgetteth foul flight altogether and hearteneth by his words him that he standeth by." Parrying an unpracticed Mantinean spear thrust with his shield, driving his own sword home, the veteran soldier and poetry reciter continues between breaths: "He that falleth in the van and loseth dear life to the glory of his city and his countrymen and his father, with many a frontwise wound through breast and breastplate and through bossy shield, he is bewailed alike by young and old . . . nor ever doth his name and good fame perish, but though he be underground he liveth evermore." Because he is engaged in close combat, the commander cannot sing the poem or move in time to it, as he has since youth, but the words tumble out. They make him feel better, and perhaps because of them, a small cadre of Brasidans begin to rally about him. Still, the enemy tide drives them rearward into their own wagon train. Tiring, knowing that if help does not arrive soon all will be lost, the commander continues, periodically raising his voice: "But and if he escape the doom of outstretched Death and by victory make good the splendid boast of battle, he hath honour of all. . . . as he groweth old he standeth out among his people. . . . all yield him place on the benches, alike the young and his peers and his elders. This is the prowess each man should this day aspire to, never relaxing from war."[46]

Suddenly, something wielded as a club strikes the commander's back. He drops to a knee, grimacing. Straining to rise, he is dealt another blow, this time speared in the same spot. He sprawls. Before consciousness ebbs away, our commander discerns through the sounds of failed combat the faint but unmistakable sound of rescue: Spartan pipes, perhaps those of the entire army, approach from the distance! This sound does more for his troops and more to undermine his enemy than his voice ever could. The din of Mantinean fury gives way increasingly to Spartan pipes and tread. Brasidans still able to do so begin to taunt the Mantineans, who take flight.

So ended the 418 B.C.E. Battle of Mantinea, with the Spartan main body coming to the rescue of its left flank. Through the general rubric of rhetoric, what more can we learn about battle exhortation by examining this reconstruction—and complementing it with more contemporary evidence?

Auditory Dimensions

Immediately we recognize that conditions complicate or constrain the rhetorical situation. The troops doubt King Agis, perhaps affecting their ability to receive, assess, or respond to exhortation. The regimental commander is wounded, perhaps affecting his ability to exhort. Overwhelmed by an angry foe, the unit begins to fall to pieces, affecting everything. And certainly there is noise from thousands of men fighting at close quarters. Once we factor in the talking, calling, singing, and piping of this battle, we cannot help but wonder what sort of impact sound has on combatants.

Terrible *sights* in war produce a range of human reactions: foreboding, numbness, rage, panic, despair. Typically, however, these reactions involve a rationale and at least a few moments to develop after seeing something. We feel or experience one thing when we see rent earth and structures. We experience something else upon seeing mangled bodies. The sight of a well-equipped, angry enemy moves us in still another way. And then we act, or react: squaring our shoulders, for example, quickly taking cover, or turning away. Beyond blinking, however, sight rarely produces in us involuntary jerking. In contrast, terrible *sounds*—cannon fire, passing jets, screeching tires, shrieking voices—make us flinch or even wince. And while experience helps some persons manage their reaction to sudden sound, Walter Ong recognizes, "Whereas sight situates the observer outside what he views, at a distance, sound pours into the hearer."[47] Unprotected by eyelid, eyelashes, or constricting pupil, unconfined by a field of vision, the ear receives sound directly and often unexpectedly. As a result, sound registers almost instantaneously throughout our body, not least of all in our virtual, sinking stomach. Of course the absence of sound can also disturb. Much of the anxiety involved in setting an ambush or suspecting one stems from the quiet that precedes the action. In our description of Mantinea, it is the necessary hushing of war songs and troop chatter that contributes to Brasidan fear.

If certain sounds or their absence produce fear or flinching, it follows that certain sounds may be particularly effective at mitigating such apprehension. Exhortation, after all, connotes encouragement *heard* more than encouragement seen. And evidence from a variety of sources suggests that there is something especially satisfying, something primal, about being encouraged audibly. When we comfort infants or pets, for example, we understand the impact of the sound of our voice. When we drive alone, without physical or phone companion, we inevitably turn on the stereo. Let us pursue this issue of encouraging auditory stimuli further.

Speech is probably the principal audible motivator on the battlefield, be that speech talk, singing, or poetry. That Sparta valued chatter within the ranks comes as no surprise, given the soldier's delight in comradeship. More contemporary demonstrations may be found in the literature of combat veterans. In *All Quiet on the Western Front* Erich Maria Remarque portrays his enlisted German narrator lost while on night patrol. The young soldier finds himself overcome by paralyzing "senseless fear" but then perceives through the darkness the muffled voices of his buddies: "At once a new warmth flows through me. These voices, these quiet words, these footsteps in the trench behind me recall me at a bound from the terrible loneliness and fear of death by which I had been almost destroyed. They are more to me than life, these voices, they are more than motherliness and more than fear; they are the strongest, most comforting thing there is anywhere: they are the voices of my comrades. . . . I could bury my face in them, in these voices, these words that have saved me and will stand by me." Such is the comforting power of the voices of one's fellows. And yet Remarque also appreciates the potency of "the word of command," the voice of one's leader on the battlefield. In one scene, only this voice, the voice of a lieutenant, reaches shell-shocked Corporal Himmelstoss, not manhandling by other soldiers. Catatonic "Himmelstoss hears the order, looks round as if awakened, and follows on."[48] Norman Mailer's *The Naked and the Dead* shows that while this reassuring voice is expected to come from a formal leader, one of higher rank than the audience, it is the properties of the command voice that matter most. Hence Mailer's Lieutenant Hearn realizes during his first combat that "he had been waiting here for [platoon sergeant] Croft to take over, waiting for the sharp voice of command that would lead him out of this."[49]

A sensibly confident voice with a credible plan is a thing craved on the battlefield. Of course the presence of a leader is important. Observing the leader's firm or even lighthearted countenance is helpful, too. An aggressive example is better still. But S. L. A. Marshall and Hannah Arendt impressed upon us earlier that physical action alone is insufficient to move humans, individually or collectively, in an environment fraught with danger. Speech connotes and contextualizes, helping troops understand subtleties. That we should run in a certain direction becomes evident when a combat leader begins running and gestures, "Follow me." But how desperately we should run and whether it is to save our own lives or to take the enemy's is revealed through the leader's speech. Beyond sheer instruction, that voice represents authority, stability, and direction in a treacherous world. Our regimental commander's decision to recite Tyrtaeus rather than attempt some sort of address is consistent with Spartan practice, privileging poetry and song over speech, but his act remains the rhetorical equivalent of a commander addressing his troops. In fact, it is probably something more.

If hearing the voice of one's commander or comrades instills confidence, how much more so when these voices are put to meter. The measured, predictable arrangement of words in song or poetry arouses in hearers an appetite to fulfill or complete that arrangement, drawing the hearers toward the lyrics and away from other concerns.[50] Our regimental commander banks on this when he first revives Brasidan courage with poetry. Spartans reveled in such lyrical dialogue, with its accompanying stamping and piping, and they knew it intimidated foes unpracticed in such a racket. The transition to war cry would only increase troops' appetite to satisfy verbal and combat requirements. So routine and successful was the Spartan practice that Xenophon suggested their war song/dance/cry could be invoked several times over the course of a protracted battle.[51] It should be no surprise, then, that Greece's first school of music was founded in Sparta or that its founder, Terpander, was a contemporary of Tyrtaeus. The meter of Terpander and Tyrtaeus produced tactical advantage for Greece's foremost war machine. Plutarch said of the Spartans, "Their songs were designed as stimulants to arouse their spirits and motivate them to wholehearted, effective action." Athenaeus explained further, "Not only do their sons learn by rote the *Embateria* or Songs of the Battle-Charge . . . but in war they themselves recite the poems of Tyrtaeus from memory and move in time to them." It became Spartan custom to sing together after supper, then have troops compete individually in their renditions of Tyrtaeus.[52] Such constant repeating of the same repertoire of songs and poetry ensured synchronization of thought and emotion, so men who might otherwise argue were cheered by their harmony.

This singing appears more common among Sparta and her allies than many of their contemporaries, but it is not a historical fluke. Today drill instructors (DIs) employ singing in the form of "ditties" (cadence calls, also known as "Jodies") as a primary means for forging recruits into a cohesive group of soldiers. For the uninitiated, the DI might appear to simply strike up a military cadence and efficiently lead a formation to its physical objective, but so much more is going on, and almost all of it stems from the cadenced sound of the DI's voice. That voice establishes rhythm, aligning everyone's left foot with verse; sets pace, determining whether the unit will march or double-time; invites rapport, pausing for the chorused reply of troops; imparts unit identity, given the DI's personalized tone and selection of ditties; indoctrinates, describing service history and traditions; and cultivates an aggressive edge, lampooning adversaries and bragging of sexual exploits. The very breathing of the troops is regulated by the DI's voice. Moreover, the sound they make in return—strong chorus, consistent synchronized tread—masks the discomfort and vulnerability of individuals. Gaggle becomes juggernaut. Add musical instrumentation, and the unit becomes psychologically unstoppable.[53]

Just how central is the sound of pipes to Brasidan morale? Thucydides has already told us that Spartan pipes were used not for religious but tactical effect, helping the troops "keep in step and move forward steadily without breaking ranks." Plutarch reported that "the resulting spectacle was both impressive and terrifying, as the men advanced in time with the pipes in a solid, unbroken phalanx, suffering from no inner perturbation, but marching up to face danger in a composed and cheerful manner to the sound of the music."[54] Instrumentation contributes to improved morale in several ways here. First, as Thucydides and Plutarch allow, by synchronizing the step of hundreds of infantrymen, the pipes produce a spectacle, a compelling visual datum that this phalanx is maximizing its lethality and defense. A second, more subtle reason for being encouraged (if you are within the phalanx) is identification, in that the pipes remind the individual Brasidan of the larger picture. To these tunes, with his comrades, the Brasidan has rehearsed and waged war for years. To these tunes his spiritual forefathers have rehearsed and waged war for generations. The Brasidan is reminded of these attachments in music's unique, emotional way, increasing the likelihood that he will fulfill his combat obligations.[55]

Experiences closer to our own time underscore the point. Witness an American cavalry officer, Bill Puntenney, preparing for World War II: "We would get back to Fort Bliss for brief periods for cleanup and resupply. I will always remember with great pride being a part of the 7th Regiment riding back across the huge parade ground with the band playing 'Gary Owen,' the Scotch melody General Custer chose as the regimental song. The tired troopers would straighten up in their saddles with pride as they heard the stirring notes of the band."[56] Likewise, a battalion commander within the Royal Scots Fusiliers remembered from the First World War, "When the men were exhausted and inclined to straggle, the effect of the pipes was most marked. The men at once pulled themselves together."[57] Failure to do so would have sullied the fine and long-standing reputation of the regiment. So it is one encouraging thing to march in step and maximize tactical advantage, and still another to be stirred through identification, tapping reserves of pride and strength that might make the difference. But there is a third consequence of pipes that makes them a combat multiplier: Muffling potentially disturbing audible stimuli or filling what might otherwise might be frightening anticipatory silences, the pipes keep hearers focused on their own world rather than the enemy's. In this sense, instrumentation synchronizes emotion as well as locomotion.

There is a final source of auditory stimulus that should be noted here: the sound of close-order drill, in other words, precision marching and manual of arms. Precise, practiced marching and handling of weapons is credited with many results. It reduces confusion and stumbling within a body of troops, whether that body be forming before the enemy or simply marching across base for lunch. It conditions troops to respond instantly to commands. It increases a unit's combat power. And it produces and helps preserve a cohesive team. William McNeill credits the exertion of keeping together in time with producing high-spirited cohesion: "I rather liked strutting around, and so, I feel sure, did most of my fellows. Marching aimlessly about on the drill field, swaggering in conformity with prescribed military postures, conscious only of keeping in step so as to make the next move correctly and in time some-how felt good. . . . 'Muscular bonding' is the most economical label I could find for this phenomenon, and I hope the phrase will be understood to mean the euphoric fellow feeling that prolonged and rhythmic muscular movement arouses among nearly all participants in such exercise."[58]

I can testify to this enjoyable feeling and attribute much of it to shared, sequenced exertion. Physiology is involved, as the brain produces endorphins in response to physical activity, the endorphins producing a sensation of well-being. Emotional calculus is involved, as one recognizes that he or she is part of a larger, many-legged whole. But there is also involved, and powerfully so, the exhilaration that results from the sound of close-order drill. Quite simply, the crunch of synchronized heels, particularly the accented left one, produces a pleasing harmony. It also provides the audible means for soldiers to keep themselves in step, since the visual means of looking down is discouraged.

The same principle applies to the manual (or handling) of arms. Whether one is a Spartan, Hapsburg, or U.S. infantryman, one learns how to carry, ready, present, and change directions with one's weapon precisely. Besides increasing the likelihood of one's survival on the battlefield and reducing the likelihood of battering a comrade, there is a pleasing corporate sound when tens or hundreds or thousands of weapons snap into place simultaneously. My drill instructor directed me to try to break the hand guards of my M-16. While such effort required the sharp movements that the DI was after, it also produced a racket—harmonized by the racket of my platoon mates. Later, in the field, we moved less exactly and more quietly, but even hushed there was a reassuring sound to Marines and their gear on the move. If there is a mus-cular bonding to close-order drill, there is certainly an audible bonding as well. And if war songs and pipes seem rather remote today, at least on the field of battle, we should remember the cheerleading, bleacher stomping, band marching, and fight songs of high school sporting events. We are not so far from Brasidan practice, employing a variety of audible, corporate stimuli to raise our spirits.

Encouraging Directions

Eric Voegelin rightly observes that "an exhortation always presupposes some-body in need of it,"[59] and through that pithy insight we may note the tight coupling between audience and difficulty in this rhetorical discourse. An audience in need of encouragement *is* the difficulty sufficiently compelling that it leads someone to utterance. What ought to be appreciated, further, is that the rank and file are not always the ones in need of encouragement, nor are commanders inevitably the ones to supply it. Downward is the classic direction of battle exhortation, most easily and often recognized in the ancient chronicles and invariably alluded to by those who have discussed the subject. But the battlefield is a complex, trying, ever-changing place. Anxiety, friction, the disquieting fog of war—all operate to varying degrees in everyone's breast, troops and commanders alike. Moreover, there are more sources from which to take some comfort than merely one's leader. For this reason it is useful to identify the half-dozen directions in which battle exhortation may flow. No doubt there is overlap, but pausing to distinguish differences heightens our appreciation of the audiences in need.

The most easily recognized direction of battle exhortation, *downward*, may take the form of a general addressing an entire army or theater or of a sergeant addressing those in his charge within a military vehicle. Audience is junior in rank to the exhorter and is believed by the senior to require encouragement. It is no accident that this is the classic course of battle exhortation. Combat leaders either have more experience than their juniors or more training and authority. They are expected to be a source of encouragement as well as direction.

It is also hard to overstate the stress most troops feel when combat is imminent. Young Marine E. B. Sledge represents generations of troops before their first combat when he remembers a heart-pounding, sleepless night; then "everything my life had been before and has been after pales in the light of that awesome moment when my amtrac started in amid a thunderous bombardment toward the flaming, smoke-shrouded beach for the assault on Peleliu."[60] Seasoned combat troops wrestle with doubts of their own. The more often they have participated in combat, the greater they have witnessed the mortality of men and the capriciousness of death and maiming, the more they tend to wonder how much longer they can "avoid the one with my name on it." The bottom-line requirement of downward battle exhortation is (as Xenophon explained) to shift the way troops are thinking, "so that instead of having in their heads the one idea of 'what is going to happen to me?' they may think 'what action am I going to take?'"[61]

Instances of downward exhortation abound. This is the primary type of encouragement reported by Thucydides at Mantinea. In our reconstruction, the Brasidan regimental commander offers it to his men via song and poetry. An actual example is when Cortés exhorted his conquistadores prior to leading them against the camp of Pánfilo de Narváez. Having tenuously secured Mexico City, Cortés led a detachment of his men back toward Veracruz to meet Narvaez, who had been dispatched by the governor of Cuba to arrest Cortés. Through a deliberative war council, Cortés had succeeded in persuading his officers and men to join him in capturing or killing Narvaez. Instructions for battle were distributed. Then, in dimming light and rain, Cortés encouraged his bedraggled force. In the words of conquistador Díaz, who was present: "Cortés said: 'I well know that the followers of Narvaez are in all four times as numerous as we are but they are not used to arms, and as the greater part of them are hostile to their captain, and many of them are ill, and we shall take them by surprise, I have an idea that God will give us the victory, and that they will not persist much in their defence, for we shall procure them more wealth than their Narvaez can. So, gentlemen, our lives and honour depend, after God, on your courage and your strong arms, I have no other favour to ask of you or to remind you of but that this is the touchstone of our honour and our glory for ever and ever, and it is better to die worthily than to live dishonoured.'"[62] Some final preparations followed; fife and drum assisted the early morning march toward Narvaez's camp, then fell silent for the sake of surprise. Discovered shortly thereafter, Cortés's force, "with the fife and drum beating the charge," defeated Narvaez's force and took the unfortunate officer prisoner.

Now because the battlefield is a fluid environment, there is not always opportunity for an address like Cortés's. For instance, when legendary, aging First Sergeant Dan Daley found Marines hesitating before enemy machine guns at Belleau Wood, the recipient of two Medals of Honor reportedly snarled, "Come on, you sons-o'-bitches! Do you want to live forever?" When Brigadier General Norman Cota found soldiers from his division crouching in the sand at Omaha Beach rather than advancing, he purportedly cajoled, "Hell, men. We're getting killed here on the beach. We might as well go a little farther in and get killed there!" When one of the machine gunners of Task Force Ranger in Mogadishu slumped back into his Humvee shot dead, panicking most of the young soldiers inside, the squad leader present commanded, "Just calm down! We've got to keep fighting or none of us will get back alive." Though cruder and briefer than Cortés, such speech from a senior to juniors offers reason to fight. Daley taunts Marines younger and less proven. In Cota there is morbidity and wry humor, but there is also military logic. The squad leader actually makes a clear argument, barking instruction, then good reason to comply. Even an exclamation as abrupt as Rear Admiral David Farragut's at Mobile Bay—"Damn the torpedoes! Full steam ahead!"—conveys a disdain for danger and a commitment to duty that invites juniors to regard the situation similarly. These exclamations are brief; they are downward; and the first two are even of dubious attribution. Daly's call is also attributed to Frederick the Great, 161 years earlier. Cota's is also attributed to a regimental commander within his division. The imprecision behind such one-liners reflects their proximity to the fight—and history's powerful expectation that leaders said *something* when the situation grew desperate.[63]

Certainly there are occasions when circumstances are so dire that symbolic action is complemented heavily by physical action. When one of Puntenney's companies met veteran German paratroopers before the town of La Trinité, he remembers, "I have never seen troops break and run in battle before or since. The shock, hysteria, and fear on the faces of the men as they came back toward the road we occupied was unbelievable. As the men came over the hedgerow we had to physically grab them and shake them to regain their senses. In some cases we had to kick some butts to get them to form a line along the hedgerow to fight back and repel the attack." Probably some speech accompanied the manhandling, but it is neither what Puntenney remembers nor apparently what got the attention of those in flight.[64]

There are also occasions when downward battlefield discourse is not rhetorical but as purely imperative as a traffic light. In our Brasidan example, the commands to left oblique and forward march are just that—commands, not encouragement characterized by good reasons. Such is also the case when Puntenney's division commander found him and a like-ranked officer discussing as equals how to try again to take a German objective: "The General said, 'Puntenney, you're in command. Get a bridgehead on the other side of the river, and get your outfit across and go make contact with the 101st Airborne.' With that he jumped in his jeep and left."[65]

One variety of downward exhortation important to note—given the size of today's strike forces, their huddle-then-hair-trigger employment, and the handiness of print-reproduction technology—is the typed message distributed for troops to read. Prototypical examples preceded the enormous, carefully choreographed invasion of Normandy. For instance, jumpmasters of the 506th Regiment, 101st Airborne Division received two packs of paper some hours before the regiment was to board C-47s for the midnight jump behind enemy lines. One pack contained printed encouragement from the supreme commander of the Allied Expeditionary Forces, Dwight Eisenhower, the other from regimental commander Colonel Robert Sink. Senior officers did circulate personally among the troops staged to cross the English Channel. Well-known U.S. Army photographs show Eisenhower addressing members of the 101st that evening.[66] But the most efficient, reasonably secure way for a commander to address a large body of separately staged troops is by having a circular put into each of their hands (as through jump masters or, today, through communications personnel managing secure electronic networks). Broadcast media is typically not an option, because it can broadcast intent and timing to the enemy.

There are tradeoffs to delivering battle exhortation in print rather than by word of mouth. There is far less control as to how the audience receives it, both physically and psychologically. Given troops' notorious black sense of humor, such discourse can be vulnerable to ridicule. At the same time, troops have some expectation for such discourse, and junior officers, closer to the front, can enforce a proper reception to some degree. Senior enlisted personnel often present colorful, reinforcing translations. Perhaps the most fundamental limitation to such battle exhortation is its inaudible nature. Many of us hear a voice in our head when we read, but it is not the voice of our commander or comrade. Unless the printed exhortation is read aloud before subordinate units, forming individual listeners into groups, readers process the text by turning in on themselves. This constrains or limits the team building and team excitement. One of Marshall's conclusions from his World War II postcombat interviews is that "no mechanical means of communicating ever given man can become a substitute for the spoken word" in the theater of war.[67]

Interactive battle exhortation, that which flows both downward and back up, encourages both troops and commander. Through this dialogue the troops signal that they are ready to answer the call for fighting. In our Brasidan example, we witness this when the regimental commander addresses his anxious regiment through song, and the regiment responds with ritualized singing and stamping. In his time Montecuccoli observed choruses of acclamation and reinforcing commentary. Many historical examples may be found in Díaz: After Cortés had finished his the-ships-are-destroyed exhortation, Díaz remembers, "One and all we answered him that we would obey his orders, that the die was cast for good fortune, as Caesar said when he crossed the Rubicon, and that we were all of us ready to serve God and the King." Later, en route to Mexico City, as the enormity of their task gave the conquistadores reason for pause, Díaz reports, "Cortés said: 'Sirs, let us follow our banner which bears the sign of the holy cross, and through it we shall conquer!' Then one and all we answered him: 'May good fortune attend our advance, for in God lies the true strength.'" Shortly after, as the enemy proved able to commit thousands of fresh warriors to the fight daily, Diaz reflects: "We certainly did not think that things looked well. . . . As we were but human and feared death, many of us, indeed the majority of us, confessed to the Padre de la Merced and to the priest, Juan Diaz, who were occupied all night in hearing our repentance and commending us to God and praying that He would pardon us and save us from defeat."[68]

Throughout Díaz's *Discovery and Conquest of Mexico,* the Spaniards precede battle with Mass and confession, perhaps the archetypes of interactive battle exhortation. During Mass the priest, representative of both field and heavenly commander, offers good reason to be strong and courageous; troops answer with choral singing and gestures of obedience. During confession the dialogue grows more intimate, encouraging the unit by unburdening individual consciences. The Holy Word, sympathetic voices, dialogue—all relieve anxieties, preparing men for abandon. While Montecuccoli argued that prayer should precede battle exhortation because it tends to quiet rather than rouse the soul, we may acknowledge both tools as encouraging prebattle speech.

Exclusively *upward* discourse, troops encouraging commander, is yet another course of battle exhortation. In our Brasidan scenario, we do not see it because a Spartiate regimental commander's entire life, his very raison d'être, would be to soldier; encouraging him to fight would not be necessary. Conceivably, however, as a younger officer he might have benefited from words of encouragement from more experienced men in the ranks. Today the discreet encouragement of lieutenants by their staff noncommissioned officers is pervasive. A young officer who has no need for it may not appreciate the risks before the unit. Even a commander as audacious as Cortés received enlisted urging. Díaz reports that "one and all we put heart into Cortés" when he was ill. Diaz also remembers when the captains lost patience with Cortés's complicated relationship with Montezuma and enjoined: "What is the good of your making so many words, let us either take him prisoner, or stab him, tell him once more that if he cries out or makes an uproar we will kill him, for it is better at once to save our lives or to lose them." Cortés himself reported an occasion when he and his chief lieutenant, Pedro de Alvarado, were each importuned by their respective assault parties to capture Mexico City's marketplace before the other. The men "held it a point of honor to take it first."[69]

It is *lateral* battle exhortation, encouragement between comrades, that Thucydides recorded so distinctly at Mantinea, the Spartans speaking "words of encouragement to each other man to man." Seventeen years later we find Xenophon recommending to members of the Greek Ten Thousand that they "call out to your comrades by name as you go. It's good to think that whoever says or does something brave and gallant now is making himself remembered among the people whom he would want to remember him."[70] It is evident among modern artillery gun crews when they bait one another to fire faster. And it is evident during lulls in combat. Sledge remembers one such episode at length. So complete in recounting need, audience, constraints, and frequency, it merits full excerpt:

> A friend came over from one of the rifle platoons that was to be in the next day's assault. We sat near the gun pit on our helmets in the mud and had a long talk. I lit my pipe and he a cigarette. Things were quiet in the area, so we were undisturbed for some time. He poured out his heart. He had come to me because of our friendship and because I was a veteran. He told me he was terribly afraid about the impending attack. I said everybody was. But I knew he would be in a more vulnerable position than some of us, because his platoon was in the assault. I did my best to cheer him up.
>
> He was so appalled and depressed by the fighting of the previous day that he had concluded he couldn't possibly survive the next day. He confided his innermost thoughts and secrets about his parents and a girl back home whom he was going to marry after the war. The poor guy wasn't just afraid of death or injury—the idea that he might never return to those he loved so much had him in a state of near desperation.
>
> I remembered how Lt. Hillbilly Jones had comforted and helped me through the first shock of Peleliu, and I tried to do the same for my friend. Finally he seemed somewhat relieved, or resigned to his fate, whatever it might be. We got up and shook hands. He thanked me for our friendship, then walked slowly back to his foxhole.
>
> There was nothing unique in the conversation. Thousands like it occurred every day among infantrymen scheduled to enter the chaos and inferno of an attack.[71]

Here we see that trepidation more than timing summons battle exhortation. Its object is to encourage others for battle, even if the fight is not until tomorrow.

Elsewhere, literally as dust settled on his most frightening combat experience of the war, Sledge remembers the helpful banter of buddies: "I tried to grin and was glad the inevitable wisecracks had started up again." Humor is the most common means by which troops encourage one another. Puntenney testifies to its purpose: "Combat is a grim affair and the consequences can be fatal, but there is always a lot of humor in a well trained outfit. Soldiers are always joking and playing pranks on each other. If it wasn't for the humor, I think many men would crack up, being confronted as they are with the daily carnage."[72]

Another less obvious course for battle exhortation is *circular*, or, put differently, when an individual needs to encourage him- or herself. We all find ourselves mumbling words of self-encouragement in one situation or another. Given the power of audible reassurance, we supply it ourselves when that is the best we can do. Sledge remembers such self-exhortation from when he participated in a frontal assault on Peleliu: "I clenched my teeth, squeezed my carbine stock, and recited over and over to myself, 'The Lord is my shepherd; I shall not want. Yea, though I walk through the valley of the shadow of death, I will fear no evil, for Thou art with me.'"[73] Psalm 23 is self-exhortation par excellence, not silent meditation in its pure form but words and meter uttered in the first person.

Because we often encourage ourselves when we encourage others, circular exhortation may apply especially to commanders. Indeed, generally regarded as self-motivated, commanders tend to receive less encouragement from others. But anxiety beyond the usual fear of failure or bodily harm might lead to it. Those in charge can feel that being present or being responsible for the impending combat requires an explanation to the troops. They might want to reveal something about themselves, even something rather intimate, given that their troops are about to risk all on their behalf. They might be anxious about unit focus or obedience. Cicero acknowledged this sort of self-soothing in his fourth Philippic: "It only remains, Men of Rome, that you stand fast in the sentiments you proclaim. So I shall do as generals are wont to do when the army is drawn up for battle: though they see that the soldiers are fully ready for the fray, they exhort them all the same."[74] Thus commanders may speak for their own sake as much as for others.

A final course for battle exhortation is actually more conventional than the general's address. Directionally we could represent it as a *starburst*, the combination and culmination of all of the other directions at once. It includes the war songs and especially the war cries that encourage self, comrades, seniors, and juniors and intimidate the enemy. Earlier we acknowledged that war songs and training ditties channel many voices and identities into a single powerful one. How much more so the battle cry. We see it as the integral complement of the ancient Greek war song (or *paean*) when Xenophon reports time after time, "the trumpet sounded and they sang the paean and then raised a shout as they brought their spears down for the attack," or "all the soldiers sang the paean and raised the battle cry," or "after they had sung the paean and the trumpet had sounded, the hoplites raised the war-cry and charged." Diaz remembers of the Mexica with a chill, "what shouts and howls and whistles they gave us, and how they came on to join us foot to foot." He remembers the conquistadores countering with their own cry, "Santiago—and at them!" Confederate forces during the American Civil War had their dreaded rebel yell. And Custer and his men perished while the Lakota "were making the tremolo and yelling, 'Hoka hey!' like a big wind roaring."[75] The battle cry is the capstone of battle exhortation, not only because it radiates in all directions but because it comes last sequentially, after the commander's speech (if there is one), after war song (if there is one), after instrumentation (if there is some). When nothing more than weapon and lungs separate the individual warrior from his enemy, it is the end of the line for rhetoric and the start of physical brutality.

Summary

In this chapter we have seen that combat may be preceded or accompanied by battle exhortation. We have taken stock of the observations and recommendations of the handful of military men and scholars who have probed the subject. We have examined a wide range of evidence, from historical reconstruction to the combat memoirs of a Spanish conquistador and two American infantrymen. With pressing need, audience, and high-level constraints in mind, I suggest the following definition: Battle exhortation is symbolic action, especially audible, most traditionally verbal, designed to brace troops for the psychological demands of combat. It provides encouraging context for physical action, as physical action provides context for speech. Traditionally the rank and file require such encouragement and the commander delivers it, but this is hardly the only scenario. Depending on who needs bracing, battle exhortation may flow downward, downward and upward, merely upward, laterally, circularly, or in all directions at once. Yet somehow, subtly, even unconsciously, we had already known much of this. We are conditioned to expect the rhetoric of combat leadership before major events, in war and elsewhere.

2
Indoctrination

In order to observe the prominence of battle exhortation in our culture and to start noting its conventions, let us examine four exemplars. The first three are classics, which cultivate the appeals of battlefield fraternity and the exceptional commander: exhortations by Plutarch's Spartan mother, Shakespeare's Henry V, and George C. Scott's Patton. The fourth, a parody by Bill Murray in the movie *Stripes,* playfully subverts topics common to battle exhortation by relying on the audience's general familiarity with them. We begin by considering the audience of such material.

Recruits All

It sometimes seems that the United States does not produce strong raw material for the battlefield. Beneficiaries of restrained politics, material wealth, oceanic buffers, and generally friendly neighbors, Americans have often focused elsewhere. In *The Naked and the Dead,* Norman Mailer's General Cummings laments to a junior: "We have the highest standard of living in the world and, as one would expect, the worst individual fighting soldiers of any big power. Or at least in their natural state they are. They're comparatively wealthy, they're spoiled, and as Americans they share most of them the peculiar manifestation of our democracy. They have an exaggerated idea of the rights due themselves as individuals and no idea at all of the rights due others." S. L. A. Marshall found Americans of the mid-twentieth century insufficiently aggressive: "He is what his home, his religion, his schooling, and the moral code and ideals of his society have made him. The Army . . . must reckon with the fact that he comes from a civilization in which aggression, connected with the taking of life, is prohibited and unacceptable. The teaching and the ideals of that civilization are against killing, against taking advantage." Marshall even pointed out that Medical Corps psychiatrists in the European theater "found that fear of killing, rather than fear of being killed, was the most common cause of battle failure in the individual." Beyond such self-criticisms, enemies of the United States have often been emboldened by what they regard as degenerate and debauched American living. Ayatollah Ruhollah Khomeini and Osama bin Laden are only among the latest to denigrate U.S. morals and take comfort in supposed American weakness. Volunteers found in recruiting stations tend to confirm the indictment. Thomas Ricks finds them to be youngsters steeped in self-gratification and self-indulgence who have reached a dead end, part-timers from broken families who require a host of induction waivers. "They are, with few exceptions," Ricks explains, "denizens of the bottom half of the American economy, or on the way there—poor kids with lousy educations, and a few wealthier ones sliding off the professional tracks their parents had taken."[1] Hence the necessity of boot camp to prepare Americans for war.

While different branches of the armed forces (and different training regimes within some) emphasize various aspects of military service, one emphasis transcends branch—the fostering of a common identity. Kenneth Burke's conception of "identification" and "division" helps us understand why this is so. Initially recruits are characterized by division. Where they are from, what they know, who they are loyal to, how they dress, speak, and wear their hair all differ, inhibiting their communion, which in turn inhibits efficiency and predictability. To compensate, the military introduces identification in the form of standardization. Recruits cannot become identical to one another, but insofar as their interests are joined at boot camp, they come to identify with one another and to be identified as "substantially one." So within a given service the process begins with common haircuts and uniforms, and the ritual of colors—the daily flag-raising and flag-lowering ceremonies that freeze everyone solemnly in their tracks. The chain of command is reviewed, repeated, and memorized, underscoring that everyone has the same senior superiors. Drill begins to equalize movement. Service dialect begins to coalesce vocabulary. Reward and punishment become collective. Paychecks become virtually the same. In time, new service personnel begin "spontaneously, intuitively, even unconsciously" to identify with one another, "even when their interests are not joined."[2]

There is still a constructive role for division. Reintroduced as interservice rivalry and small-unit competition, it underscores identification within one's platoon or squad. One learns to respect the authority of the commander-in-chief, and to call oneself a Soldier, Sailor, Airman, or Marine, but it is typically for a small-unit buddy that one goes back during an endurance run or obstacle course. This subordination of individual interest—imposed initially but soon ingrained—does more than produce like-minded troops. It germinates the nearly impenetrable emotional norm that makes them stick together and fight together when every objective consideration urges them to scatter and hide. "When, through military reverses or the fatiguing and often horrible experiences of combat, the original purpose becomes obscured," Glenn Gray explains, "the fighter is often sustained solely by the determination not to let down his comrades. . . . Such loyalty to the group is the essence of fighting morale."[3]

For those headed to military specialties that require killing, especially the most traditional and personal kind, there is additional reprogramming, that which imbues the "warrior ethos." Whereas previously aggression resulted in grounding, detention, expulsion, or arrest, now it is for timidity and inaction that recruits are punished. Boot camp instructors lecture on combat power and combat multipliers, the desirability of maximizing violence, and the virtue of being ruthless. Bayonet drill helps recruits get in touch with their outside (shouting) voice and used to the idea that they are in a grisly new line of work. The rifle range follows, more practically. Perhaps the exercise of "pugil sticks," where two recruits must violently confront one another within a ring, most dramatically signifies the transformation from civilian to warrior. Troops will never face a real enemy sporting a great Q-tip, diaper, and football helmet. (The look and weaponry are ridiculous.) But passage through pugil sticks compels a psychological crossing-over into the world of violence. For many in the ring, it is the first time in their lives that they are told to attack someone physically and the first time they themselves face physical attack. Not only are the equipment and ring unfamiliar, but so is the surrounding commotion as instructors and peers holler for blood. The adrenaline of fight or flight, so carefully mitigated back home, fills their veins. For those from more violent neighborhoods, or at least used to contact sports, the emotionality is more familiar, but the ethics are still new. Here the law does not discourage clubbing but encourages it. Here, until the whistle, there are no cheap shots or forbidden blows. Initiates swing away civilian inhibitions and get a taste of sanctioned combat.

And yet the adjustment of young Americans for war may not require as much training as it first seems. Americans have always been surrounded by messages, images, and practices of contest, physical and spiritual, from the earliest sermons preached in the New World to the latest gun-toting movies to the daily news. Illustrations abound in literature and cinema. Mark Twain charged that Sir Walter Scott's gallant Waverley novels precipitated the American Civil War. Others have laid similar charges on the imperialistic prose of Rudyard Kipling for World War I, and the tough-guy acting of John Wayne for Vietnam. Though the charges go too far, there is something to them. For instance, during intense 1944 combat in the Pacific, Marine Captain Joseph Buckley moved his company forward with the quip, "Okay, pals. Let's do it, just like in the movies."[4] Appealing for combat valor, Buckley did not allude to military training but to standard Hollywood fare. He might have done equally well referring to sports.

Competitive sports have evolved into one of the dominant customs of American society. From holiday bowls to daily ESPN, Little League play to corporate sponsorships, "the thrill of victory" to "the agony of defeat," we love the arena and the struggle that takes place within it. In 1825 Daniel Webster could declare politics and government "the master topic of the age," but today he would have to concede sports as at least a master metaphor. We routinely allude to events unrelated to athletics as slam dunks, home runs, and fumbles. "Sport is one of the most popular cultural practices in American society," George Sage agrees. "Indeed, involvement in sport, as either a participant or a spectator, is considered almost a public duty."[5]

Moreover, Americans prefer hard-hitting, high-stakes contests over the more gentle variety. Some wish it were otherwise, as does Harry Edwards, who deplores the inclination while acknowledging its depth: "America would gain far more than she would lose through the initiation of . . . an alternative sport structure . . . in which the younger generation can be socialized with values stressing cooperation rather than antagonism, participation and self-actualization rather than confrontation and domination."[6]

Others celebrate the rough-and-tumble, even seeing it as a substitute for violence, as in the film *Knute Rockne, All American*. In one scene the Notre Dame football coach (depicted by Pat O'Brien) defends collegiate sports before a congressional committee: "Games such as football . . . are an absolute necessity to the nation's best interest. Every red-blooded young man in any country is filled with what we might call the natural spirit of combat. In many parts of Europe and elsewhere in the world this spirit manifests itself in continuous wars and revolutions. But we have tried to make competitive sport serve as a safer outlet for the spirit of combat. I believe we've succeeded."[7]

Less naive about America's penchant for war, more practical about how to get ready, Douglas MacArthur composed the following quatrain as superintendent of the U.S. Military Academy and had it carved onto the stone entrance of the gymnasium:

> Upon the fields of friendly strife,
> Are sown the seeds
> That, upon other fields on other days,
> Will bear the fruits of victory.[8]

But George Patton made the argument most directly (as he was wont to do). Steeling unit after unit of his untested troops before D-Day, he lectured: "Men, this stuff we hear about America wanting to stay out of the war—not wanting to fight—is a lot of bull-shit. Americans love to fight—traditionally!

All real Americans love the sting and clash of battle. When you were kids, you all admired the champion marble player, the fastest runner, the big league ball players, the toughest boxers. Americans love a winner and will not tolerate a loser."[9]

We shall return to Patton shortly, but the point here is that Patton's well-known ability to inspire men stemmed in part from his choosing to speak directly to their experience. For younger troops especially, games and sports have far more relevance than abstract matters such as Nazi tyranny or al-Qaeda terror networks. *Hearts and Minds,* the 1974 award-winning antiwar documentary, indicts the United States with the same premise, juxtaposing tragic Vietnam War footage with footage of Americana such as high school football.[10]

Americans may fancy themselves a peace-loving people, but in truth our hypercompetitiveness, honed by our sports, entertainment, free-market economy, and adversarial legal system, makes us the Spartans of our age—even before military training. While our youngsters do not recite Tyrtaeus' war poetry, they are swamped by Little League and televised athletics, much of which are quite gladiatorial. They do not dance, as the Spartans did, with "motions like someone dodging a javelin or throwing one, leaping up from the ground and skillfully brandishing a shield," but they do manipulate the controls of various screen-based games, trouncing opponents. Everywhere (theater, television, home video, computers, arcades) they see Hollywood heroics. If, as Francis Fukuyama suggests, "there is a side of man that despises a riskless life, that seeks danger and heroism and sacrifice," then the United States ensures that this side is well developed long before boot camp.[11]

Perhaps a culture that valued only individual contests (one-on-one combat) could operate without battle exhortation, but in America, where adversarial group situations are widespread, the question is moot. We are surrounded not only by aggressive institutions and martial metaphors but also by countless instances of leaders calling on groups to perform as teams to overcome threats. In the aggregate these examples are indoctrinating, creating in us at least two significant expectations.

We are so familiar with battle exhortation as a type of speech that we feel a need for it in team situations; that is, we recognize it as a legitimate, even necessary forum, whether we are the would-be exhorter or audience. When exhorters draw upon their previous exposure to such speech, we see just how prevalent and reciprocal it is. Groping for the means to rally his demoralized platoon, S. L. A. Marshall's platoon sergeant (in chapter 1) determines "to talk it up, as a man might do in a football game." Going the other direction, football players enter stadiums shouting war cries. Besides being explicitly encouraged to do so, the players have witnessed such cries and the situations that precipitate them elsewhere. Audiences expect and assess battle exhortation the same way. E. B. Sledge regards his platoon commander's words and actions moments before landing on Peleliu as "just like they do in the movies!"[12] Indeed, leaders who do not encourage their troops or teams before a contest risk disappointing their followers' expectation to be so addressed. As well as needing emotionally to be appreciated and inspired, such audiences have a conditioned craving for this sort of speech-act. It is not because the majority have served in the military and experienced battle exhortation there. It is because all of us partake, to varying degrees, in the sports, television, cinema, and literature of our general culture, and our culture is replete with battle exhortation.

The other expectation developed by this subtle but pervasive indoctrination, beyond anticipation for the speech-act itself, is anticipation for its conventions. As Lloyd Bitzer explains, when a situation recurs with some frequency, a certain type of discourse tends to address it, establishing "a special vocabulary, grammar, and style" for that speech genre. In fact, a distinct "form of discourse is not only established but comes to have a power of its own— the tradition itself tends to function as a constraint," limiting potential departure from the template.[13] If we consider the texts of presidential inaugurals, for instance, we find substantial agreement among them: solemnity, a call for reconciliation, and the charting of new direction. Eulogies have their own consistency, offering remembrance, consolation, and closure. What is regarded as appropriate or inappropriate in such circumstances is influenced largely by what we have heard previously. Done skillfully, such speeches may offer some departure, but for the most part differences between inaugurals or eulogies reflect choices within their larger established vocabulary, grammar, and style. To begin observing such conventions from popular renditions of battle exhortation, we turn, first, to antiquity.

Fraternal Standing in Plutarch's Spartan Mother

Plutarch, the first-century Greek biographer, is best known for his *Parallel Lives*, in which he describes notable Greek and Roman leaders. There is battle exhortation in some of these biographies, but more resides in his collection of moral essays titled *Moralia*. A bit unexpectedly, the sources of some of this exhortation are the tough mothers of Sparta, who provide us a glimpse into a perfectly martial society. Only one of these laconic exhortations really endures. Portrayed by Louis Jean François Lagrenée's eighteenth-century painting *Spartan Mother and Son,* in which the mother is handing her panoplied son his shield and gesturing toward it, the memorable saying is "Come back either with your shield or upon it."[14] Today, after marveling at such maternal severity, we wonder about the exact meaning of the words. Clearly the mother is encouraging her son to excel on the battlefield, and her approval is contingent upon his returning with the shield. But why that focus? Might it be because the emblem of Sparta would be painted on the shield, and leaving that on the field would be akin to deserting the national colors? Might she be appealing for individual courage or skill? Based on the tactics of the day and other maternal exhortations preserved in Plutarch, it seems instead that the mother is admonishing her son on the grounds of fraternal standing —the reputation for standing beside brothers in the most difficult circumstances.

In Greece, when private duels between free-running and riding knights gave way to massed phalanx fighting, the more heavily armored, more widely enfranchised infantryman or "hoplite" began carrying a new shield. Wooden, it offered more protection than earlier cowhide shields, but it was also heavier, and it could not easily be slung over the back to protect soldiers in flight. This general awkwardness, and the shield's uselessness to those on the run, led to it being the first piece of gear discarded on the battlefield. This act was sufficiently common across Greece that reference to it became a charge, one associated with cowardice. Aristotle included "throwing away one's shield" in his list of acts that were shameful. This kind of shame or cowardice meant more than failing an individual test in battle. It meant the hoplite had also forsaken his comrades. As Victor Davis Hanson explains, those accused of tossing away the shield "were assumed to have been among the first to have abandoned their friends in an effort to save their own lives during a general collapse of the phalanx; that is, they had endangered the men who had kept their arms and were not able, or had no desire, to make good such an ignoble escape."[15]

This is the context in which Spartan mothers warned their sons to return with their shields or dead upon them. Tactics and equipment of the day, particularly the shield, worn on the left arm, made each infantryman dependent upon the man on his right for a complete defense. The hoplite who discarded his shield to make easier his escape exposed the right side of the warrior to his left. He violated the standard observed by Plutarch—and attributed by him to a Spartan king—that each hoplite donned his helmet and breastplate for his own sake, "but the shield for the common good of the whole line."[16] Beyond physical protection, then, the shield in classical Greek warfare served as a symbol of disciplined fraternity. In essence, a hoplite without his shield was not a citizen-soldier but an individual who had abdicated his communal responsibilities. Thus the Spartan mother's exhortation firmly grounds acceptable battle conduct in a concern for fellow warriors. No public-spirited mother wanted her son to return without this practical, visible badge of comradeship.

As tactics of the day help us appreciate the shield-to-shield, shoulder-to-shoulder fidelity that the pithy words cited are demanding, so too does the context of other sayings attributed to Spartan mothers. Of the more than two dozen maternal sayings, all are concerned with the combat reputation of sons, and each has considerable edge. One mother, upon hearing that her son may have survived battle through flight, writes to him, "You've been tainted by a bad reputation. Either wipe this out now or cease to exist." Another confronts sons who have run off by demanding, "In making your escape, vile slaves, where is it you've come to? Or do you plan to creep back in here where you emerged from?" And with this she pulled up her garment, apparently exposing her belly or pudendum. Time and time again we see that the reputation for disciplined battlefield conduct—"fighting bravely in the battle line"; "right at his place in the line"—is of paramount concern. In some cases, mothers kill deserter sons rather than exhort them or share in their shame. What is the higher good behind such severity? What would lead a mother to interrupt one son describing the noble death of another (his brother) by asking, "Isn't it a disgrace, then, not to have gone on such a fine journey with him?"[17] The higher good is fraternal standing: The reputation that every Spartan hoplite was asked to live up to was of standing by his brothers in the heat of battle, thereby standing by Sparta at large. Nothing better signified success or failure in this regard than whether one returned from battle with his shield.

True, this battle exhortation is uttered not by a military commander but by a mother, and addressed not to a military unit but to one son, but this maternal call for combat steadiness would have been commonplace. The relatively small and tight-knit Greek city-states sent forth phalanxes made of real brothers, fathers, sons, nephews, and uncles. Consequently, very much was at stake when phalanxes marched to war. Perhaps this is another reason the Spartan mother speaks to defensive rather than offensive armament. She would well understand that the object of combat was to punish, even kill the soldiers of other armies. But their dying would not affect her or her sisters in the same way dying Spartan husbands and sons would. Her exhortation focuses on preserving life rather than taking it, and in this respect she is more like a modern-day mother than her exhortation first suggests.

It is also true that there is some question as to the authenticity of the "Sayings of Spartan Women" and to Plutarch's authorship. Because Plutarch was known to have collected adages, believing them important insights into character, the material of others worked its way into his wide-ranging *Moralia*. But from the perspective of socialization or transmission of values, who said what is far less important than what audiences believe to have been said. In the case of the sayings attributed to Spartan women, Richard Talbert points out, "their value lies . . . in the demonstration they offer of how Sparta's admirers from the fourth century [B.C.E.] onwards (Plutarch among them) liked to dream of her citizens in bygone days—bold, wise, just, free, unworldly."[18] Ascetic Sparta has inspired spiritual descendants throughout history. When admirers become soldiers, or educate soldiers, the fact that they are working from the reports of Plutarch, Thucydides, and others rather than what was actually said is of small consequence. It is little different from Mason Locke Weems leading generations of Americans to believe that George Washington once told his father "I cannot tell a lie" or William Wirt claiming that Patrick Henry exclaimed before the Virginia Convention, "Give me liberty, or give me death!" These biographers did not report verbatim speech but reflected and shaped what Americans regarded as good morality.

Our memory of the Spartan mother's exhortation may have dimmed, but the exhortation has echoed its way to us in a variety of ways. History has memorialized the heroic last stand of Spartan king Leonidas, who bought greater Greece time to organize before the invading Persian emperor Xerxes. Today the military of our diverse nation-state carefully cultivates a shared identity that produces a surrogate brotherhood, as acknowledged earlier. Coaches of team sport endeavor to create the same. "Whether it be a military battle or Notre Dame football," Lou Holtz would tell his teams, "we can only enjoy success when we realize that we must be able to count on one another."[19] We expect the well-coached, media-sensitive athlete to speak in terms of the team rather than him- or herself. We quickly think less of the athlete who speaks otherwise.

Uniforms in sport and the military may be one of the closest parallels we have today to the classical Greek shield. Besides helping to distinguish friend from foe, simplifying matters of supply, and offering some degree of physical protection, the uniform attests that one is on the team, subscribing to its interests and defending them. It symbolizes the promise to stand by comrades and imbues the wearer with that unselfish standing, complete with certain privileges and protections. Egregious departure from the team's interest leads one to be stripped of the uniform, that reputation, and its perks. Desertion, basically hiding the uniform, is an unconscionable offense. Perhaps most Spartan-like is the practice concerning uniforms at the mortuary of Dover

Air Force Base (Delaware), where American war dead are prepared for burial. Every casket leaves the mortuary containing the deceased's dress uniform, even when the uniform cannot be fitted onto the remains and Dover recommends that the casket not be reopened. Released caskets are escorted from the mortuary to the receiving funeral home by a uniformed member of the deceased's branch of service.[20] A bugle may yet signal "Taps," and the national flag may yet be folded and pressed into the arms of the bereaved, but these burial practices are primarily for the larger, nonmilitary audience, addressing its need for closure with pathos and dignity. For the military, attention to the uniform is the more deep-seated gesture. It is the phalanx's soft-spoken tribute that the fallen perished while standing shoulder-to-shoulder with comrades. In effect, the deceased is returned home on his or her shield, sign of the selfless soldier.

Fraternal Standing in Shakespeare's *Henry V*

Spartans valued brief discourse. The characterization that terse speech is "laconic" is derived from Laconia, the geographic homeland of ancient Sparta. It should not be surprising, then, that the exhortation we have just considered is a single, short sentence. For an eloquent and extended battle exhortation reflecting a wider culture, we must look elsewhere. Nowhere is staying and fighting—for the sake of brothers and for the reputation of doing so—more memorably stated than in Shakespeare's play *Henry V*.

The battle between English and French forces at Agincourt in 1415 is uncommonly well recorded for the Middle Ages. At least four eyewitnesses, two from each side, wrote about the battle afterward. From these accounts, several secondary historical accounts arose, one of which is in Raphael Holinshed's sixteenth-century *Chronicles of England, Scotland, and Ireland*. Shakespeare used Holinshed's *Chronicles* as the main historical source for his plays, including *Henry V*. Now what twenty-eight-year-old Henry V said at Agincourt is a question of history. How directly Holinshed may have drawn from eyewitness or other descriptions to render his own account is a question of historiography. From a rhetorical perspective, however, what is of greater import is how Shakespeare adapted Holinshed's Henry to his play and which words of Shakespeare's Henry we best remember. For it is Shakespeare's eloquent warrior king, not Holinshed's historical one, that moves us with his "band of brothers" appeal.[21]

If book and movie titles are not sufficient proof of the power of Shakespeare's artistry, the battlefield act of Brigadier General Thomas Draude is. During the United States's first war against Saddam Hussein (Operation

Desert Storm), the First Marine Division conducted a frontal attack on Iraqi forces in Kuwait, starting through belts of Iraqi mines at night. The prior afternoon, as light armored vehicles pulled up to gather Draude, who was assistant division commander, and the others who would serve as the forward command post, there was a pause. Everyone present was serious and focused. At the time they believed they were headed into a terrific and protracted fight, since across the minefields waited far greater numbers of Iraqi troops, tanks, artillery—and chemical weapons. (Back in Delaware, Dover Air Force Base was quietly prepared to process fifty thousand American dead.) Draude himself had strong premonitions of death, although he had survived three combat tours in Vietnam. At this tense moment, with comrades about to part and head into the vagaries of war, he asked everyone, including the division commander, to wait a moment and went to his tent. Upon his return, Draude, nicknamed "Sage" by First Division staff, explained that there seemed parallels between their own outnumbered, "coughing and hacking" force and another in history. He alluded to the relative youth of their own division commander (who was younger than Draude) and the youth of this other commander. Draude noted that encouraging words were shared when the officers of this other force parted to assume their places for battle. And then he read aloud Shakespeare's memorable battle exhortation.[22]

As rendered by Shakespeare, Henry's speech at Agincourt is a towering, potent example of the genre, impressing upon us first that commanders address their troops prior to combat and suggesting to us, second, that they summon foremost the fighting motivation of fraternal love. In fact, the prominence of this topic stems from choices Shakespeare made while writing his play and choices we make when remembering it.

Shakespeare took considerable liberty with Holinshed's material when he crafted Henry's battle discourse. Holinshed recorded only one battle exhortation by Henry during his 1415 campaign in northern France. It took place at Agincourt, where a much larger and rested French force precipitated the battle by blocking the English's withdrawal to Calais. At the earlier siege of Harfleur, the primary English objective of the campaign, where the English prevailed but lost thousands to combat and illness, Holinshed's Henry was silent. Shakespeare took the one battle exhortation documented by Holinshed and created two, splitting it where Holinshed recorded an interruption by someone wishing for more English troops. Shakespeare then transported much of the essence of the historical Agincourt speech to Harfleur and invented an entirely new speech for Agincourt, still responding to the wish. It is this fabricated exhortation that we best remember, not the one more historically grounded. We also tend to remember the topic of fraternity more than the other within his Agincourt creation. Let us explore why.

The exhortation of Holinshed's (historical) Henry is truly a fighting speech. The king calls on his troops to behave "manfully," reminds them of the justice of their cause, and recalls that their ancestors regularly defeated this foe. Henry concludes, or rather first concludes, by portraying himself as a fierce fighting man, assuring his men that he shall neither be captured nor ransomed but shall gain fame either through victory or death. It is at this point that Holinshed's Henry overhears a wish for more English troops. To this muttering—an open recognition that the English are gravely outnumbered— Henry grows stern, long-winded, and makes an argument from what we might call "divine calculus." Referring to God five times, compared to his one reference earlier, he contends that the smaller his army the better. If it is lost, then England loses fewer men. If it prevails, then they cannot help but ascribe the victory to God's will and the justice of their cause. This half of Henry's exhortation is so effective, and French taunting (from the other end of plowed Agincourt farmland) so annoying, that Holinshed reported the king was interrupted by his host crying, "Forward, forward!"[23]

In his play Shakespeare preserves this belligerent mood for his exhortation at Harfleur:

> Once more unto the breach, dear friends, once more;
> Or close the wall up with our English dead!
> In peace there's nothing so becomes a man
> As modest stillness and humility;
> But when the blast of war blows in our ears,
> Then imitate the action of the tiger:
> Stiffen the sinews, conjure up the blood,
> Disguise fair nature with hard-favored rage;
> Then lend the eye a terrible aspect:
> Let it pry through the portage of the head
> Like the brass cannon; let the brow o'erwhelm it
> As fearfully as doth a gallèd rock
> O'erhang and jutty his confounded base,
> Swilled with the wild and wasteful ocean.
> Now set the teeth, and stretch the nostril wide,
> Hold hard the breath, and bend up every spirit
> To his full height! On, on, you noble English,
> Whose blood is fet from fathers of war-proof;
> Fathers that like so many Alexanders

Have in these parts from morn till even fought
And sheathed their swords for lack of argument.
Dishonor not your mothers; now attest
That those whom you called fathers did beget you!
Be copy now to men of grosser blood
And teach them how to war! And you, good yeomen,
Whose limbs were made in England, show us here
The mettle of your pasture. Let us swear
That you are worth your breeding; which I doubt not,
For there is none of you so mean and base
That hath not noble luster in your eyes.
I see you stand like greyhounds in the slips,
Straining upon the start. The game's afoot!
Follow your spirit; and upon this charge,
Cry, "God for Harry, England and Saint George!"[24]

Fiery and pious, this address is more faithful to the historical record than the one Shakespeare devises for Agincourt: Holinshed's Henry appealed to the troops "to play the men" and acquit themselves "manfully"; Shakespeare's Henry artfully appeals for the same thing (tigerlike fierceness). Holinshed's Henry remembered ancestral victories; Shakespeare's Henry makes much of being worthy of fathers proven in war. Shakespeare dresses up the historical record still further, his Henry identifying the troops with England and concluding with a bestial simile and battle cry.

And yet this is the less popular of Shakespeare's two battle exhortations. (Nor is it the one Draude read aloud in the Saudi desert.) Is its lesser prominence because Shakespeare was in any less command of his craft here? Does his vocabulary, syntax, or meter somehow falter? Hardly. Shakespeare intended to fire his audience in this brief scene, and one cannot read or witness it without being so moved. We must examine the Agincourt address, and compare it to the one above, to appreciate why the second address prevails.

At Agincourt, Shakespeare's exhortation departs entirely from Holinshed's, other than using the wish for more English troops as the point of departure:

What's he that wishes so?
My cousin Westmoreland? No, my fair cousin.
If we are marked to die, we are enow
To do our country loss; and if to live,
The fewer men, the greater share of honor.
God's will! I pray thee wish not one man more.

By Jove, I am not covetous for gold,
Nor care I who doth feed upon my cost;
It earns me not if men my garments wear;
Such outward things dwell not in my desires:
But if it be a sin to covet honor,
I am the most offending soul alive.
No, faith, my coz, wish not a man from England.
God's peace! I would not lose so great an honor
As one man more methinks would share from me
For the best hope I have. O, do not wish one more!
Rather proclaim it, Westmoreland, though my host,
That he which hath no stomach to this fight,
Let him depart; his passport shall be made,
And crowns for convoy put into his purse;
We would not die in that man's company
That fears his fellowship to die with us.
This day is called the Feast of Crispian;
He that outlives this day, and comes safe home,
Will stand a-tiptoe when this day is named,
And rouse him at the name of Crispian.
He that shall see this day, and live old age,
Will yearly on the vigil feast his neighbors
And say, "Tomorrow is Saint Crispian."
Then will he strip his sleeve and show his scars,
And say, "These wounds I had on Crispin's day."
Old men forget; yet all shall be forgot,
But he'll remember, with advantages,
What feats he did that day. Then shall our names,
Familiar in his mouth as household words—
Harry the K⸍   nd Exeter,
W⸍   ury and Gloucester—
b   ⸍hly rememb'red.
T⸍   ⸍n teach his son;
An⸍   ⸍e'er go by
Fro   of the world,
But   ⸍ered—
We f⸍   ⸍nd of brothers;
For h⸍   ⸍lood with me
Shall t   ⸍'er so vile,
This da   ⸍lition.

1.05

And gentlemen in England, now abed,
Shall think themselves accursed they were not here;
And hold their manhoods cheap whiles any speaks
That fought with us upon Saint Crispin's day.[25]

Dispensing with Holinshed's belligerent tone and his topics of just cause, past reputation, and divine calculus, Shakespeare spins a more sentimental yarn grounded entirely in future reputation and fraternity. Whereas Holinshed's Henry snapped at the wish for more troops, Shakespeare's Henry is tender, asking who has made the request, then gently correcting his "fair cousin" Westmoreland. Whereas Holinshed's Henry preferred fewer Englishmen to check human pride and minimize potential English loss, Shakespeare's Henry reasons contentedly, "The fewer men, the greater share of honor." Almost the entire rest of the theatrical speech relishes the honor and fame that comes from facing great odds. Henry even suggests to Westmoreland that rather than wishing for more men, his cousin should find the fainthearted in their midst and send them home (an unlikely historical prospect). Noting that the day happens to be the "Feast of Crispian," a remembrance of two martyred Christians, Henry then constructs a vivid future where the holiday has evolved into the cherished anniversary of what is about to occur on the field of battle. Yes, he explains confidently, our names, this story, "shall the good man teach his son," and soldiers that make it home "will stand a-tiptoe when this day is named." Then come the eight concluding lines, which encapsulate the vision of fame/honor with an appeal for fraternity:

Verse	Topic
We few, we happy few, we band of brothers;	Fraternity
For he today that sheds his blood with me	Fraternity
Shall be my brother; be he ne'er so vile,	Fraternity
This day shall gentle his condition.	Honor
And gentlemen in England, now abed,	Honor
Shall think themselves accursed they were not here;	Honor
And hold their manhoods cheap whiles any speaks	Honor
That fought with us upon Saint Crispin's day.	Fraternity

Less exclamatory and more sentimental than the verse at Harfleur, these eight lines are the best known from *Henry V.* Yet they represent but one-sixth of the Agincourt battle exhortation. Add the speech at Harfleur, and they represent but one-tenth of the battle exhortation in the play. How is it that this speech has come to epitomize battle exhortation? Because, I suggest, its blending of fraternity and fame is more consistent with our contemporary standards than are such concepts as ancestral performance and divine calculus.

Shakespeare's insertion of fame and fraternity into *Henry V*—for Holinshed's Henry employed neither topic—reflects a shift of powerful normative currents in Western society. When we note that upon Henry's return to London a month after Agincourt, victory singing proclaimed "Give thanks to God, England, for the victory," we ought to believe that Holinshed's pious Henry was close to the historical mark.[26] Writing almost two hundred years later, however, Shakespeare seemed to recognize that he could stir his audience at least as well with secular concerns. He did not do away with God. Shakespeare's Henry still prays before Agincourt: "O God of battles, steel my soldiers' hearts." To his men, his last words before the fight are "Now, soldiers, march away; And how thou pleasest, God, dispose the day!" When he learns the French have surrendered, he exclaims, "Praised be God, and not our strength for it!" But within the battle exhortation itself, the climax of the play, Shakespeare's Henry delivers forty-nine lines of verse with only two fleeting references to God. Shakespeare chose instead a speech about honor and fame with a fraternal tie at the end. When Henry then asks Westmoreland whether he still desires help from England, the now inspired cousin bawls, "God's will, my liege!" But it is as if Westmoreland has heard another speech or heard Holinshed's Henry rather than Shakespeare's. The celebrated speech does not submit to God's will but relies on honorable men fighting as brothers, a proposition much easier for us to accept today.

Similarly, Shakespeare's different treatment of reputation in his Harfleur and Agincourt exhortations probably contributes to the latter's popularity today. At Harfleur, Shakespeare's Henry inspires his troops by referring to the fame of their ancestors. In essence the speech reflects an older obsession with good breeding and birthright. At Agincourt, Shakespeare turns the concern for celebrity on its head, painting a future in which the troops themselves become renowned. This more closely aligns with our contemporary preference for self-made persons and our own sense of glory. Perhaps most powerfully, Shakespeare's forward-facing focus on honor aligns with the metamorphosis of medieval chivalry.

Earlier, chivalry had been characterized by the ideal of the knight-errant, the individual warrior with his own arms and coat of arms, roving the countryside to uphold justice and protect the weak. By Shakespeare's late sixteenth century, however, advances in military technology, tactics, and finance had driven the military aristocrat to become an officer and gentleman, the commander of a larger unit, fighting enemies of the state under the state's flag. Many traditions of medieval chivalry had disappeared. Jousting, for example, no longer reflected the techniques and equipment of the day. An obsession with honor remained, but its basis had become less entrenched in the past and individuality. Whereas proper heraldry and a fine suit of armor counted for much in centuries past, even masking the brutality of many knights, honorable repute had become more contingent upon one's conduct, and that within a more fraternal milieu.[27] This is precisely the normative shift that Shakespeare's Henry acknowledges and augments at Agincourt. Where he imitates the raw pugnacity of Holinshed's Henry, that battle exhortation, at Harfleur, is less fashionable.

One scholar fairly assesses Shakespeare's Agincourt exhortation in this way: "Harry covets honor in his heart and would have his soldiers do so with him; and this is his battle cry."[28] The first 80 percent of the speech concerns honorable conduct and its resultant fame. Even where fraternity is mentioned, in the exhortation's conclusion, only four of the last eight lines address it. And yet by introducing fraternity in this manner Shakespeare seems to apply worthy frosting to a rich cake. Much like Plutarch's Spartan mother, Shakespeare's Henry suggests that the repute of being a good brother is the epitome of battlefield glory. Face the odds with him, shed one's blood with him, and such courage shall "gentle" even the lowest combatant, ennobling him to the status of brother-in-arms with the king of England. This is the eloquent outcome of Shakespeare's craft, and it is not difficult to understand why Draude or the rest of us relish the "band of brothers" sentiment as opposed to the more prevalent references to honor. Put another way, desire for renown is a powerful combat incentive, but obsession with it can lead to hubris. (J. Huizinga points out that the conception of honor is "formalized pride.")[29] Similar to fighting for a just cause, in accordance with God's will, or because the ancestral record portends victory, fighting for reputation's sake is dangerous business. All battle appeals are either goods vulnerable to vice or necessary evils—save fraternity. Fraternity is the necessary good always. We can never love our brother too much, especially our brother in arms. The balder truth, the majority of the exhortation, may be that we wish to be *recognized* for our love, but Shakespeare enables us to savor the love itself.[30]

Ethos Matters: George C. Scott's Patton

There is subtlety in the previous two exemplars. At first hearing, the Spartan mother seems concerned with the national emblem or her son's individual gallantry. Initially Shakespeare's Henry V seems focused on battlefield glory.

Only through further investigation do we find both prizing the status forged when men at arms draw together. By contrast, there is nothing subtle about George C. Scott's portrayal of George S. Patton Jr. in the 1970 motion picture *Patton*. The battle exhortation of Scott's Patton is overwhelmingly about himself, the commander.

Historically the address of Scott's Patton is based on the series of exhortations that the actual general delivered to his Third Army on the eve of its employment in northern France. (The physical terrain covered by Henry V in 1415 would be plied by the Canadian First Army in World War II, not the U.S. Third.) In fact, the makers of *Patton* went to considerable effort to render an informed portrayal of the general during the period March 1943 to September 1945. They drew heavily from Ladislas Farago's biography *Patton: Ordeal and Triumph* and employed as consultants Omar Bradley, once Patton's junior, peer, and senior, and Paul Harkins, Patton's deputy chief of staff and annotator of his *War as I Knew It*. Neither the producers nor viewers could regard the movie with the same relative detachment from history as they might Plutarch's Spartan mother or Shakespeare's Henry V, because the historical Patton is more familiar. We have photographic images of the man, commentary from close associates, Patton's own writing, and numerous biographies. Anyone with sufficient interest to watch the movie would know that Patton led American GIs in World War II, and did so with panache. Such basic historical understanding is context for the movie, and we cannot escape it. At the same time, the majority of Americans are acquainted with Patton primarily through Scott's Oscar-winning portrayal of him. (The film won seven Academy Awards in all.) Moreover, Patton's opening battle exhortation is the most famous scene in the film.

There are two significant qualities to the motion picture rendition. First, it is remarkably accurate historically. If one is familiar with what the editor of *The Patton Papers*, Martin Blumenson, calls Patton's "famous speech to the troops," or what biographer Carlo D'Este simply terms "The Speech,"[31] one cannot help but be impressed by how faithfully Patton's words are woven into Scott's script by screenwriters Francis Ford Coppola and Edmund North. Although Farago's biography (in a sense, the "Holinshed" of *Patton*) does not include the speech, the movie's makers did not need to go far for renderings, because there are many. The trouble is their variability. In May 1944 the general delivered his exhortation repeatedly, visiting many units of his Third Army. Because he spoke extemporaneously, there is no prepared text among his papers, so every recorded version varies somewhat.[32] Even had Patton used a manuscript, there would likely be multiple versions recorded, because, as one regimental commander put it, Patton's discourse was "so fantastic that the best of us could not give a good report of just what was said."[33] Thus the second feature of the movie rendition, especially from a socializing perspective, is its fixed text. Scott's performance minimizes differences in historical versions, inserts a few dictums Patton used elsewhere, and provides us a single, reasonable, memorable account.

Before examining this exemplar closely, it is useful to take stock of some more rhetorical theory. Aristotle found rhetoric to have three fundamental means of persuasion: logos, pathos, and ethos. Put simply, he believed that orators persuaded audiences to belief and action by engaging their rational sense, their emotional sense, and their sense that the speaker could be trusted. He thought the orator must do reasonable justice to all three means. In Aristotle's words: "The orator must not only try to make the argument of his speech demonstrative and worthy of belief [through logos]; he must also make his own character look right [ethos] and put his hearers, who are to decide, into the right frame of mind [pathos]."[34] Wayne Booth helps us appreciate the importance of that proper balance by tracing the problems of unbalanced discourse. Too much logos, or nearly exclusive attention to subject matter, and a rhetorical audience is likely to be bored by pedantry. Such discourse may be appropriate within a scientific community, where instruction is the end, but within the realm of practical human affairs it is unlikely to sway voters, jurors, or troops. Similarly, too much pathos or pandering to the audience's appetites and the audience may grow suspicious, as if facing slick advertising. Commercials sell merchandise, but risk and sacrifice require something more. Too much ethos or personality and the audience may be charmed but left unpersuaded, unwilling to do more than enjoy the presence of their host.[35]

We need only this basic understanding to recognize that the *ethos* of Scott's Patton in the opening scene of the movie is over the top. We, the cinematic audience, sitting where a supposed army of soldiers would, face an outsized and perfectly displayed American flag. We are apparently on our own time, because we hear the low-grade din of hundreds of soldiers talking among us, but suddenly we are called to attention. Now we are on someone else's time, and we wait silently, anticipating an entrance. Scott's Patton comes into view, ascending steps and striding front and center. He shares the stage with no one: no invocation-delivering chaplain; no division or corps commander. Initially Patton is dwarfed by the flag, but only momentarily. As the general brings himself to attention and renders a salute, "To the Colors" is sounded by a bugle offstage. This provides us our first opportunity to soak up the details of his person, for while the bugle sounds and the general holds his salute, the camera bears in on different quadrants of him. We see manly rings on muscular fingers; a riding crop and gloves clenched tightly in the general's non-saluting hand; medals, sashes, and a host of other decorations; a sidearm with the initials *GSP* on its ivory handle; and the Army rank of three stars. Here is a man of significant grade in full, personalized regalia, a curious mix of riding boots and britches, dress uniform, and steel helmet. He holds us, figuratively, at attention and wraps himself, figuratively, in the flag. Before we can come to our own conclusions about this spectacle, the general puts us in our seats and starts supplying his conclusions.

Part of the reason Patton's ethos explodes from the screen is because he is presented without a cinematic introduction. In truth this entrance is not too far from how the real general materialized before his men. A young enlisted eyewitness wrote home how Patton stood "three steps above us . . . and when the drum, ruffles, and bugles sounded the General's March, we stood transfixed upon his appearance . . . that towering figure impeccably attired." A young officer wrote about doors being "thrown open" and "a strange officer" walking out in a "performance" probably "carefully staged."[36] Still, there was always the backdrop of looming combat. In our case, without preceding frames, without clues about date or location (in other words, without pressing need, observable audience, or perceptible environmental factors), there is no immediate context for this man and his message. As the film progresses, we grow accustomed to Patton's outrageousness—his contention to General Bradley, for instance, that "two thousand years ago, I was here," or his telling a Russian general through an interpreter that "I do not care to drink with him or any other Russian son of bitch." So too we come to realize that a chronological time line would place the battle exhortation almost exactly in the middle of the film. Presented out of temporal frame, however, Patton's grand, profane, unapologetic speech astounds:

Now I want you to remember that no bastard ever won a war by dying for his country. He won it by making the other poor dumb bastard die for his country.

Men, all this stuff you've heard about America not wanting to fight, wanting to stay out of the war, is a lot of horse dung. Americans, traditionally, love to fight. All real Americans love the sting of battle.

When you were kids, you all admired the champion marble shooter, the fastest runner, the big league ball players, the toughest boxers. Americans love a winner and will not tolerate a loser. Americans play to win all the time. I wouldn't give a hoot in hell for a man who lost and laughed. That's why Americans have never lost and will never lose a war. Because the very thought of losing is hateful to Americans.

Now, an army is a team. It lives, eats, sleeps, fights as a team. This individuality stuff is a bunch of crap. The bilious bastards who wrote that stuff about individuality for the *Saturday Evening Post* don't know anything more about real battle than they do about fornicating.

Now we have the finest food and equipment, the best spirit, and the best men in the world. You know, by God I actually pity those poor bastards we're going up against. By God, I do. We're not just going to shoot the bastards. We're going to cut out their living guts and use them to grease the treads of our tanks. We're going to murder those lousy Hun bastards by the bushel.

Now, some of you boys, I know, are wondering whether or not you'll chicken-out under fire. Don't worry about it. I can assure you that you will all do your duty. The Nazis are the enemy. *Wade* into them. Spill *their* blood. Shoot *them* in the belly. When you put your *hand* into a bunch of *goo* that a moment before was your best friend's *face,* you'll know what to do.

Now there's another thing I want you to remember. I don't want to get any messages saying that we are holding our position. We're not holding anything. Let the Hun do that. We are advancing constantly and we're not interested in holding onto anything—except the enemy. We're going to hold onto him by the nose, and we're going to kick him in the ass. We're going to kick the hell out of him all the time, and we're going to go through him like crap through a goose!

Now, there's one thing that you men will be able to say when you get back home, and you may thank God for it. Thirty years from now, when you're sitting around your fireside with your grandson on your knee and he asks you, What did you do in the great World War II, you won't have to say, "Well, I shoveled shit in Louisiana."

All right, now you sons-of-bitches, you know how I feel.

Oh. I will be proud to lead you wonderful guys into battle anytime, anywhere.

That's all.[37]

Patton's presentation is not devoid of logos and pathos. It is just that he reasons and emotes so distinctively that they are part and parcel of his ethos. From a rational perspective, for example, we know that effective battle exhortation supplies intellectually good reasons to fight, despite the dangers of death, injury, capture, failure, embarrassment, and so forth. Patton supplies reasons to fight, but his reasoning is so spectacular—for example, "When you put your *hand* into a bunch of *goo* that a moment before was your best friend's *face* . . ."—that it has more to do with him than with the listening soldier. Moreover, every reason for fighting is straddled by a statement of method, instruction in Patton's signature doctrine of advance, attack, disrupt. Presumably he is exaggerating when he explains the enemy will not only be shot but used "to grease the treads of our tanks," but it is remarkable just how bellicose he seems. What if the American soldier becomes fainthearted from shellfire? Shake it off and start killing. When is defense acceptable? Never. Fix the enemy ("hold onto him by the nose") and maneuver to his flank or rear ("kick him in the ass"). Such tactical doctrine is not unique to Patton, but the impetuousness with which he expresses (and practices) it is. Patton's experience, like Montecuccoli's, had taught him that timidity cost more lives than it saved. In letters of instruction to his commanders, he explained such lifesaving logic. Exhorting the rank and file, however, Patton presupposes "that you will all do your duty" and concentrates instead on what that duty looks like. In his mind this audience does not require careful argument to overcome reservations. Trained and equipped, it need only hear the dynamic intent of the commanding general.

The emotional response of a rhetorical audience is often shaped by the style and delivery of discourse. We question the sincerity of an apology if the apologizer does not look us in the eye. We more quickly give our confidence to the police officer who is dressed crisply and speaks in measured tones. Typically the key to putting an audience in what Aristotle called "the right frame of mind" is appropriateness—respect for the constraints of the occasion, audience, and speaker—but Patton aims beyond the appropriate. In dress, although Patton is a modern, even pioneering mechanized warrior, he is dressed in the part of a cavalryman. Cynics might think the old man cannot let go of a beloved, obsolete form of warfare, but the outfit is of deliberate design. That it is characterized from the waist down by equestrian fashion is not so important as that it is distinctive, even from other general-grade officers. For Patton strongly believed that troops take heart from the presence of their general on the battlefield, and a general who adheres to a single, distinct type of dress is readily recognized.[38] In speech, Patton breaks almost all of the rules for a high-ranking officer, from whom decorum and reserve is expected. He demonstrates a mastery of what traditionally would be regarded graces of language, but he corrupts them with profanity, pigheadedness, and a joy of killing. Take alliteration, where the initial consonant of adjacent words is repeated. Patton employs it when he says, "I wouldn't give a hoot in hell for a man who lost and laughed," but consider the subject matter: it is another case of the general summarily dismissing someone who does not see the world as he does. The general's syntax is nuanced, but his way of thinking is not. In his remarks about advancing rather than holding, he employs anaphora, stringing the phrase "we're going to" across the beginning of four successive clauses. Raising his voice, gesturing with his riding crop, and taking an oblique step forward with every clause reinforces the aggressiveness. General Bradley thought this bombastic style might be an attempt by Patton to compensate for "a voice that was almost comically squeaky and high-pitched."[39] That Scott renders Patton in a deep, guttural voice makes the character that much more domineering, as does his alternating between softer tones and bellowed fire. One moment he seems to be sharing a secret of war, as a father might with sons. The next he is shouting obscenities and orders, as if an angry drill instructor facing recruits. It is a mercurial, mesmerizing show.

One soldier who witnessed a real Patton performance spoke of being "transfixed" by the "hypnotizing" presentation.[40] An observer of Scott's rendition cannot help but feel some of that, and the soldier's choice of words is telling. To be hypnotized is to be psychologically captivated by a stimulus so fantastic or monotonous that competing stimuli melt away. The hypnotized can then be induced to follow instructions or endure conditions they might otherwise not. Patton's dominating ethos serves the same purpose as a pocket watch swinging on a chain. While Booth warns that ethos-dominant discourse can leave an audience entertained but unmoved, the problem does not seem to apply in Patton's case. History testifies that his men would follow him, even once the fog of war rolled in.

Why? Patton is not unmindful of his audience. While he dramatically develops his own ethos, he also addresses the reputation of his men. Like Shakespeare's Henry V and Plutarch's Spartan mother, Patton recognizes that part of the appeal of being a soldier is enjoying a soldier's reputation, the repute of admirable conduct in the face of adversity, of being part of something larger than oneself. But naturally there is the Patton twist. "Thirty years from now," he explains in his extraordinary treatment of future celebrity, ". . . you won't have to say, 'Well, I shoveled shit in Louisiana.'" How different in style but similar in vein is this to Shakespeare's Henry V foreseeing his veteran's boast: "These wounds I had on Crispin's day." It can offend, not least those from farms and Louisiana, but it also secures a fundamental concern for significance and honor. If troops are nervous about the coming combat, at least it will save them from the scorn of missing the action.

Patton provides an abbreviated version of the historical battle exhortation. Although the general opted himself for shorter speeches to foster his energetic persona, Hollywood condenses things further to suit the tastes of a cinematic audience. Moreover, the opening scene of the film serves to hook the audience rather than develop Patton at length. The rest of the three-hour picture does that. So the exhortation of Scott's Patton takes only five minutes and drops discussions about the relevance of drill, the secrecy of Patton's command of the Third Army, and his wanting to get on to Japan. One topic still included, but dramatically abbreviated, is Patton's treatment of comradeship.

Neither the historical Patton nor Scott's Patton mention the words *brother* or *brotherhood*. In both cases Patton's metaphor for the fellowship of soldiers is the "team." The historical Patton greatly emphasized teamwork, devoting more than 25 percent of his exhortation to the topic. Through it he made the point that a modern army requires first-rate performance from a host of specialties. This is why he took exception with the *Saturday Evening Post*. To correct the record, Patton conducted a colorful roll call of contributors. There was the truck driver, who stayed behind the wheel even as shells rained in about him; the ordinance man, who kept the guns supplied with ammunition; the quartermaster, who brought up food and clothes; and the kitchen soldier, who boiled the water to prevent diarrhea. "Even the chaplain is important, for if we get killed and he isn't there to bury us, we would all go to hell."[41] Elsewhere within his exhortation the historical Patton elaborated with detailed vignettes: one about a communicator fixing wire at the top of a telephone pole amid murderous fire; another of a lieutenant fighting a German with nothing more than his helmet; a third of "magnificent" truck drivers driving forty consecutive hours. For all of his tough talk about killing, Patton's historical roll call and vignettes featured support roles. (Only the lieutenant kills somebody.) By contrast, Scott's Patton makes only passing reference to this discussion. He notes that "an army . . . lives, eats, sleeps, fights as a team," but that is as far as he goes, quickly segueing to his abuse of the *Post*.

Why is this material about teamwork absent from the film? It probably does not make the cut for inclusion for several reasons. First, a team of specialized, interdependent professionals cut from the same basic cloth (GI-issue) does not stir the heart like a "band of brothers." It is the nuts and bolts of modern warfare, resistant to adventure or romance. Second, in an abbreviated cinematic production that has to make choices, removing teamwork leaves room for more extreme metaphors (for example, wading into the enemy) that more dramatically portray Patton's fighting spirit. Third, by removing the roll call and the vignettes, writers eliminate characters that might distract from Patton himself. Similar to having no one else on the rostrum

and no rousing music in the background, the opening scene of the film is all
—and exclusively—commanding general.[42]

Why does Patton speak in terms of the team rather than brotherhood? As
mentioned earlier, his allusion to his audience's experience as sports- and
game-loving Americans seems an astute rhetorical choice. His unbloodied
audience might not yet be moved by appeals to combat comradeship, but all
could identify with athletics. Without digressing into psychological analysis,
we may also note that Patton probably knew more about sports than brotherhood. Throughout his youth, military training, and significantly into his
career, he was an avid sportsman, even an Olympian. In contrast to this ath-
leticism, Patton did not have a biological brother, and he had few close friends.
An aristocratic upbringing, a smothering aunt, and the social challenges of
dyslexia all combined to make him a relative loner. Even within his beloved
sports, he excelled more in individual than in team contests.[43]

If, loosely speaking, ethos amounts to reputation, Scott's Patton carefully
manages the play between his own and his troops'. On the one hand, his personalized uniform, rank, and grandstanding establish him as a senior officer
far removed from the experience of other men. This distance is developed
over the course of the film, as the general sleeps in chateaus, travels with his
own dog (Willie, the bull terrier), and slaps a shell-shocked soldier, whom he
regards as a malingerer. Throughout, the supporting cast seems to marvel at
how spectacularly different Patton is from the rest of them. On the other
hand, Patton's exhortation addresses issues pertinent to the combat uninitiated, and he speaks in coarse, enlisted terms. He is not selling apple pie, as
some generals are wont to do, but speaking candidly about unpleasant, necessary business. This lack of political correctness would count for much
among those experiencing the harsh realities of army life and anticipating the
fearsome realities of combat. For these reasons the troops can identify with
and appreciate him.

Patton's difference or distance is accentuated by the frame that producers
of *Patton* put around the opening speech. At the start, while Patton holds his
salute "To the Colors," we notice that the general is surveying his audience.
His facial expression is so severe that it borders on scorn. Then, once he puts
his audience in its seats, he opens unkindly: "Now I want you to remember
that no bastard ever won a war by dying for his country. He won it by making the other poor dumb bastard die for his." Only after this insinuation that
we, the troops, are poor dumb bastards does Patton refer to us more endear-
ingly as "men" and start reminding us of our childhood heroes. Similarly, at
the very end of the speech, after forceful explanation of method and colorful

assurance that there will be something to tell the grandchildren, the general exclaims—seemingly caught up in his own harangue—"All right, now you sons of bitches, you know how I feel." But with this he catches himself. His eyes flit down, and as they come back up, he says, "Oh." Recasting in more fashionable language, he closes again: "I will be proud to lead you wonderful guys into battle anytime, anywhere." As he begins to turn away, however, it is clear that he still regards the audience as sons of bitches. Indicating "That's all," he keeps his eyes on the audience just a moment longer, and the look is unmistakably that of contempt. In Sir Walter Scott's *Ivanhoe*, there is a scene where the heroic Black Knight and the villainous Maurice de Bracy exhort their respective followers about the flame-engulfed castle. The Black Knight (actually Richard the Lion-Heart) addresses his men as "friends" and asks them to "follow me boldly across," while De Bracy chides, "Dogs! . . . Let despair give you courage or let me forward."[44] Scott's Patton manages to play both roles in a single speech.

Is such derisiveness a fair representation of the historical speech-act? Perhaps. Many in Patton's large audiences would not have been able to see the subtleties about his eyes, but at least a couple recognized the general "looking them over and at first saying nothing" or surveying them "grimly." None of the historical recordings of the speech include the opening comment about poor dumb bastards, but in his diary Patton does remember, "I tell them that it is fine to be willing to die for their country but a damned sight better to make the German die for his."[45] More significantly from a conditioning perspective, the movie audience of Scott's Patton must come to terms with this frame of contempt. Some might find it proof that Patton has little respect or concern for those under his command, that they are simply a means to an end for him. From this perspective, Patton is a psychopath addicted to war and war glory, who speaks to troops only to better manage the cannon fodder. (A scene toward the end of the film reinforces this interpretation. Having been relieved of command for impolitic comments to the press, Patton struggles to bid his staff officers goodbye. Once again it is only as an afterthought that he pays homage to the "privilege" of command.) Others viewers, however, may interpret particularly the insincere, self-correcting "oh" at the conclusion of the opening speech as further reason to embrace Patton's warrior ethos. Coming at the end of a frank talk about what it takes to win at war, a more polite idiom simply rings hollow. Reference to leading "wonderful guys" into battle offers no prescriptions for survival and success against the murderous Nazis. Only determined "sons of bitches" driven by a master SOB are likely to prevail.

Bill Murray's Parody in *Stripes*

Before considering a parody of battle exhortation, let us review what we know about its genuine common topics. Among the students of battle exhortation surveyed in chapter 1, the most experienced soldier, Montecuccoli, best recognized the multiple dimensions of the genre. He recommended to the battle captain flamboyant dress, wit, and the occasional sword-wielding example so that troops gained confidence from his character. He advocated the display of national symbols, the coining of heartening passwords, and even the allocation of alcohol because of their emotional boost. First and foremost, however, Montecuccoli enumerated arguments that "can incite soldiers to fight well." These discursive reasons for pulling together and fighting are the most obvious feature of battle exhortation, particularly when we witness the exhortation through text alone, where nonverbal subtleties are lost. These are what sometimes bother more contemporary observers, because the topics can sound stilted, the work of romantic historians. But we are beyond such concerns for historical accuracy, understanding that discourse from fictional, analogical (for example, athletic), and bona fide battlefields inform one another. Real or figurative, battle exhortation has a conventional repertoire of moves, similar to any recurrent situation.

The table below catalogs nearly two dozen topics of battle exhortation, consolidating four lists found elsewhere and adding two topics: "Get it over with" and "proper authority." "Get it over with" has probably not been identified previously for a number of reasons. It is not a particularly glorious or dramatic appeal, so it may tend to be eclipsed by more memorable topics or ones that better lend themselves to theater. It may also fail to be articulated as often as it should be, because officers undervalue its appeal. (In a War Department study of World War II combat incentives, enlisted veterans identified "ending the task" almost three times more often than any other incentive, while officers thought it fourth most important in keeping their men fighting.)[46] Yet "getting it over with" is readily observed in the slogan "The shortest route home is through" Berlin, Tokyo, or Baghdad. Reference to "proper authority" is discussed in chapter 4. The point here is that we have a catalog of topics uttered with some frequency. They are not the only topics raised in battle exhortation but are the more common ones.

When trying to understand a phenomenon, examining its parody offers several advantages. First, parody confirms the existence of the very thing being made fun of. By definition a parody is an artistic work that imitates the characteristic or conventional form of some other work but in a humorous

Common topics within battle exhortation

Topic	Elaboration
Auspices favorable	Oracles or signs make it evident that God will help us.
Commander	The commander is competent, superior, or beloved.
Consequences of defeat	The consequences of defeat preclude failure as an option.
Death is a release	Should we die, it will end our suffering, sinful nature, etc.
Death is glorious	Should we die, a glorious death is preferable to shameful survival. Martyrdom.
Defense	Defend yourself, your buddies, outfit, family, property, country, or God. Duty demands or love requires it.
Dismiss the danger	This threat is easily overcome (often delivered as a quip).
Do not dismiss the danger	Be careful and not overconfident.
Enemy	Evils of this enemy warrant our challenge or revenge.
Flight invites destruction	Standing and fighting increases the odds of survival.
Follow	Follow me, my example, or my plan.
Force comparison	A comparison of forces proves that we have the advantage (not always in numbers or material but in valor, virtue).
Get it over with	The shortest route home is through this fight.
Here, now	Here is the battle we have sought.
Just cause	Our cause is just, be it national, ideological, religious, etc.
Magnitude of the occasion	We should contribute, given the stakes, others' effort, etc.
Previous loss does not apply	This time we are not handicapped as we were last time.
Proper authority	Combat has been authorized by the proper authority.

Common topics within battle exhortation (*continued*)

Topic	Elaboration
Punishment	There will be punishment for those who fail to do their duty.
Reputation, fame, honor—*future*	At stake is one's future standing as a man, country man, brother in arms, or passer of "the test."
Reputation, fame, honor—*past*	Past personal or ancestral conduct portends victory (sometimes considers win-loss record with this enemy).
Reward	To the victor goes the spoils, commendation, and other rewards.
Unit is ready	We are well prepared for this fight.

Note: This table includes but is not limited to topics identified by Bliese, "Rhetoric and Morale," 220; Burgess, *Epideictic Literature,* 212–13; Pritchett, "The General's Exhortations in Greek Warfare," 102–5; and Montecuccoli, "Concerning Battle," 130–36.

way, exaggerating it or applying it to unconventional circumstances. Had we not at least a basic understanding of the characteristic form, we would not recognize the parody's hyperbole or incongruity, which makes us laugh. That comedic battle exhortation exists popularly proves that the majority of Americans, not merely veterans, are exposed to the rhetoric of combat leadership and grow sufficiently familiar with it that they recognize gag versions. A second advantage to considering a phenomenon through the parody it inspires is that mocking vehicles are impious, reminding us how our object of study can be regarded by others. Being mindful of "not x" or "ridiculous x" can enlighten what otherwise might be a moral blind spot in the "x" student's field of view. In the case of battle exhortation we should not lose sight of the fact that such discourse can produce—in additionon to goods such as teamwork and selflessness—vices such as chauvinism and harm. A third advantage to considering a type of discourse this way is that it can be fun.

Quite a few examples are available: the sequential, contradictory exhortations of Sergeant Croft and Lieutenant Hearn in Mailer's *The Naked and the Dead;* the combined, figurative exhortation of John Belushi and Tim Matheson in *National Lampoon's Animal House;* and the Animals' antiwar song "Sky Pilot," to name a few.[47] Here we pursue the caricature within the 1981 motion picture *Stripes,* starring Bill Murray. It is the work of a well-known artist, and it mischievously overturns a third of battle exhortation's common topics.

The scene that prompts Murray's battle exhortation in *Stripes* is this: John Winger's (Murray's) recruit platoon is the unit that basic-training company commander Captain Stillman (John Larroquette) has come to hate. After the platoon's most recent transgression during liberty, the captain threatens to have the men repeat basic training should they disrupt the graduation parade the next day. Winger and his friend Russell Ziskey (Harold Ramis) return to the barracks later that night, after antics of their own, and learn of the situation. They find the rest of the platoon thoroughly demoralized, having practiced manual of arms and drill much of the night without improvement. So Winger and Ziskey bring the platoon to the motor-pool Quonset hut to practice further. Ziskey tries leading first but fares poorly. At one point he says, "Come on, rhythm. Hut, two, three, four. Black guys, help the white guys," and a brawl ensues. Winger breaks it up and then, with the unit on the brink of dissolution, offers the following counter-exhortation:

> We're all very different people. We're not Watusi. We're not Spartans. We're *Americans,* with a capital *A,* huh? Do you know what that means? Do ya? That means that our forefathers were kicked out of every decent country in the world. We are the wretched refuse. We're the underdog. We're mutts! Here's proof. [He touches a comrade's nose.] His nose is cold. But there is no animal that's more faithful, that's more loyal, more loveable than the mutt. Who saw *Old Yeller*? Who cried when Old Yeller got shot at the end? Nobody cried when Old Yeller got shot? I'm sure.

Winger raises his hand, then others go up. When he concedes, "I cried my eyes out," more hands are raised and there are mumbles of concurrence.

> So we're all dog faces. We're all very, very different. But there is one thing that we all have in common. We were all stupid enough to enlist in the Army. We're mutants. There's something wrong with us, something very, very wrong with us, something seriously wrong with us. We're soldiers. But we're *American* soldiers. We've been kicking ass for two hundred years. We're ten and one.
>
> Now we don't have to worry about whether or not we've practiced. We don't have to worry about whether Captain Stillman wants to have us hung. All we have to do is to be the great American fighting soldier that is inside each one us. Now do what I do . . . and say what I say . . . and make me proud.[48]

With this Winger commands, "Fall in!," the platoon responds with a concerted "Yeah!," and he begins leading an inspired session of practice. We do not see it but witness its result, once the platoon reaches the graduation parade just in time. The platoon's routine is slick and most unorthodox.

When we ask ourselves why this speech is funny, and filter out Murray's delivery (what the *New York Times* calls "a sardonically exaggerated calm"), we find that the script violates every battle exhortation topic it addresses. Certainly its first and main topic is past reputation, typically the recognition of previous renown on the part of the audience or the audience's ancestors. It is commonplace, particularly in older exhortations. For instance, Shakespeare's Henry V wields it at Harfleur: "On, on, you noble English, / Whose blood is fet from fathers of war-proof; / Fathers that like so many Alexanders / Have in these parts from morn till even fought / And sheathed their swords for lack of argument." One of many treatments within Thucydides' *History of the Peloponnesian War* finds the Athenian general Nicias entreating "those who had an established and brilliant reputation not to betray that reputation now, and those whose ancestors were famous men not to deface the great deeds of their forebears."[49] Now a logician or military historian might challenge whether the combat performance of previous generations is predictive of future performance and therefore a good reason to fight, but Murray's Winger challenges the topic in another way. He denies for himself and his comrades any relation to warriors. They are instead descendants of the "wretched refuse" that was deposited at the foot of the Statue of Liberty. The idea of "the underdog" permits him to segue not only to a dog metaphor but to that of a mongrel dog, warming the platoon to the idea that it is a collection of sensitive, poorly bred strays.

After developing this wry treatment of past reputation, the speech shifts to the topic of future reputation, typically as a fighter, brother, man, countryman, or passer of "the test." Probably the most common topic of all, it is why Spartans must return with their shields and why Shakespeare's Henry V rejects the idea of reinforcements. The historical Patton made much of this. His roll call of contributors and vignettes of honor aimed to inspire comparable feats from soldiers desiring comparable reputations. He half-seriously worried about the Marines getting all the credit in the Pacific. Both the historical Patton and his cinematic double imply that it is more desirable to face the perils of combat than to shovel manure back home because one promises celebrity and the other, disgrace. In Patton's case, because of the seriousness of his profession, such wit sometimes produced scandal. By contrast the comedy of Murray's Winger allows him to plunge headlong into the assertion that choosing to soldier is wrong, stupid, even freakishly original. Beyond mutts, which resemble their parents, Winger and his comrades are *mutants*, decidedly new and different from their parents. No sooner has he denigrated their prospects, however, than he circles back to take some pride in ancestry. They are, at least, American soldiers, and American soldiers have been "kicking ass for two hundred years." With a national record of "ten and one," the platoon just might amount to something.

Rhetorical topics can intermingle, and they do so here in several instances. In citing America's record of victories and losses, Winger is not only referring to past reputation but implying, as another conventional topic does, that a recent loss or setback is of no consequence. Of course the record actually has no bearing on the fate of this still ungraduated mob. Citing the record draws more attention to America's loss than to its wins, particularly six years after the fall of Saigon. But this is part of what's comical. Winger bumbles into several other topics when he says the platoon need not "worry about whether Captain Stillman wants to have us hung": the prospect of punishment for poor performance; vilification of the enemy; the commander is competent or beloved; even magnitude of the occasion. Because the commander is also the enemy and he threatens official punishment, Winger is able to dismiss this host of potential fears in a single sentence. Combined with the preceding sentence about not needing practice (which undermines the conventional topic that the unit is competent and ready), Winger deliberately diminishes the crisis.

Quantifying the consequences of combat is a delicate rhetorical matter. On the one hand, troops need to appreciate that something serious is afoot, something that requires their best effort. We see this in Richard Tregaskis's *Guadalcanal Diary* through Colonel Hunt's mimeographed exhortation: "The coming offensive in the Guadalcanal area marks the first offensive of the war against the enemy involving ground forces of the United States." It is also evident in the motion picture *Gladiator* when Roman general Maximus (Russell Crowe) reminds his cavalrymen, "What we do in life echoes in eternity." On the other hand, if too much is made of the moment, the stakes and responsibility might overwhelm the audience. Hence the value of the battlefield quip and why Maximus counterbalances his warning with humor: "If you find yourself alone riding in green fields with the sun on your face, do not be troubled, for you are in [Paradise], and you're already dead!"[50] In the case of *Stripes*, there are no serious stakes, but Winger manages them just the same. He diminishes practice, punishment, ancestry—but he stops short of discounting everything.

In his conclusion Winger abruptly shifts from the preposterous to the reasonable. When he alludes to future reputation here, it is with some gravity, suggesting that all the members of the platoon really need to do is live up to the ideal American soldier within each one of them. Then, dispensing with his jocular tone, he closes with slow and sober instruction: "Now do what I do . . . and say what I say . . . and make me proud." With this, the exhortation is set right. Troop reputation suddenly matters. Leadership suddenly matters. Affection by and for Winger, the de facto commander, suddenly matters. Shared risk, so important to authentic battle exhortation, emerges. There *are* reasons to pull together and best the threat. Moments before a brawling mob, the platoon responds.

Had the screenwriters wished, they could have continued the parody right to the end of the scene. The response to Winger's exhortation might have been cynical silence, laughter, or the sound of someone passing gas. But responses such as these would undermine his leadership, comedic as it is. Moreover, the successful (albeit unorthodox) performance of the platoon in the following scene would be difficult to explain. So instead, the suddenly reasonable exhortation is followed by the decidedly traditional reply. When Winger utters the command "Fall in!," platoon members shout "Yeah!," consistent with Montecuccoli's observation, "When the senior officers have finished with their utterances, the multitude replies by clamoring 'yea' in unison."[51] What can we say about such a response? First, it is not particularly cerebral, as was the grudging participation in Winger's poll about Old Yeller. It is spontaneous, visceral. Second, it contains elements of interactive, lateral, and self-exhortation. For in this response, troops hearten (1) their commander, by assuring him that his appeal has not been in vain, (2) each other, by demonstrating mutual commitment, and (3) themselves, by participating in the ritual. Outcry rattles larynx and viscera, loosening inhibitions that might otherwise interfere with the work at hand. Outcry envelops the group and seals its union. Were the enemy (Captain Stillman) present, he might be intimidated by such verve and singularity of purpose. The shouted cry of approbation is a fitting close to a spoof turned genuine article.

Summary

In this chapter we have considered the conditioning influence of general culture on nonmilitary and premilitary audiences. Americans are, because of our dominant institutions, a competitive or combative people. We are also, because of the way our contests tend to read or play out (very often involving teams), a people accustomed to battle exhortation. We recognize this type of speech, expect it, and are familiar with its conventions.

Through dictums such as that of Plutarch's Spartan mother, or narratives such as the Agincourt speech in Shakespeare's *Henry V,* we come to value not only the tactical advantage of fraternity but the reputation or standing for doing so. Through cinematic depictions such as George C. Scott's opening address in *Patton,* we come to appreciate the central role of the commander. Through parodies such as Bill Murray's in *Stripes,* we realize just how pervasive our socialization into battle exhortation is. If these exemplars represent our indoctrination, it is time to move to the front line. As Patton observed, "Battle is much more exigent than football."[52]

3

Tensions

Certain tensions are necessary for battlefield enterprise. They are tonics within a difficult environment that otherwise can leave military units to disintegrate, revolt, rampage, or sit idly by. These tensions are not synonymous with the many indoctrinating topics we observed in the previous chapter, although topics contribute to them. Neither do these tensions characterize the pressing need that prompts battle exhortation (the need to be braced for combat), because they are means to that end. These tensions are distinctive because, though instituted by the establishment, they are particularly susceptible to the exhorter's personal style, personal character, and understanding of troop psychology.

Rhetorical management of these tensions is the subject of this chapter. For clarity's sake I examine each separately, starting with the foremost and that which most involves release: reputation. The others have to do with the careful maintenance of tension: The distance between troops and commander, for instance, must be preserved but not overextended. Troops must be violent on the battlefield but not berserk. There is even the potential for love of the commander, if the commander balances certain responsibilities.

Managing Reputation: George Washington versus Daniel Morgan

An obvious tension on the battlefield would seem to be courage, in other words, whether an individual will carry out his duty despite his fear. If war was fought without an audience—without comrades, seniors, juniors, home front, or enemy—this tension would primarily be a matter of conscience. But because war is a communal affair, the more fundamental issue is a matter of reputation, whether one's degree of courage will merit honor or dishonor, fame or shame. Ardant Du Picq observed that of all the combat incentives on the battlefield, "self-esteem is unquestionably one of the most powerful," for troops "do not wish to pass for cowards in the eyes of their comrades." Bewildered figures on the battlefield "have no longer the eyes of their comrades or of their commander upon them, sustaining them."[1] Many agree with this observation, that one's reputation is perhaps the master tension experienced by the combat soldier. John Bliese finds it first among the appeals recorded in medieval chronicles. Shakespeare's Henry V obsesses over it, although he enwraps it pleasingly with fraternity. Indeed, while some armies have marched especially for booty, and others especially because of physical coercion, all armies have marched for the sake of reputation. Even the soldier unconcerned about national interest is concerned about how he is regarded by someone: a sweetheart, a parent, or immediate peers. And the first means by which such persons embrace or reject the soldier is by offering or withholding respect. "The satisfaction we derive from being connected to others," notes Francis Fukuyama, ". . . grows out of a fundamental human desire for recognition."[2] This affects every combatant at some level. Most formally, the recognition sought is for chivalrous virtue (martial, manly, at least somewhat sacrificial), but it includes or can be eclipsed by other dignities. The motivational trick is in the tension. For reputation's sake, troops want to be asked to do much, but not too much. If there is nothing at stake, or perhaps if no one is watching, there is no honor to be won, so exertion is not worth the bother. If, on the other hand, there is too much at stake, too terrible a risk, the promise of respect can prove insufficient stimulus. Limbs may not respond to former imaginings of valor. Psyches can snap.

An excellent place to see how reputation is rhetorically managed is the American Revolutionary War. More than any of America's subsequent conflicts, this one depended upon hortatory discourse in the field. Only "a mixture of threats, cajolery, and artful persuasion" could have kept the fledgling Continental Army in the field against the British Empire.[3] During this period the American officer corps was sorting out what it meant to be gentlemen in a society that placed no premium on birthright. Charles Royster refers to this as the "extra freight of gentlemanly ideals," the interest in being refined, removed, honorable, and sufficiently honored. Whereas European officer-gentlemen felt secure in their station by virtue of their social class, American officers felt an insecurity that required heroic demonstration. Hence, Royster suggests, American officers "freed their audacity."[4] We may suppose that they freed their lips as well, to justify their own conduct and to influence their men's. In what follows, a weighing of battle exhortation between George Washington and Daniel Morgan, I find Morgan's superior because of his better management of the tension of troop reputation.

In Philadelphia on July 2, 1776, the Second Continental Congress accepted Richard Henry Lee's proposition that the "United Colonies are, and of right ought to be, free and independent States." In New York, on the same day, George Washington was bracing the new Continental Army for the landing and assault of tens of thousands of British regulars. Only days before the fleet carrying British General William Howe and his army had appeared dramatically in New York's lower harbor. (Ten thousand Hessians would arrive shortly.) Washington, short of weapons and disciplined men and undermined by local Tories, faced the difficult task of defending an area laced with waterways from an enemy with ample sea power. News of recent American failures in Canada only darkened the pall. Nonetheless, resolved to make a stand, Washington endeavored to hearten his troops. He admonished them on July 2 through posted and read-aloud general orders:

> The time is now near at hand which must probably determine, whether Americans are to be, Freemen, or Slaves; whether they are to have any property they can call their own; whether their Houses, and Farms, are to be pillaged and destroyed, and they consigned to a State of Wretchedness from which no human efforts will probably deliver them. The fate of unborn Millions will now depend, under God, on the Courage and Conduct of this army—Our cruel and unrelenting Enemy leaves us no choice but a brave resistance, or the most abject submission; this is all we can expect—We have therefore to resolve to conquer or die: Our own Country's Honor, all call upon us for a vigorous and manly exertion, and if we now shamefully fail, we shall become infamous to the whole world. Let us therefore rely upon the goodness of the Cause, and the aid of the supreme Being, in whose hands Victory is, to animate and encourage us to great and noble Actions—The Eyes of all our Countrymen are now upon us, and we shall have their blessings, and praises, if happily we are the instruments of saving them from the Tyranny meditated against them. Let us therefore animate and encourage each other, and shew the whole world, that a Freeman contending for LIBERTY on his own ground is superior to any slavish mercenary on earth.
>
> The General recommends to the officers great coolness in time of action, and to the soldiers a strict attention and obedience with a becoming firmness and spirit.
>
> Any officer, or soldier, or any particular Corps, distinguishing themselves by any acts of bravery, and courage, will assuredly meet with notice and rewards; and on the other hand, those who behave ill, will as certainly be exposed and punished—The General being resolved, as well for the Honor and Safety of the Country, as Army, to shew no favour to such as refuse, or neglect their duty at so important a crisis.[5]

At first this discourse, the middle section of Washington's general orders for the day, might seem to be sounding all of the right notes. It features numerous topics common to battle exhortation: magnitude of the occasion, future reputation, just cause, self-defense, comparison of forces, instruction, reward and punishment (see table, chapter 2). Despite the wide scope of appeals, however, a particular self-consciousness dominates them. The audience cannot help but feel that it is being watched. There are more than nine references to parties and entities, watching or involved, beyond Washington's and Howe's forces. God, the whole world, countrymen, unborn millions, the honor of the country are all implicated in the coming struggle. The exhortation suggests that each of these will affect or be affected by the mettle of American soldiers. Thus repulsing the British is one thing, but equally important is earning the title of brave fighting men. Blessings and praises or shame and infamy hang in the balance.

Toward the end of the exhortation, the shift in voice from first-person plural to third-person singular individuates the self-consciousness for the audience. References to "our" and "us" shift to recommendations that officers should do this and soldiers do that, and then finally to the statement that "any officer or soldier" distinguishing himself will be duly rewarded or punished. Thus the onus of duty and honor, of standing and fighting, of winning praise or blame is placed squarely on the individual fighting man. Washington makes this his primary rhetorical appeal—assuming that his troops hold their reputation as dear as he holds his. As Joseph Ellis explains, Washington had a "tendency to regard each engagement as a personal challenge to his own honor and reputation," and he would sooner go down fighting than have these sullied.[6]

Washington's position improved for a while after he issued the above exhortation. Within days it became clear that Howe did not plan an immediate assault. The arrival a week later of a copy of the Declaration of Independence "sliced through innumerable tangles that had previously been Gordian knots." But when Howe launched massive attacks the following month, Washington's outnumbered and poorly trained forces were routed repeatedly. In some instances Washington was simply outsmarted. In others he would ride among his men and try to rally them, but too often he was unsuccessful. He was learning about his "Young Troops," as he reported to the president of the Continental Congress, John Hancock, in the midst of the New York campaign, "The honor of making a brave defence does not seem to be a sufficient stimulus, when the success is very doubtful, and the falling into the Enemy's hands probable." More strategist than tactician, reserved aristocrat than battle orator, Washington was better suited for leading Greek phalanxes, where tempered veterans' "one worry was not to turn fainthearted in front of lifelong companions-in-arms." He was ill-equipped to rally a younger, inexperienced force, where individualistic farmers and tradesmen were happy to return to their primary occupations when the battlefield situation grew bleak.[7] This does not diminish Washington's stature as the indispensable man during America's fight for independence, keeping an army in the field against all odds and snatching victories when and where he could until Britain grew weary. It simply recognizes one of his limitations.

For a more capable battle orator and tactician, we turn to Brigadier General Daniel Morgan and specifically to his fight at Cowpens, South Carolina. Here, almost a half-decade after Washington's frustrations in New York, Americans won their clearest battlefield victory against regular British forces. And "though battlefield oratory was not uncommon in the patriot army," Don Higginbotham acknowledges, "seldom did it bring more striking results than at Cowpens." Because Morgan exhorted his men over the course of perhaps fifteen hours—and his discourse is more sensitive to immediate context than Washington's—greater tactical detail is necessary to appreciate his rhetorical choices.[8]

By 1780 the British had shifted their efforts to suppress the American rebellion to the southern states. With British general Charles Cornwallis occupying the South Carolina seaboard, the new head of the American southern command, Major General Nathanael Greene, decided to divide his army. He remained with the bulk of his forces between Cornwallis and North Carolina. To the southwest he dispatched a light corps under Morgan to raise the spirits of those sympathetic to the cause, check Loyalists, and harass Cornwallis's left flank should the British general move northward.

Uncomfortable with Morgan's movement, Cornwallis divided his own force, ordering Lieutenant Colonel Banastre Tarleton to give chase. Tarleton, only twenty-six, was notorious in America for his brutality. As he hurried his own force after Morgan, the elder fell back, bolstered in number by militia but also bothered by their lack of discipline.[9] On January 17, 1781, Morgan was forced to give battle. Before sunrise the opposing forces faced each other at Cowpens, an open-wooded area where Carolina farmers grazed their cattle before sending them east to market. Each force numbered about a thousand men, but the British were entirely regulars, and they had more cavalry and cannon.

When Morgan decided to make his stand at Cowpens, he was determined that his militiamen not have to face open-field volleys and bayonet fighting. Militia tended to bolt in such circumstances, and Morgan knew it. He thus devised a fire-and-fall-back battle plan that would make the most of their marksmanship without requiring them to stand toe-to-toe with the enemy. He would deploy his infantry in three consecutive lines, each about one hundred yards behind the other, each twice the number of men in the preceding line. The first two lines would consist entirely of militia and be permitted to withdraw once they had fired several rounds (a minute's worth of combat) each. The third line, making up the majority of Morgan's force, his regulars and former regulars, would stand its ground and face, he hoped, a disrupted British attack. To the rear, behind the crest of the gently rising pasture, would stand Morgan's reserve of cavalry and re-formed militia.

Very briefly, the fighting proceeded in this way: Once the British began their advance, Morgan's first and second lines performed according to plan. But the situation quickly turned dicey when British cavalry disrupted the withdrawal of the second, larger line. Panic among the militiamen jeopardized their re-forming to be employed again. To make matters worse, although the third American line initially stalled the British advance, trading volley for volley, it soon began withdrawing itself, owing to misunderstood orders shouted in the din. With two American lines having given way entirely, and the third appearing ready to break, the British advanced with increasing confidence—and carelessness. Meanwhile, because his main body was falling back in good order, Morgan sensed an opportunity. He prepared these seasoned men to face about and discharge a sudden volley at their pursuers. When he gave the word, only ten paces separated the still formed Americans and the now disordered, surging British. The volley staggered the latter. As the American main body followed up with a bayonet charge, Morgan directed his re-formed militia to fall upon the British left, and his cavalry to fall upon the British right. The result was a well-timed double envelopment, every ground commander's wish. Surrounded, the great bulk of the British infantry threw down its arms. To the rear Tarleton persuaded about sixty of his reserve cavalry to charge the Americans with him, but he soon fled, following the couple hundred cavalry who would not counterattack.

In the end Morgan had produced one of those lopsided victories, losing but a handful of his own men but killing and capturing nearly a thousand of the enemy. The loss so infuriated Cornwallis when he learned about it the next day that he decided to pursue Morgan with his entire command. This attempt to destroy Morgan and recover captured troops and equipment ultimately exhausted Cornwallis's army, leading in no small part to its surrender at Yorktown.

Now familiar with the disposition and movements at Cowpens, we can better appreciate Morgan's exhortation, presenting his discourse in its entirety before commenting. It is recounted in the memoirs of multiple participant witnesses.

The night before the contest Morgan made a point of circulating among the militia, lightheartedly helping them with their equipment and sharing his battle plan: "Just hold up your heads, boys, give them three fires and you will be free. And then, when you return to your homes, how the old folks will bless you, and the girls will kiss you for your gallant conduct." Likewise, he assisted militia officers in rousing their men before dawn: "Boys, get up, Benny's coming; and you that have sweethearts or wives or children or parents, must fight for them, and above all you must fight for liberty and your country."[10]

At dawn, with the Americans just in position, the British emerged from the heavy wood and began to array themselves for battle. Since they were out of small arms range and Morgan had no artillery, the Americans could only watch in awe the precision with which the British swung into position. Morgan, however, was not about to let this demonstration unnerve his men. Mounted, he galloped first to his skirmishers, those closest to the enemy, hand-picked militia sharpshooters from Georgia and North Carolina. Playing on this regional difference, Morgan challenged them: "Let me see which are most entitled to the credit of brave men, the boys of Carolina or those of Georgia."[11]

Riding back to his second line, the bulk of the militia, Morgan spoke a little longer. According to Henry Lee's *Memoirs,* "He extolled the zeal and bravery so often displayed by them, when unsupported by the bayonet or sword; and declared his confidence that they could not fail in maintaining their reputation, when supported by chosen bodies of horse and foot, and conducted by himself. Nor did he forget to glance at his unvarying fortune, and superior experience; or to mention how often, with his corps of riflemen, he had brought British troops, equal to those before him, to submission. He described the deep regret he had already experienced in being obliged, from prudential considerations, to retire before an enemy always in his power; exhorted the line to be firm and steady; to fire with good aim; and if they would pour in but two volleys at killing distance, he would take upon himself to secure victory."[12]

Now Morgan rode to the highest ground of Cowpens, to his third and largest line, over four hundred men. To these seasoned troops "he was very brief. He reminded them of the confidence he had always reposed in their skill and courage; assured them that victory was certain if they acted well their part; and desired them not to be discouraged by the sudden retreat of the militia, *that* being part of his plan and orders. Then taking post with this line, he waited in stern silence for the enemy."[13]

When the British began their advance at a trot and with a battle cry, Morgan shouted above them: "They give us the British halloo, boys—give them the

Indian whoop." Finally, once the militia's planned withdrawal was upset by some of Tarleton's cavalry, Morgan galloped after the terrified men, urging: "Form, form, my brave fellows. . . . Old Morgan was never beaten."[14]

The first thing to be said about Morgan's exhortation is that he speaks at every critical juncture before and during the battle: as his men retire the previous evening, as they are awakened, as they watch the enemy embattle, as the enemy starts for them, as militiamen begin to flee. By revealing his limited demands in advance and breaking anxious silences generally, Morgan prevents fear from overwhelming his men.

More important, Morgan's discourse complements his tactics of minimizing what he asks of his men. In this he differs sharply from Washington. Morgan, a backwoodsman with the speech and manners of the ranks, does not address his troops through stiff, apocalyptic general orders. He mingles easily with his men and casts the upcoming fight in terms of kisses from sweethearts, not the fate of unborn millions. He asks them "to pour in but two [or three] volleys," not to resolve to conquer or die. He refers to the enemy in mockingly diminutive terms, as "Benny," not as unrelenting and cruel, as Tarleton was. Indeed Morgan is quick to inject levity and identity at the very moment of truth. When he shouts "give them the Indian whoop," he spiritedly reminds his men of their North American heritage and the intimidating barbarism that the redcoats associated with it. Morgan's buckskin attire reinforces the connection.

Rhetorically Morgan embraces his troops, presupposing their skill and bravery and offering them his own. He does so complementarily. For instance, he calms his skirmishers by transforming the imminent fight into a marksmanship contest between fellow militias. Once he has extolled the bravery of the next line of militia, he refers to his own record and takes on the lion's share of responsibility, promising that if they do their brief part, "he would take upon himself to secure victory." To his regulars and former regulars he is cursory, underscoring in form his professed faith in their steadiness. He addresses them only long enough to convey that he has mapped out the events of battle cleverly. His careful disposition of troops reinforces the claim nonverbally.

Morgan does not belittle his men but shores them up at every turn. This is evident from the very first words of exhortation we have recorded. "Hold up your heads, boys," he cheers the militia the night before. Whether they are smarting from the previous days' withdrawal, from being asked to fire only several rounds, or because they were self-consciously self-doubting, Morgan encourages them to take pride in their role. Compare his style with that of a junior officer trying to rally the militiamen once they start scattering during the fight. The lieutenant cries, "You damned cowards, stand and fight; there is more danger in running than fighting, and if you don't stop and fight, you will all be killed."[15] This is good reason to stop running, and it is a common battle topic (flight invites destruction; see table, chapter 2), but the young officer delivers it as a rebuke. Morgan shouts instead, "Form, form, my brave fellows. . . . Old Morgan was never beaten," presupposing troop courage and keeping the onus of the fight on himself. Morgan does not threaten his men, either. Washington promised "to shew no favour to such as refuse, or neglect their duty at so important a crisis," elaborating on another occasion "that if any man attempt to skulk, lay down or retreat without Orders he [should] be instantly shot down as an example." But Morgan's appreciation for positive appeals enabled him, as Russell Weigley says, "to draw from his troops battlefield performances unexcelled and perhaps unequalled by any other officer of the American cause."[16]

This juxtaposing of Morgan's and Washington's discourse brings into sharp relief different approaches for summoning masculine virtue. To "be a man" is a common appeal on the battlefield because combat has traditionally been a rite of passage to manhood. David Gilmore finds such a rite near universal: "Among most of the peoples that anthropologists are familiar with, true manhood is a precious and elusive status beyond mere maleness, a hortatory image that men and boys aspire to and that their culture demands of them as a measure of belonging. Although this stressed or embattled quality varies in intensity . . . true manhood . . . frequently shows an inner insecurity that needs dramatic proof. Its vindication is doubtful, resting on rigid codes of decisive action in many spheres of life: as husband, father, lover, provider, warrior. A restricted status, there are always men who fail the test."[17]

One of the reasons that Morgan's militiamen may pass "the test" better than Washington's is because, to hear Morgan speak, they are well on their way to passing it. Ever addressing the immediate tactical situation, Morgan reduces what it will take for them to escape the battlefield honorably. Moreover, he tends to address them as "boys," keeping the matter lighthearted and sporty. Even if we concede that the salutation "boys" enjoyed more frequent usage in Morgan's day, his use of it connotes affection and perhaps a hint that father is nearby. The tension within bearable, his troops heed their commander's leadership, even in the face of the notorious Tarleton.

In contrast, when Washington demands his troops "acquit yourself like men"—and he tends to withhold the honorific masculine title, more often using *we* or *us*—he only makes the test loom larger. For him the honor of "manly exertion" in a cause of vast significance dictates steadiness regardless of battlefield circumstance. But this flies in the face of Vegetius' dictum: "Never lead forth a soldier to a general engagement except when you see that he expects victory." Magnified conditions also tend to make Washington's general orders sound the same. Invariably his soldiers are in the fishbowl, expected to stand up to whatever the enemy has to offer. For many of Washington's troops—unduly watched and pressured—this is just too much. The glint of thousands of smartly aligned British bayonets overcomes their concern for a manly reputation. As any overextended material snaps, his troops bolt.[18]

After reputation, there are other, lesser, but still important tensions on the battlefield. Let us look at them in turn: distance, violence, and love.

Managing Distance at Second Manassas and San Juan Heights

The separation between commissioned officers and enlisted personnel in the military is sanctioned by regulation, reinforced by symbolism, and happens naturally. The separation is sanctioned in that officers attain their rank by political appointment, which usually demands certain standards of wealth or education. They are then assigned responsibilities and enjoy pay, privileges, and courtesies that enlisted personnel do not. Military codes add force to the differences, empowering officers over enlisted and discouraging fraternization between the two. This separation is reinforced at every turn symbolically to preserve the chain of command, especially during periods of great stress. As David Kertzer explains, "Through symbolism we recognize who are the powerful and who are the weak, and through the manipulation of symbols the powerful reinforce their authority."[19] Thus enlisted personnel initiate and hold salutes until officers conclude them. The former rise to their feet in the presence of an officer until the officer allows "seats." Enlisted insignia are often painted matte black; officers' are polished silver or gold. Traditionally the lower ranks walk and officers ride. Enlisted carry rifles and officers, side arms. Enlisted eat on the mess-decks, and officers eat in the wardroom. There is great unspoken meaning in these arrangements, making it especially noteworthy when an officer chooses to carry a rifle or march with the troops. Finally, the separation between officers and the others happens naturally because they often do possess different interests and habits, even speech patterns. For the differences in wealth and education that influence selection also influence deportment (to what degree it can be shaped by the egalitarian or elitist character within society at large). The higher ranking the officer, the greater the divide.

The practical result of all of this social distance is twofold: it prevents something in enlisted personnel, and it prevents something else in officers. In the former it discourages the casual attitude that can attend familiarity. It is more difficult to dismiss someone we rarely see and who has the authority to discipline, decorate, and transfer us. When a person appropriately removed and official tells us to do something, we tend to do it. In the officer the distance tends to prevent becoming so attached to one's troops that one dare not risk them in combat. In other words, the military divide tries to ensure that armies behave and fight rather than dissolve or hide.

For the routine administration of armies, noncommissioned officers (NCOs) bridge the gap between officers and troops. The bridge is crucial, because it permits the officer and enlisted realms with their respective focuses to exist in parallel. The bridge works because NCOs have access to officers and often have more experience, but NCOs have the manners of the ranks. Thus NCOs may make tactful suggestions to officers, while officers may embrace the experienced counsel, lend their own authority to it, and allow the NCOs to effect it. NCOs then leave "officers' country," where they are permitted but do not dwell, and return to their own realm, where they are in charge. This realm is guarded jealously by most NCOs, and most officers know not to enter it routinely. Here what needs to be done is articulated in enlisted terms, preserving the compulsion of rank but increasing identification and so the receptiveness of the audience. Not that increased identification leads to coddling. NCO eloquence features a blunt attention to detail that never equivocates about who is in charge. But there is also a been-there-done-that informality that suggests (1) "We can get this done without resorting to commissioned officer protocol," and (2) "If you put in enough time and do well enough, you can have my job." Witness a sergeant calling for better aim in the central Pacific: "OK, you guys, line 'em up and squeeze 'em off. You don't kill 'em with the noise. It's the slugs that do it. You guys couldn't hit a bull in the ass with a bass fiddle." The instruction is clear, and it reportedly produced results—without the intervention of a platoon or company commander.[20]

Before premeditated combat or that of particularly high stakes, however, officers often address their troops directly, appealing through extraordinary means for extraordinary effort. While the divide gives officers room for rhetorical maneuver—that is, the ability to discipline, decorate, and transfer troops increases one's power of persuasion—it also poses a special challenge. Suddenly officers must span the divide sufficiently for troops to identify with them and their goals. If there is too much distance or division, battle exhortation is in vain, and the only resource left to move troops is raw coercion. The sum of this complex relationship: Troops respond best to commanders who are neither too distant nor too familiar.

A clear example of a commander failing to get close enough to his troops may be found in the exhortation of Major General John Pope, upon taking command of the newly formed (Union) Army of Virginia in July 1862. President Abraham Lincoln, impatient with General George McClellan's war effort in eastern Virginia, created this new army further west and brought Pope from Ohio to lead it. Pope, intent on distinguishing his command from McClellan's and putting his troops in an aggressive mood, issued the army an open letter:

> By special assignment of the President of the United States I have assumed the command of this army. I have spent two weeks in learning your whereabouts, your condition, and your wants, in preparing you for active operations, and in placing you in positions from which you can act promptly and to the purpose. These labors are nearly completed, and I am about to join you in the field.
>
> Let us understand each other. I have come to you from the West, where we have always seen the backs of our enemies; from an army whose business it has been to seek the adversary and to beat him when he was found; whose policy has been attack and not defense. In but one instance has the enemy been able to place our Western armies in defensive attitude. I presume that I have been called here to pursue the same system and to lead you against the enemy. It is my purpose to do so, and that speedily. I am sure you long for an opportunity to win the distinction you are capable of achieving. That opportunity I shall endeavor to give you. Meantime I desire you to dismiss from your minds certain phrases, which I am sorry to find so much in vogue amongst you. I hear constantly of "taking strong positions and holding them," of "lines of retreat," and of "bases of supplies." Let us discard such ideas. The strongest position a soldier should desire to occupy is one from which he can most easily advance against the enemy. Let us study the probable lines of retreat of our opponents, and leave our own to take care of themselves. Let us look before us, and not behind. Success and glory are in the advance, disaster and shame lurk in the rear. Let us act on this understanding, and it is safe to predict that your banners shall be inscribed with many a glorious deed and that your names will be dear to your countrymen forever.[21]

The unambiguous tenor of this discourse, along with Pope's sound defeat just six weeks later, leads historians to agree that this is a "snide," "patronizing," "singularly inept document," and that "more unfortunate words John Pope never wrote."[22] Its defamation of eastern troops in general and of their leadership in particular flies in the face of the master tension of reputation. The practical result was that officers within Pope's command and McClellan's, including McClellan himself, dawdled when Pope urgently needed reinforcements to win the Battle of Second Manassas. But rhetorically more than reputation is unbalanced here. There is too much distance.

Even in the introductory paragraph, Pope's language conveys expanse. By "special" (not routine) assignment, "the President of the United States" (not the War Department) has provided him command. He has spent "two weeks" (not mere hours or days) learning his army's "whereabouts," strewn as it is across northern Virginia. These labors "nearly completed" (but not yet), he is "about to join" his men in the field, which is to say he is still miles away in Washington. This removed, messianic introduction complete, Pope suggests a shared understanding is necessary, but he again portrays expanse. He has come "from the West," a place where warfare is practiced differently by Federal forces. Instead of identifying himself with his new army, Pope sets himself in opposition to it, referring to himself or his former unit sixteen times and the new army—in terms of "you" or "your"—eighteen. He only mentions "us" and "our" on seven occasions, and usually as if lecturing children (for example, "Let us understand each other"). Pope's address insinuates that his audience is not just underperforming, but it is of an altogether different caliber. Even his conclusion suggests that the army look to and fro (expansively) rather than within.

At first, a modern auditor might hear a bit of George C. Scott's Patton when Pope disparages strong positions, lines of retreat, and bases of supply. But a fundamental difference between the discourse of the generals is a matter of distance. Patton, recall, keeps his audience at arm's length through spectacle more than language. He speaks in the idiom of his troops. He is also more vague than Pope in his censure, at least before large groups. When Patton pointedly explains, "I don't want to get any messages saying that we are holding our position. We're not holding anything. Let the Hun do that," he denigrates a practice rather than a practitioner, maintaining rapport with his audience. Pope's language, in contrast, clearly distances the general from his own army: "I desire you to dismiss from your minds certain phrases, which I am sorry to find so much in vogue amongst you." Moreover, knowing the president is frustrated with McClellan's cautiousness, Pope distances himself even from the logistics-minded terminology of his peer. The stiff-arm was so plain and public that McClellan wrote his wife, bristling: "the paltry young man who wanted to teach me that art of war will in less than a week either be in full retreat or badly whipped. He will begin to learn the value of '*entrench-ments, lines of communication & of retreat, bases of supply*, etc.'"[23]

Pope's distancing himself from McClellan rhetorically would not have been lost on Robert E. Lee any more than the physical distance between the two Union armies. As Lee wheeled his forces from facing McClellan to facing Pope, he must have taken comfort from the manifest antipathy between his two antagonists. It further reduced the likelihood that the Union armies could combine before he dealt Pope a serious blow.

Contributing to Pope's discursive distance from his army was his admitted physical distance from it. His fifty-one thousand men received the address while enduring the hardships of the field. He would not leave Washington and join them for another two weeks. "His absence," notes John Hennessy, "did nothing to instill in the army a sense of identity or esprit de corps. Instead the three corps [constituting Pope's army] lay spilled across northern Virginia and the lower Shenandoah Valley, each the domain of its corps commander only."[24] Pope made little time for cultivating the relationships that leave men wanting to fight for one another and knowing how each will operate under fire. Inevitably, his army was soon trudging northward in retreat. Pope felt so little attachment to his men that he preceded their withdrawal rather than stiffen the rearguard. Small wonder that the army cheered his relief once that word worked its way along the retreating column.

In Pope we see at the start of the campaign of Second Manassas an officer who mismanages the tension of distance by never getting close enough to his men to inspire desired results. We should remember, however, that greater identification does not necessarily correlate with hortatory success and division with failure. As noted earlier, there is some distance between the ranks by design. Once the fight that Pope is spoiling for commences, the Union's "Iron Brigade" and Confederacy's "Stonewall Brigade" trading blows, we get a glimpse of too much identification through Major General "Stonewall" Jackson. Although the Confederates would soon roundly defeat the Federals at Manassas, this part of the engagement was proving a stalemate, much to the chagrin of the decisive Jackson. Increasingly agitated by the lack of progress his men were making against the smaller, less experienced enemy, he flew into a rage. According to one staff officer: "[I] met Gen'l. Jackson near a gate trying to rally some stragglers, more excited and indignant than I ever saw him, riding rapidly about among them and threatening [them] with his arm raised. It made [me] feel a little qualmish as to the result—to see such conduct on his part, such evidence of uneasiness."[25] Here a general ordinarily regarded even

by his own staff as remote compromises his station by behaving more like a
sergeant or lieutenant. Excited, abusive, concerning himself with stragglers
rather than the battle at large, he no longer seems Lee's favorite corps commander. He is too close to his men, too involved with immediate circumstances, undignified and unbecoming of his rank. Rather than inspired, the
witness is left "a little qualmish" by the display.

A commander conscious of the tension of distance may be found a quar-
ter-century later when Teddy Roosevelt led his "Rough Riders" in their famed
charges through the San Juan Heights of Cuba. Having assumed command of
the volunteer regiment only the day before, his predecessor, Leonard Wood,
being promoted to brigade command, Lieutenant Colonel Roosevelt was particularly manic on July 1, 1898. Mounted, he hastened his regiment to the
base of the Spanish-occupied heights, driving his unmounted men forward
through the intense heat by "joking with some and swearing at others, as the
exigencies of the case seemed to demand."[26] Roosevelt had orders to support
the regular regiments in their assault on the heights, but upon finding these
regiments inert, he spiritedly led the Rough Riders through the regulars' lines.
His eloquence and pugnacity inspired elements of the regiments he bypassed,
meaning that soon the force following him consisted of a mix of Rough Riders and regular troops. So impetuous was Roosevelt's advance that those wit-
nessing it from afar, including foreign attaches, figured it to be a mistake due
to botched orders. Moreover, in the words of one correspondent, "No one
who saw Roosevelt take that ride expected him to finish it alive. As the only
mounted man, he was the most conspicuous object in the range of the rifles
. . . only 200 yards ahead."[27]

At this daring moment, however, Roosevelt is carefully negotiating his distance from those that follow him, particularly his Rough Riders. To no small
degree he embodied the regiment. A Harvard-graduated New Yorker who
nonetheless spent a great deal of time pursuing "the strenuous life" out West,
Roosevelt had with Wood raised the volunteer regiment, an exotic combination of Ivy Leaguers and frontiersmen. The ranks were composed, as Roosevelt's executive officer would later write, of those "accustomed to adventure"
and those "looking for it, so there was no man in the whole organization who
was not anxious to face hardship and brave death." These men identify with
Roosevelt's pluck and want to keep up with him as he works his horse forward, then pauses to holler rearward, "Come on!"[28]

Well up this first hill, soon to be dubbed Kettle Hill, Roosevelt makes his
first mistake—and amends—in managing distance between himself and his
men. As they encounter a barbed-wire fence, which momentarily checks their

progress, enemy fire becomes particularly effective. A dozen men crumple to the ground dead or wounded as they wait for the wire to be cut. Forced to dismount, Roosevelt must fear that momentum and nerve are beginning to ebb from the troops. As soon as the wire is cut, he pushes past it, turning and shouting: "If any man runs I'll shoot him myself." This threat visibly stings the Rough Riders around him. As much proud volunteers as the colonel, they had no intention of running. The suggestion that they might be less daring or duty-bound suddenly causes a rift, the appropriate distance spooling out to a chasm. Sensing this, Roosevelt adds: "And I won't have to shoot any of my own men either." Together again, he, his Rough Riders, and the regulars drive the surviving Spaniards from their trenches atop Kettle Hill. As if to prove there is little difference between himself and his men, Roosevelt waves a bleeding hand at one wounded Rough Rider and jokes, "You needn't be so damned proud."[29]

As the battle continued, Roosevelt lost his balance with his men once more. Atop Kettle Hill, he observed U.S. troops working their way up the remaining, larger ridge, San Juan Hill, from the left. At first he directed rifle and machine-gun fire at the Spanish trenches atop the hill, but soon he determined upon another charge. Picking his way through more barbed wire, the eager colonel shouted a challenge, then began running down into the small valley that separated the ridges. But only a handful of the throng atop Kettle Hill noticed. Two of the five men who gave chase were shot within the first hundred yards of the bungled advance. Realizing that he no longer had his makeshift brigade with him, Roosevelt returned to it, fuming. In his own words, "I ran back, jumped over the wire fence, and went over the crest of the hill, filled with anger against the troopers, and especially those of my own regiment, for not having accompanied me."

No sooner does Roosevelt begin to berate the men, however, than he realizes again that they are kindred spirits: "They, of course, were quite innocent of wrong-doing; and even while I taunted them bitterly for not having followed me, it was all I could do not to smile at the look of injury and surprise that came over their faces, while they cried out: 'We didn't hear you, we didn't see you go, Colonel; lead on now, we'll sure follow you.'"[30] Roosevelt paused to better coordinate the charge, then executed more successfully. By nightfall the heights were completely in American hands, Santiago lying before them.

Roosevelt, Jackson, and Pope each show us the challenge of finding the right rhetorical distance from one's troops. Roosevelt twice doubts the commitment of his men, and both times this doubt stings them. In his case, familiarity is not the hazard. Roosevelt's role, rank, and reputation—to say nothing of his distinct manner—see to that. Disparity is. In both instances Roosevelt quickly reels himself back within a constructive distance of his Rough Riders, and he is probably permitted these recoveries because he is right there, risking his life with his men. In Jackson we catch sight of a senior commander too closely resembling his men. Troops appreciate a general who remembers their names and personal circumstances in garrison. In action, however, they are not reassured by a general who "sweats the small stuff." They know that more junior officers or noncommissioned officers should police the ranks, and generals ought to be concerned with the big picture. Pope, for his part, never attempts to balance. Deliberately, consistently aloof, he so antagonizes his officers that they contribute to his failure, and even the ranks cheer his relief. Had Pope been more successful at Second Manassas, it is still unlikely the sentiments would have been very different. For all of his military genius, even Douglas MacArthur would be dubbed "Dugout Doug" by his troops. There is something insufferable about distance that exceeds visibility.

Managing Violence in the Fifty-fourth Massachusetts

Carl von Clausewitz defined war as "an act of violence intended to compel our opposition to fulfill our will." Submission of the enemy is the object, violence the means. He was not impressed by "self-imposed restrictions" to the violence of war, boundaries that today take the shape of rules of engagement (for specific operations) and the general law of war (the Hague Conventions and Geneva Conventions). For him, "War is an act of violence pushed to its utmost bounds," each side egging the other on, "which logically must lead to an extreme."[31] The advent of nuclear weapons has necessarily kept humanity from carrying war to its logical extreme, but even in Clausewitz's day, competent warfare required curbs to violence. Without checks, without tension, there would be neither enemy left to surrender nor captured treasure left to enjoy. Moreover, one's troops would not execute their mission smartly but operate as unrestrained savages, an incendiary mob. Spartan war songs and pipes, Plutarch reminded us, not only emboldened the scarlet-cloaked hoplites but guarded them against "excessive rage."[32] With this sort of tension in mind, Garry Wills characterizes the psychological state that commanders must engender in troops prior to combat: "To overcome combatants' inhibitions against facing death, against inflicting death, against massive violence, leaders must create a kind of psychic explosion in each soldier, but a *controlled* explosion. All the discipline of drill, uniforms, codes of conduct are meant to ignite and yet contain the forces that can keep up this unnatural psychic game of risk and wrath."[33] Where might we find an exemplar of violent ardor being carefully managed, a mix of spur and bridle? The Fifty-fourth Regiment of Massachusetts during the Civil War.

The Fifty-fourth Massachusetts is one of the Civil War's more famous regiments because its ranks comprised the first free black troops enlisted in the North, it was formed with great fanfare by the abolitionist establishment, and it faced dramatic challenges on and off the field. Fascinating personalities were involved: Frederick Douglass, as recruiter and father of two of the regiment's members; governor of Massachusetts John Andrew, official champion of the regiment and the principles behind it; Sergeant William Carney, remembered for his gallantry during the regiment's first major action; and Colonel Robert Gould Shaw, the regiment's young commanding officer, virtually deified in New England upon his death at the head of his unit. The 1989 motion picture *Glory* has helped educate modern audiences about the regiment. Its story, a microcosm of the nation struggling to become worthy of its philosophical principles—capped by a climactic battle—is well-suited for cinema.

The exhortative climax of the Fifty-fourth took place at the start of its climactic battle, the regiment's first major combat. Immediately prior to assaulting Fort Wagner, South Carolina, Colonel Shaw faced his men and urged, "Now I want you to prove yourselves men," reminding them that "the eyes of thousands" watched "the night's work."[34] Without further appreciation of the context, besides battle being imminent and the Fifty-fourth being regarded as a test case for black troops, this appeal sounds like one with which we have become familiar: Be a man in this fight, self-consciously; recognize that should you behave cowardly, you will face the derision not only of comrades here but of skeptics, champions, and loved ones back home. On the surface Shaw sounds very much like Washington, staking his appeal overwhelmingly on the matter of reputation. But just as there is something deeper to Pope's discourse than reputation-robbing condescension (that is, too much distance), there is something deeper to Shaw's discourse than reputation chasing. It is the tension of violence.

In the 1860s there was something particularly momentous about "the arming of negroes."[35] By then American slaveholders had been worried about slave uprisings for nearly two hundred years. Some believed that though white America introduced a measure of civilization to the Negro, his savage instincts were only barely restrained. Others recognized that it would be perfectly natural for blacks to be violently angry toward those who enslaved and visited arbitrary violence upon them. The disturbances of Nat Turner and John

Brown heightened such fears. Another opinion held that Negroes could not or would not soldier—the possibility of battlefield gallantry crippled by generations of slavery or by the promise of summary execution if captured by the South. And why should they risk life and limb? Even many Northerners would sooner abuse blacks than pay them wages equal to white soldiers, promote them to the commissioned ranks, or permit them crack military assignments. Within American society, North as well as South, that Negroes would willingly shoulder rifles, bravely work them, and carefully attend to military protocol seemed far-fetched.

In March 1863, beleaguered by casualties, expiring enlistments, and resistance to the draft, Abraham Lincoln suggested to the military governor of Tennessee (eventually his second-term vice president, Andrew Johnson): "The colored population is the great *available* and yet *unavailed* of, force for restoring the Union. The bare sight of fifty thousand armed, and drilled black soldiers on the banks of the Mississippi, would end the rebellion at once." In that second sentence Lincoln acknowledged a psychological impact larger than the tapping of a new source of manpower. If it were simply a question of logistics, he could have said "fifty thousand black soldiers," period. By including the phrase "armed and drilled" Lincoln recognized just how demoralizing it would be for Confederates to see blacks officially armed and skillfully soldiering. Such a sight would shake Southern prejudices at their foundation, especially (as the *Lynchburg Virginian* put it) the "natural distaste of seeing negroes clothed in regimentals with arms in their hands."[36]

A few months earlier, in his Emancipation Proclamation, Lincoln had managed this tension of Negro violence publicly. In the two paragraphs that immediately follow his order freeing slaves within the Confederacy, he spoke directly to the new freemen, concurrently discouraging them from random violence but encouraging them to participate in the organized, legitimate variety:

> And I hereby enjoin upon the people so declared to be free to abstain from all violence, unless in necessary self-defense; and I recommend to them that, in all cases where allowed, they labor faithfully for reasonable wages.
>
> And I further declare and make known, that such persons of suitable condition, will be received into the armed service of the United States to garrison forts, positions, stations, and other places, and to man vessels of all sorts in said service.[37]

Shaw, explicitly recruited by Governor Andrew to lead the Fifty-fourth, was a good choice for managing the tension that would be the big question surrounding the regiment. A Harvard-educated patrician of the New England establishment, Shaw had already seen his share of combat. Handsome, even delicately so, he was nonetheless a strict disciplinarian. Abolitionist poet John Greenleaf Whittier saw something both "beautiful and awful" in him. Perhaps the best proof of balance comes in Shaw's own writing once he reached the Southern theater. Initially attached to the brigade of Colonel James Montgomery, he was appalled by how Montgomery employed "contrabands," former slaves hastily impressed into Federal military service in the South. During raids about the Georgian coast, Montgomery would indiscriminately bombard towns and then have the contrabands fall out of formation, loot, and set fire to property. When Montgomery ordered a company of Shaw's troops to participate in the mayhem, Shaw let loose a fusillade of frustrated, protesting correspondence. To the assistant adjutant general of the Southern department, he requested clarification on the lengths of Montgomery's orders. To his wife, he lamented, "I do not like to degenerate into a plunderer and a robber. . . . All I complain of is wanton destruction." To Governor Andrew he reported the incident in detail and worried that "such a course is sure to bring discredit on the coloured troops if persisted in. . . . The destruction seemed to me perfectly useless if not barbarous." At nearly the same time Shaw was protesting random violence, however, he was appealing up the chain of command for assignment to a set-piece, front-line fight. To Brigadier General George Strong he argued that "my men are capable of better service than mere guerilla [sic] warfare." Having trained the Fifty-fourth from its inception, Shaw had the utmost confidence in its ability to fight—with discretion.[38]

Shaw did not have to wait long. Two weeks later, when the Fifty-fourth was moved to operations south of Charleston Harbor, General Strong sent for it. Upon receiving Shaw, Strong explained that Federal forces would attempt to take Fort Wagner (again) that evening. His own brigade would spearhead the assault, and he offered the Fifty-fourth the opportunity to lead the brigade. Shaw accepted the mission enthusiastically, even though skirmishes, illness, hunger, and fatigue had begun to take their toll on the regiment. At dusk on July 18, 1863, the Fifty-fourth finally found itself at the center of a conventional battle.

Remembering that encouragement on the battlefield comes in many guises, it is important to take stock of the significance of colors (that is, national, state, and unit flags) during the Civil War. Their advance, retreat, fall, or capture conveyed how the fight was going, often leading to behavior that we would regard as foolhardy today. Should the flag bearer be shot down—and typically he was targeted—another man would immediately seize the staff and silk, knowing full well this made him the next obvious target. Often a long line of men would fall endeavoring to keep the colors aloft. Medals were generously awarded for it. In cases where capture of the flag seemed imminent, a color-bearer might strip the flag from its staff, stuff it in his shirt, and race from the field. On occasions when the enemy had managed to rip the flag from its staff, soldiers would sometimes still rally around their naked pole as if it exuded resolve. Perhaps no soldier on the battlefield better typified the tension of violence than the color-bearer. Where he advanced, violence to the enemy followed, and yet the bearer himself did not work a weapon. The colors of the Fifty-fourth were regarded with this sort of reverence, and we may trace it from the day the colors were presented to the regiment.

Exactly two months before the assault on Fort Wagner, Governor Andrew had presented the regiment with its flags amid great fanfare, near Boston. Formally addressing Shaw, but also speaking to the troops, guests, and sponsors, the governor began by framing the general situation. He acknowledged the unique composition of the regiment, identified his own honor with its fortunes, and promised a home audience of "anxious eyes." Moreover, he expected nothing less than vindication of the "manly character" (read *discretion*) and "manly zeal" (read *aggression*) of "the colored citizens of Massachusetts, and of those other States which have cast their lot with ours." The governor was unable to remember "when, in all human history, to any given thousand men in arms there has been committed a work at once so proud, so precious, so full of hope and glory." He then presented Shaw four flags by explaining the origin of each, charging them with symbolic import. Regarding the national and state colors, which would be carried into battle, he was grave. The white stripes of the American flag, he admonished, had better "be red with their blood before it shall be surrendered to the foe." As for the standard of Massachusetts, still unsurrendered in battle, "You will never part with that flag so long as a splinter of the staff or a thread of its web remains within your grasp." For administrative marches the governor also offered two "emblematic banners," one rather reserved, bearing the image of the Goddess of Liberty and the motto "Liberty, Loyalty, and Unity," the other unabashedly aggressive, bearing the image of a cross and the Latin slogan "In hoc signo vinces" (In this sign thou shall conquer). Both of these had come from committees of interested citizens.[39]

Would these four standards sustain the Fifty-fourth on the march and in battle? Absolutely. Even if the ideological principles they represented rang somewhat hollow to the ranks, these flags symbolized the sponsorship of home and a shared trust that the Fifty-fourth would fight, fight well, and bring the flags home. Shaw's response to the governor reflects this: "Your Excellency: We accept these flags with feelings of deep gratitude. They will remind us not only of the cause we are fighting for, and of our country, but of the friends we have left behind us, who have thus far taken so much interest in this regiment, and whom we know will follow us in our career. . . . May we have an opportunity to show that you have not made a mistake in entrusting the honor of the State to a colored regiment."[40]

Two months later, before Fort Wagner, the forceful act of one of Shaw's company commanders demonstrates this commitment. "Unfurl those colors!" he commands, stabbing toward them with his sword. As the Fifty-fourth had been assuming its place at the head of General Strong's brigade, Confederate cannoneers on nearby James Island had tried to disrupt things. Fearing that the American and Massachusetts flags were attracting undue attention, their bearers had begun to roll them up on their staves.[41] By today's standards, presenting a less obvious target to enemy gunners reflects excellent sense, but during the Civil War it represented the first sign of timidity. If the colors were not flying, the color-bearers were more concerned about the violence being directed at them than the violence their brothers were about to unleash. Such fearfulness was contagious. The sight and snap of the flags would help remind the regiment that it needed to fight its way home.

In the remaining hour, as dusk turns to twilight and General Strong's brigade finishes aligning behind the Fifty-fourth, the tension of violence within Shaw's regiment is carefully managed. First, the men are ordered to load their muskets but not cap them (that is, not apply firing caps), to affix bayonets, and to lie down. This makes their weapons semilethal and reserves their strength for the coming fight. (Coincidentally, incoming shellfire continues but is ineffective.) Next, Shaw directs the bearer of the state flag to fall out of the color company, one of his forward-most companies, and take a more rearward position with the regiment's executive officer.[42] The significance of this move would have been lost on no one. All knew Shaw would lead the regiment in its assault, and the national flag would be but a few paces behind him. Sending the state flag to the rear indicated that the colonel wanted a second rally point available to the regiment. Expecting a stiff fight, Shaw was not about to overextend his unit. Finally, called again to its feet, the regiment hears the gallop of approaching horses. True to form, a few words of encouragement are spoken.

General Strong rides dashingly before the regiment on a spirited gray charger. Accompanied by two aides and two orderlies, the brigade commander is in full uniform with a yellow handkerchief around his neck. The appearance is immediately that of a man in command. Mounted, he sits head and shoulders above the Fifty-fourth. At liberty to wear a bright personal bandanna, he is easily distinguished from the others on horseback and seems unimpressed by the skill of Confederate sharpshooters. His entourage suggests that the general is well prepared to control the brigade and to be assisted in any personal matter. At the same time that Strong seems fierce and remote, however, he speaks in endearing terms, identifying with the regiment, recognizing its hardship, and determining the odds in its favor: "Boys, I am a Massachusetts man, and I know you will fight for the honor of the State. I am sorry you must go into the fight tired and hungry, but the men in the fort are tired too. There are but three hundred behind those walls, and they have been fighting all day. Don't fire a musket on the way up, but go in and bayonet them at their guns." Thus the general demands the most grueling type of fighting from these men: hand-to-hand. To ensure they are in the proper spirit, Strong calls the national color-bearer forward and asks: "If this man should fall, who will lift the flag and carry it on?"[43]

Now Shaw, whose reputation for silence and discipline imbued him with a distance and fierceness of his own, speaks. Coolly taking the cigar from his mouth, he answers: "I will." This expression of solidarity electrifies the men, and they cheer their regimental commander loudly. As Strong and his party gallop away to coordinate the brigade's advance, Shaw reins his men in again. Calmly, silently, dressed impeccably, he walks up and down his line. Finally, in the words of the regimental historian, an officer eyewitness: "[Shaw's] manner, generally reserved before his men, seemed to unbend to them, for he spoke as he had never done before. He said, 'Now I want you to prove yourselves men,' and reminded them that the eyes of thousands would look upon the night's work."[44] With a fuller understanding of the situation, we perceive this exhortation to summon black manly "character" and "zeal." Far beyond a commander's general concern about the reputation of his troops, this is a test of the black man's ability to fight in a disciplined manner.

Shortly thereafter Shaw provides the measured combat instruction that epitomizes the tension of violence: "Atten-*hut!* Move in quick time until within a hundred yards of the fort, then double quick, and charge. Forward *march!*"[45] In other words, stand straight and still, even amid shellfire; let us walk, then trot, then storm, without firing our weapons. These orders are the last steps in an elaborate endeavor to produce that "psychic explosion in each soldier, but a *controlled* explosion."

Tactically this battle soon proved a Union disaster. Part of the lattice of Confederate defenses for Charleston Harbor, Fort Wagner was heavily fortified, within range of supporting Confederate fires, and (poised near the northern tip of Morris Island) approachable only via a long strip of infirm beach. Unknown to Federal commanders, the preliminary bombardment of the fort had been ineffective, and there waited inside probably more than 1,000 Confederate soldiers, rather than the estimated 300. As Shaw led 600 of his men to the obstacles and ramparts of the fort, its defenders answered vigorously, along with the batteries of Fort Sumter, James Island, and Sullivan's Island. Shaw was shot to death on the fort's parapet, which his men actually contested before being repulsed. Enemy artillery fire kept supporting regiments at bay until the Fifty-fourth fell back, reduced to nearly half its assault strength. By the time the rest of Strong's brigade and a second brigade moved forward and were repulsed, total Union casualties exceeded 1,500. Strong himself was mortally wounded.[46]

Strategically and symbolically, however, the battle proved an abolitionist success, the *Atlantic Monthly* proclaiming that "the manhood of the colored race shines before many eyes that would not see." Because the Fifty-fourth had demonstrated that black troops were capable of being as well trained and as well disciplined under fire as white troops, the Lincoln administration pressed ahead with creating additional Negro regiments, compensating for increased white resistance to the draft.[47]

What became of the colors that terrible evening? Both of the Fifty-fourth's were planted on Fort Wagner's parapet momentarily. As the decimated regiment began to ebb, however, Sergeant Carney snatched the Stars and Stripes and carried them back along the beach to the first officer he found still alive and functioning. Because darkness rendered the flag an ineffective rally point, the officer directed Carney to carry it further to the rear for safety. Seriously wounded, the sergeant staggered on, mumbling that the flag had never touched the ground. As for the state flag, it was torn from its staff by the enemy but—as the official report of the battle explained—"the staff remains with us." Responding to the deliberate leadership of Shaw and Strong, the men of the Fifty-fourth had measured up to their day's standard of structured violence.[48]

Managing Love: Julius Caesar and the Tenth Legion

Within his epic *Caesar: A Biography*, Christian Meier is taken, in passing, by the Roman general's battle exhortations. "Caesar's descriptions of his dealings with the soldiers are sometimes striking," writes Meier. "He often praises their bravery, experience and steadfastness. Yet again and again they display fear and regain their courage only through his intervention." Were we to consider these exhortations alone, Meier suggests, it would seem that Caesar treats his men "a little like overgrown children." Consider the exhortations within their cultural milieu, however, and "they correctly reflect the much greater openness with which the soldiers—and the Romans generally—expressed their emotions." Meier then contrasts modern-day emotionality with that of the ancient world: "The particular emotional control that we have inherited from early modern times, which sets up official channels, as it were, between emotions—good and bad—and their expression, arose only with the modern state and the particular civilization it engendered. Fear then came to be regarded as a base emotion. In the Roman soldiers, however, courage and fear probably manifested themselves more directly; they did not need to conceal them and therefore reacted more naturally. It was thus possible to address them more openly."[49]

While it is certainly true that cultures vary in how emotive they are, that Romans soldiers did not regard fear as a base emotion and were unconcerned about concealing it are unlikely reasons for troop volatility before Caesar. Indeed, they are unlikely at all. Caesar regularly calls for courage, like Tyrtaeus before him and Patton afterward, because courage has always been more highly valued than its alternative. As for the need of its concealment, fear on the battlefield jeopardizes not just one man's performance. If plain, his fear jeopardizes the performance of those around him like a contagion. It also telegraphs emboldening information to the enemy. A more likely explanation for the volatility of Caesar's troops is their love for him.

There are, of course, many types of love: paternal, maternal, fraternal, romantic, divine. There are many typologies of love, as psychiatrists, clergymen, and Plato demonstrate. We need only reflect on our spouse, children, and close colleagues to realize that we are committed to them in different ways. The common thread is that when our love for them becomes threatened, we become volatile. Jilt a lover, betray a brother, threaten a mammal's young, and you have a storm on your hands. So it is with troops before a beloved commander.

The refrain is heard often enough, that troops feel so much affection for a certain leader that they would follow him "to hell and back." To better understand this devotion, let us consider a contemporary example sensitively stated by E. B. Sledge, our young Marine in the Pacific theater during World War II. Sledge recalls of his company commander, Andrew Allison Haldane, that during preparations for the assault of Peleliu "we were thankful that Ack Ack was our skipper, felt more secure in it, and felt sorry for other companies not so fortunate. While some officers . . . thought it necessary to strut or order us around to impress us with their status, Haldane quietly told us what to do. We loved him for it and did the best job we knew how." Once Haldane is slain, Sledge's loss is palpable, even as he writes forty years later: "Never in my wildest imagination had I contemplated Captain Haldane's death.... Now his life had been snuffed out. We felt forlorn and lost. It was the worst grief I endured during the entire war. The intervening years have not lessened it any." What Sledge and his buddies feel they have lost identifies the nature of the love we are discussing: "The loss of many close friends grieved me deeply on Peleliu and Okinawa. But to all of us the loss of our company commander at Peleliu was like losing a parent we depended upon for security—not our physical security, because we knew that was a commodity beyond our reach in combat, but our mental security."[50]

If "mental security" is a somewhat amorphous good, it clearly emanates from a senior who, in Sledge's words, "commanded our individual destinies under the most trying conditions with the utmost compassion."[51] This affection, then, is not for the commander who never puts his troops at risk. War entails casualties, and commanders wage war. Mature troops understand this. But they deeply appreciate the commander who puts their lives and reputations at risk *judiciously*. It follows that the commander who misspends blood and treasure is feared or hated. Such waste may stem from inexperience—from the new lieutenant, so to speak—but surely troops' most intense loathing would be reserved for the experienced commander who squanders just the same. The key here, as elsewhere, is in the tension. The commander who balances mission accomplishment with troop welfare is the commander whose troops will follow him to hell and back.

While Haldane strikes the appropriate balance at the relatively small-unit level in the twentieth century, Caesar struck it on a grander scale two thousand years earlier. The balance is evident in his *Commentaries*, his third-person autobiographical accounts of his military exploits, and in Suetonius, the impartial Roman biographer of Caesar. Drawing from these sources, let us examine three instances where Caesar addressed his men in perilous circumstances.

In the first year of his governorship in Gaul, Caesar hurried several legions and hundreds of local allies to the township stronghold of Vesontio (now Besancon in eastern France), determined to get there before Ariovistus. Several years earlier Ariovistus had settled his Germanic tribe on the Gallic side of the Rhine. Gallic tribes had since persuaded Caesar to challenge him. Once Caesar made camp at Vesontio, however, panic engulfed his army, spurred by rumors of Germanic ferocity. Roman administrative officials began feigning reasons to take their leave. Some opted to stay but remained in their tents, wanting, in Caesar's words, to "conceal their fearful expressions" and "avoid the taint of cowardice." (So much for the supposition that Romans did not frown upon or try to conceal fear.) Military officers began voicing concerns about the next route of march, the terrain, and supplies. They even suggested that their troops might not break camp, given dread of the enemy.

Caesar responded by calling his officers together. At this point we may conjecture that he was still a relatively unknown quantity to them. They would have known Caesar to be a patrician of significant rank and influence in Rome. They might have been aware of his achievements as a junior officer early in his military career. They would have had an initial glimpse of his ability during their first joint campaign against the Helvetii. But most of Caesar's demonstrations of military genius and personal bravery lay before him. So too did most demonstrations of his legendary commitment to his men and his absolute intolerance for shirkers. This meeting foreshadows that personal style for which he would become loved.

Caesar's account of his discourse here is too lengthy to quote in its entirely, but the crux may be ascertained through generous excerpts, and the crux is a skilled combination of edge and attentiveness. Facing all of his officers, Caesar first "severely reprimanded them, primarily for thinking that it was their business to inquire or think about either the direction or the strategy of the march." Then, slackening a bit, he amplifies his trustworthiness and discounts the threat that Ariovistus poses: "Why did they despair of their own courage, or of his anxious concern for their well-being? The danger posed by this enemy had already been experienced in the time of our fathers, when the Cimbri and Teutoni were expelled by Gaius Marius. . . . The Germans were the same people who had often clashed with the Helvetii—and the Helvetii had frequently beaten them, not only within their own borders but also in Germany itself— and yet the Helvetii had proved no match for our army. . . . Perhaps, he went on, some of those present were disturbed by the defeat and flight of the Gauls. But if they took the trouble to inquire. . . . not even Ariovistus would pin his hopes on the success of such tactics as a means of beating our army." Caesar repeats this cycle of stick and reassurance on the issues of food and route of march: "As for those who shifted the blame for their own fear on to a pretended anxiety about corn supplies or the narrowness of the route, they were doing so out of presumption. After all, they apparently either doubted their commander's commitment or they were dictating it to Caesar. Yet his attention was taken up with all these things: the Sequani, the Leuci, and the Lingones were supplying corn, and the crop was already ripe in the fields—as for the route of their march, in a short while they would themselves decide it." Caesar now works his way toward a stern challenge. But even in the challenge there is a final stroking, at least for one of the legions:

> On the subject of their declared intention not to follow orders and raise the standards, it did not trouble him at all. He was well aware that whenever an army had disobeyed its commander in the past, it was either because fortune had deserted him, as proved by his failure on the field, or because he had been discovered in some crime and found guilty of rapacity. That he, Caesar, was guilty of no crime was evident from the whole course of his life: that he was a man who enjoyed good fortune was evident from his campaign against the Helvetii.
>
> And so, Caesar concluded, he would do at once what he had intended to put off till a later date. The very next night, during the fourth watch, they would strike camp. Then he would know as soon as possible whether their sense of shame and duty was stronger than their fear. Moreover, even if no one at all followed him, then he would still set out, with only the Tenth legion, for he had no doubts about *its* loyalty. Indeed, it would in future serve as his bodyguard.[52]

Clearly there is displeasure and temper in this exhortation. There is flattery and division, too, as Caesar presupposes fidelity from his most veteran legion. Several topics common to battle exhortation are manifest (competent commander, past and future reputation, comparison of forces; see table, chapter 2). Most striking, however, is the tension between Caesar the careful administrator, purportedly safeguarding his troops from behind the scenes, and Caesar the aggressive warrior, ready to lunge headlong at the enemy, under strength if need be. He is the consummate balanced commander.

Caesar reports that upon concluding his speech, "the change of attitude was quite remarkable." Not only does the favored Tenth immediately pledge its readiness for service, but the remaining legions fall into line denying any initial doubt or panic. This is the harangue and transformation that catches Meier's notice. But even if most of the officers do not love Caesar yet—it is too early; indeed, they tread near mutiny—they respond to a delicately balanced, albeit harshly stated, exhortation. Neither should we forget Caesar's oratorical prowess. Cicero and Suetonius say he was unsurpassed in his time.[53] Thus it is not so surprising that Caesar's legions soon drove Ariovistus fleeing across the Rhine and laid waste to his army and family.

Before long Caesar's disciplining/coddling approach does produce affection. Suetonius tells us that he treated his men "with strictness and indulgence in equal measure," vigorously prosecuting desertion and mutiny but also, after significant victories, permitting his men "to indulge themselves as they pleased." In other words, legionaries profited by following the ever offensively minded Caesar. "By these means," says Suetonius, "he made his men utterly loyal to him and supremely brave as well."[54] An example of their devotion may be found on the banks of the Sambre near its headwaters (in modern-day France, just beyond Belgium) in 57 B.C.E.

There Caesar marched eight Roman legions and thousands of allies to subdue the Germanic tribes he termed collectively the Belgae. Learning that three tribes had resolved to fight and had encamped in the woods on the far side of the Sambre, Caesar directed his army to make camp on the near side. As the legions lumbered into the vicinity, he sent his more lightly armed allies ahead to probe the enemy. What Caesar did not realize was that while the allies began their skirmishing across the shallow river and his men became involved in foraging for materials and erecting earthworks, the majority of the enemy was forming in the woods for a large-scale surprise attack.

All at once they explode from the woods, in a frightening scene that Caesar describes vividly: "The enemy . . . ran at astonishing speed down to the river, and so seemed—almost at one and the same moment—to be near the woods, then in the river, and now already upon us. With similar speed they made their way up the hill to our camp and attacked the men who were working on the fortifications."[55]

The allies are scattered. The Romans, needless to say, are startled. But by now Caesar is the beloved commander, his troops tested, and his officers developed in his own image. They have learned of the premium that Caesar places on "force protection." They have learned further that he prizes initiative and bravery. So by the time Caesar finishes some emergency signaling and hurries forward to lend moral support, the legions are already fighting proficiently.

A crisis does develop, however. The two leftmost legions are able to throw back the Belgic tribe they face and drive it across the river, and the two center legions are able to repulse the Belgic tribe they face and drive it to the river, but the two rightmost legions begin to buckle. They face the Nervii, the especially fierce and brave tribe leading the Belgic resistance to Rome. Moreover, the advance of the other legions had permitted the rightmost to be flanked. Caesar works his way to the troubled right only to find most of its officers dead or wounded, the standards lost, and men in the rear starting to leave the fight.

At this point the outcome of the battle rests, in Caesar's words, "on a knife-edge." Grabbing a shield and plunging forward, he begins to command, as

Sledge said of Haldane, "individual destinies under the most trying conditions with the utmost compassion." According to Caesar's commentary, he is personable and at the same time deft in starting to get these men out of their predicament: "There he called upon the centurions by name and encouraged the men, ordering them to advance and open ranks, so they could use their swords more easily. His coming gave the men fresh hope and heartened them; each one was eager of his own accord to do well in his commander's sight, even at great personal risk—and the enemy assault was checked a little."[56]

If the reaction of troops nearest Caesar does not sufficiently reflect their affection for the man, the act of the Tenth Legion does. Although clear across the width of the battlefield, clear even across the Sambre, the Tenth is picked by Caesar's executive officer to go to Caesar's and the right's rescue. This selection is almost assuredly not happenstance. Favored by Caesar, the Tenth would continually wish to repay his goodwill. Other legions would continually be trying to supplant its special standing. Thus it comes as no surprise that the Tenth swoops down as if protecting a struggling loved one: "When the men of the Tenth discovered from the fleeing cavalry and orderlies where the fighting was, and the extent of the danger which now threatened the camp, the legions, and their commander, they left nothing undone in terms of speed. Their arrival transformed our fortunes."[57] Before long the Nervii warriors were nearly annihilated.

Let us close by observing Caesar and the Tenth Legion a final time. In this case the account is reported by Suetonius rather than Caesar, and it must have taken place eleven years later, during the civil war with Pompey. Although the battlefield was still far away, this is the most remarkable instance of troops being "as if transformed" by the speech of their beloved commander. It demonstrates most clearly that when love is involved, even a turn of phrase can produce dramatic results. Suetonius reports: "When the men of the tenth legion demanded retirement and bonuses at Rome, threatening serious harm against the city, at a time when the war was raging in Africa, he did not hesitate to go to them, though his friends advised against it, and disband them. But with one word—addressing them as *citizens* rather than *soldiers*—he won them over and brought them round, for they at once replied that they were his *soldiers* and, although he asked them not to, they followed him to Africa of their own accord. Even then he imposed on the most troublesome a fine of a third of the booty and the land which they had been due to receive."[58] With a single redefining word, then, Caesar transformed mutineers into warriors. He generated combat motivation in them even as he dismissed them.

At the most superficial level, Caesar's rebuke appears to be a matter of reputation. But surely these men would not have responded to the same rebuke from a different man the same way. A different man might have been killed, or offered the Tenth what it wanted, or only sent messengers. Instead Caesar appears dramatically before the mob, supremely confident in his ethos of the beloved commander. In the past he has called these men not just soldiers but comrades, made them rich, and entrusted them with his life. On other occasions, he stood "in the way of those who were fleeing, laying hold of each soldier, even grabbing them by the throat and turning them round to face the enemy."[59] These men cannot endure the censure of such a commander.

Lest we think Caesar is too hard on the Tenth, we should note (from Suetonius' account) that he ultimately accepts its service, fines only "the most troublesome" characters within it, and fines even these only "a third" of what they are due. Thus even when their relationship is most strained, Caesar strikes a balance with the Tenth that is both sternly mission-oriented and in the end kindhearted. Neither abused nor pampered, the men love him.

Summary

In this chapter we have seen that certain tensions inherent to the battlefield can be reflected in battle exhortation quite personally. To earn a favorable reputation, troops like to be asked to do much but not too much. Daniel Morgan struck this balance better than George Washington by speaking more directly to the tactical situation and keeping tolerable what he asked of his men.

To respond best to their commanders, troops must find them neither too distant nor too familiar. John Pope, emphasizing distance through his speech and physical absence, inspired few followers. Stonewall Jackson, temporarily forgetting his place and policing the ranks personally, engendered doubt. By contrast, Teddy Roosevelt ever sought the sweet spot between remoteness and familiarity. He was sensitive enough to detect and correct his rhetorical imbalance.

To fight effectively troops must be both enthusiastic and restrained in their violence. While training and symbolism promote this in all armies, the requirement received special attention in the case of the Fifty-fourth Massachusetts, the United States' first regiment of free black enlisted men.

To appreciate—nay, love—their commander, troops like to be both pushed and indulged. Julius Caesar epitomized the demanding, devoted commander. The Tenth Legion, most clearly the object of his method, responded with great loyalty.

How these tensions are resolved varies. Reputation involves a release, as it is attained once some requirement is fulfilled; the strain is greatest before one's first combat and within irregular outfits (such as militia). Distance and love are more continuous tensions, each perpetuated by hard edge and soft touch. Violence involves a release of sorts but must never get wholly out of hand. Understanding and addressing such tensions are hallmarks of the effective combat commander.

4

Evolutions

The tensions discussed in the previous chapter are inherent to the battlefield and influenced quite personally by the exhorting commander. Broadening our focus, let us now consider how environmental and audience concerns affect the discourse. To enable greater depth of treatment, I choose an era and place most familiar: U.S. battle exhortation from the past two generations. The first four sections of this chapter compare the exhortation of theater commanders over sixty years, starting with Dwight Eisenhower. This survey identifies, through war-specific and societal influences, a general evolution of the discourse from the fierce to the mild. The remaining section identifies differences in exhortation engendered by combat arm. In other words, when addressing audiences more specific than the theater at large, commanders tend to motivate troops differently. To illustrate this I compare examples from across a multifaceted (combined-arms) expeditionary group during a single operation.

Eisenhower on D-Day

As the supreme commander of the Allied Expeditionary Force in Europe during World War II, Eisenhower had to contend with the usual problems of theater command but on a massive scale. Responsible for the entire invasion of Normandy, he had to serve the interests of multiple nations and balance towering egos. In addition, he felt it his and his commanders' business to cultivate high morale among the troops. One of his criteria in selecting commanders, in fact, was that they "appreciated the importance of morale and had demonstrated a capacity to develop and maintain it." While he recognized that "methods employed by successful leaders in developing morale differ so widely as to defy any attempt to establish rules," he felt that the principal means was personally visiting with the troops, and he insisted that he and his commanders do so. "Soldiers like to see the men who are directing operations," Eisenhower would explain in his war memoirs. "They properly resent any indication of neglect or indifference to them on the part of their commanders and invariably interpret a visit, even a brief one, as evidence of the commander's concern for them. Diffidence or modesty must never blind the commander to his duty of showing himself to his men, of speaking to them, of mingling with them to the extent of physical limitations." Contrary to "Dugout Doug" MacArthur or distant John Pope, Eisenhower personally visited twenty-odd divisions, twenty-odd airfields, and a host of warships, depots, and other installations over the four months that preceded D-Day.[1]

At the same time, he began preparing a traditional exhortation with the help of his staff. It would be distributed as a one-page order to all participants of the invasion shortly before the Allied armada got underway:

Soldiers, Sailors and Airmen of the Allied Expeditionary Force!

You are about to embark upon the Great Crusade, toward which we have striven these many months. The eyes of the world are upon you. The hopes and prayers of liberty-loving people everywhere march with you. In company with our brave Allies and brothers-in-arms on other Fronts, you will bring about the destruction of the German war machine, the elimination of Nazi tyranny over the oppressed peoples of Europe, and security for ourselves in a free world.

Your task will not be an easy one. Your enemy is well trained, well equipped and battle-hardened. He will fight savagely.

But this is the year 1944! Much has happened since the Nazi triumphs of 1940–41. The United Nations have inflicted upon the Germans great defeats, in open battle, man-to-man. Our air offensive has seriously reduced their strength in the air and their capacity to wage war on the ground. Our Home Fronts have given us an overwhelming superiority in weapons and munitions of war, and placed at our disposal great reserves of trained fighting men. The tide has turned! The free men of the world are marching together to Victory!

I have full confidence in your courage, devotion to duty and skill in battle. We will accept nothing less than full victory!

Good Luck! And let us all beseech the blessing of Almighty God upon this great and noble undertaking.   [Signed Dwight D. Eisenhower][2]

An eye for indoctrinated topics and personally adjusted tensions finds many here:

First and last there is the magnitude of the occasion, characterized by the order's opening ("Great Crusade") and its conclusion ("great and noble undertaking"). The stakes are sufficiently high that "the hopes and prayers of liberty-loving people everywhere" accompany the force, and numerous contributors are involved: "brave Allies and brothers-in-arms on other Fronts."

The audience's future reputation is at stake. "The eyes of the world" are upon them, and an ambiguous "we" promises to "accept nothing less" from them than full victory.

The enemy is vilified, responsible for tyranny "over the oppressed peoples of Europe." More immediately relevant to the combat solider, the enemy is promised to "fight savagely."

The audience is also cautioned against underestimating the danger. For all of the resources and practice behind them, their task will "not be an easy one," given the enemy's own training, equipment, and experience.

These attention-getting matters are balanced with more encouraging ones:

A comparison of forces foretells "the destruction of the German war machine." The enemy, fearsome as he is, has in the last several years experienced "great defeats, in open battle, man-to-man." While Allied airpower continues to reduce him, the Allied home front has generated overwhelming reserves of weaponry and troops. "The tide"—surging and inexorable— "has turned" in favor of the GI.

The justice of the cause is implied through terms loaded with ideological significance: "liberty-loving people," "free men," "security . . . in a free world." Instead of enumerating injustices of "Nazi tyranny," the text condemns them by this subtle contrast.

The commander himself is present (through this order, if not a personal visit), competent (reflected by the document's professionalism), superior (exhibited in the Supreme Headquarters letterhead), and perhaps loved. For while he orders his audience into danger, he has cared enough to address them, and he has "full confidence" in their character and skill.

Finally, there is the hint that the auspices are favorable as the commander, supreme as he may be, acknowledges "Almighty God" and entreats His blessing.

Were Eisenhower and his staff cognizant of the traditional strategies of battle exhortation? Probably, at least subconsciously, they had been indoctrinated like the rest of us, before their years of practical military experience. But even if the officers were not, the prebattle situation naturally called for certain matters to be addressed. When the exhortation was first drafted for Eisenhower, his assistant chief of staff explained:

An effort was made . . . to tell the soldier, in simple, direct language:
What he is about to do.
What it is expected to accomplish.

About his enemy.
That he can defeat that enemy.
That the world is watching him.
That you have confidence in him and in the outcome.[3]

This is a practitioner's catalog of essentially the same topics and tensions identified above, with one exception. Justice of the cause is not explicitly listed, and probably with good reason.

Studies in social psychology after World War II found that the three most stringent norms within U.S. Army combat units were proving oneself a man, proving loyalty to one's buddies and outfit, and avoiding "any talk of a flag-waving variety." Seasoned combat troops typically regarded "idealistic exhortation" as "bullshit," inconsistent with "the combat man's hard-earned, tough-minded point of view."[4] Patriotic newsreels might lead civilians to volunteer for military service or heed the draft. The movie series *Why We Fight* might ensure that recruits understood the official rationale for war. But as combat grew nearer or more familiar, troops were motivated by more immediate concerns such as personal rather than national reputation.

The Eisenhower exhortation hedges in this regard. On the one hand it is brushed with a handful of abstract, idealistic terms; on the other, it does not make a detailed argument about the cause. Because the initial draft of the message has not survived, it is impossible to know whether the idealistic terms are the assistant chief of staff's or Eisenhower's, but we may speculate. We do know that Eisenhower made some changes. ("I've changed this a bit.")[5] We know that he had come to regard the war as a contest between "a completely evil conspiracy" and "human good and men's rights. . . . a crusade in the traditional sense of that often misused word."[6] This conviction influenced the title of his wartime memoirs, *Crusade in Europe,* so it seems likely that it led him to add "Great Crusade" and possibly other idealistic language to his exhortation. Still, instinct, space, or the desired tenor of the message kept Eisenhower from turning it into an ideological argument. The exhortation's focus remains on the impending event—closely watched combat across the beaches and countryside of northern France—and a favorable comparison of forces.

When we consider the tenor of this discourse, it is important to remember what Eisenhower is asking his audience to do. He has ordered the flower of Allied youth into the very teeth of the enemy, and he is asking them to rise to the occasion. Many would soon jump from planes into the dark, heavily laden, and descend into unfamiliar, hostile territory. Many more would jump from landing craft into the sea, heavily laden, and slog across fire-swept

beaches. Some would ride gliders down onto countryside unsuitable for landing. Others would deliver all these infantry while facing antiaircraft or shore
battery fire. Still others would pound the enemy with heavy weaponry of their
own. The audiences of this message were about to participate in the most vulnerable and physical type of combat, and though there had been months of
practice, there would be but one opportunity to get it right.

The frame of mind required to participate in such an operation is boldness, and boldness is what Eisenhower's exhortation endeavors to inspire. Fully
one-third of its sentences are punctuated by exclamation marks, including
four of the last six. Many words are capitalized beyond convention (for example, *Great Crusade* and *Victory*). At the top the letterhead of Supreme Headquarters, Allied Expeditionary Force, features a flaming sword. At the bottom
the supreme commander's heavy signature conveys a substantive, personal
touch. Moreover, the message is distributed to individual combatants, carefully designed to be carried by the individual as a good-luck or boldness
charm.[7] Eisenhower's exhortation is very much within the emotional tradition of the classical harangue. As Victor Davis Hanson explains: "In Greek
warfare, which by convention was battle for a day, the prebattle environment
—the yelling and singing that went on within the phalanx, the drink of wine
before battle, the expectation of a speech by their leader—was more con-
ducive to attack than to defense. This accustomed activity before battle was
aimed at rousing the hoplite to advance, rather than calming him in an effort
to keep steady, stay put, and wait for the enemy's charge."[8]

But Eisenhower's exhortation also reflects adaptation to modernity. Rather
than a spontaneous or extemporaneous act, it was painstakingly prepared,
a corporate effort more than a month in the making. While it is true that
some generals before Eisenhower relied on others to draft encouraging words
(Washington comes to mind), many more did not. It is difficult to imagine,
for instance, Caesar, Montecuccoli, or Morgan commissioning a battle exhortation. Technological advances are evident, as well. In addition to exhorting
the age-old soldier and sailor, Eisenhower addresses a newer warrior in "airmen" and attributes much of the shift in Allied fortunes to an "air offensive."
Even more obvious is the means by which Eisenhower delivers his message.
Printed exhortative circulars were not particularly novel by 1944. Eighty-one
years earlier, as Union and Confederate armies converged on Gettysburg,
Major General George Meade issued a printed circular to his subordinate
commanders within the Army of the Potomac. (In it Meade requests "that
previous to the engagement soon expected with the enemy, corps and all
other commanding officers address their troops." He even offers "fitting terms"

for them to use.)[9] The difference by Eisenhower's time is that print-reproduction technology and logistics have so advanced that the supreme commander intends to put a copy of his circular into the hands of every Allied participant, even (or especially) junior enlisted men, although they far outnumber those of Meade's command. Subordinate commanders might reinforce the message in their own way, but Eisenhower addresses every contributor personally. With broadcast radio he might have reached a great many audibly, but that would have compromised the secrecy and surprise being practiced against the enemy.

While these elements of modernization affect Eisenhower's discourse around the edges, his exhortation is consistent with the practice of millennia. Employing traditional strategies—common topics and tensions—the commanding general aims to invigorate his audience.

Ridgway's Turn

In contrast to the Second World War's general tides, where the Axis powers expanded at length before the Allies slowly pushed them back, the Korean War produced a front that raced down and up the Korean peninsula for its first six months. Within this context of desperate seesawing, the commander of the majority of the U.S. and UN ground forces, Lieutenant General Walton Walker, was killed in a motor vehicle accident, December 23, 1950. Immediately Douglas MacArthur, supreme commander for the Allied Powers in the Pacific, sent for Lieutenant General Matthew Ridgway to replace him. As Ridgway raced from Washington to Tokyo and onto the battlefield, his new command was fleeing (again) down the Korean peninsula. The stage was set for a dramatic rallying of troops.[10]

Ridgway did not fancy battlefield oratory. Reflecting on his primary audience, he had concluded, "American soldiers do not like rhetoric. They react with either ridicule or indifference." Instead Ridgway preferred pointed communications. This is evident from the first two messages he dispatched to his army while pausing in Tokyo. In the first he commemorated his fallen predecessor, wishing the eulogy to have its own "separate identity, unmingled" with the thoughts he planned to share upon formally taking command. In the second message, for distribution as he reached Korea, Ridgway aimed "in one simple, brief, sincere statement" to assume command and convey his confidence that the Allies could best "the Chinese horde that had sprung so suddenly from beyond the Yalu." This general order (which Ridgway directed "be read as soon as practicable by every officer" and "made known to as many of the men as may be practicable," including "prompt translations") reads:

I have with little notice, assumed heavy responsibilities before in battle, but never with greater opportunities for service to our loved ones and our nation in beating back a world menace which free men cannot tolerate.

It is an honored privilege to share this service with you and with our comrades of the Navy and Air Force. You will have my utmost. I shall expect yours.[11]

Although the order was but four sentences, Ridgway had spent considerable time crafting them during his flights westward.[12] This language, he believed, would set the tone for his command. There would be no windy speeches. There would be heavy responsibilities; beatings for the enemy; honorable service and fraternity; and most of all—conveyed through his concluding, staccato sentences—there would be no slackers. Ridgway was a hard-bitten, old-school commander, having led the Eighty-second Airborne Division into Sicily and Normandy during World War II. Though assumption of command is typically (or preferably) a rhetorical situation distinct from battle exhortation, Ridgway combined the two, echoing Eisenhower's D-Day discourse in the process. For instance, while Ridgway's order is more self-centered (not unfitting as one assumes command), it at the same time tersely frames an ideological war. His reference to "a world menace which free men cannot tolerate" sounds very much like Eisenhower's "elimination of Nazi tyranny . . . and security for ourselves in a free world." The order is more nationalistic than Eisenhower's, with its explicit references to "our Nation" and "our comrades of the Navy and Air Force," but distribution to all units serving with the U.S. Eighth Army made for an Allied audience. Knowing that Ridgway would in four months become Supreme Allied Commander himself, we sense already an Eisenhower-like poise, a fitness for full theater command. Most significantly, Ridgway's order closes in such a way that cannot help but quicken the pulse of its audience. All are put on notice that the new commander expects their "utmost."

But what Ridgway found on the ground sobered him. As he hurriedly acquainted himself with units in the field, he was struck by their lack of confidence and alertness and an atmosphere of "gloomy foreboding." He concluded that his "was a bewildered army, not sure of itself or its leaders, [with troops] not sure what they were doing there, wondering when they would hear the whistle of that homebound transport." Recognizing his forces "were simply not mentally and spiritually ready" to return to the offensive, he embarked on a multifaceted course of action to restore his army to "a fighting mood."[13]

Strategically, Ridgway arranged for the Allies to retire to "strong, deep, fortified positions," from which they would make their stand. Tactically, he required his commanders to return to the business of securing high ground, getting off the roads, and maintaining intelligence-generating contact with the enemy. There would be, Ridgway made clear, no more abandoning of units to be overwhelmed and destroyed; neither would there be further abandoning of equipment, which had been shipped to them from so far away. Symbolically, to encourage the ranks through the physical presence of their commander, Ridgway became "ubiquitous," invariably sporting a grenade on the right side of his chest. He ordered up for the troops more chow (*hot* chow), more stationery for writing home, and more gloves. As for "glib," confidence-robbing commentary from some quarters of the United States that intervention in Korea was ill-advised, he had a special response.[14]

On January 21, 1951, still less than a month after his arrival, Ridgway issued an uncharacteristically lengthy communiqué intended for every individual under his command. Through it, we see the beginning of a shift in U.S. theater battle exhortation:

MEMORANDUM FOR: Corps, Division, Separate Brigade or RCT Commanders, and Commanding General, 2d Logistical Command

SUBJECT: Why We Are Here

1. In my brief period of command duty here I have heard from several sources, chiefly from the members of combat units, the questions, "Why are we here?" "What are we fighting for?"

2. What follows represents my answers to those questions.

3. The answer to the first question, "Why are we here?" is simple and conclusive. We are here because of the decisions of the properly constituted authorities of our respective governments. As the Commander-in-Chief, United Nations Command, General of the Army Douglas MacArthur said publicly yesterday: "This command intends to maintain a military position in Korea just as long as the Statesmen of the United Nations decide we should do so." The answer is simple because further comment is unnecessary. It is conclusive because the loyalty we give, and expect, precludes any slightest questioning of these orders.

4. The second question is of much greater significance, and every member of this command is entitled to a full and reasoned answer. Mine follows.

5. To me the issues are clear. It is not a question of this or that Korean town or village. Real estate is, here, incidental. It is not restricted to the issue of freedom for our South Korean Allies, whose fidelity and valor

under the severest stresses of battle we recognize; though that freedom is a symbol of the wider issues, and included among them.

6. The real issues are whether the power of Western civilization, as God has permitted it to flower in our beloved lands, shall defy and defeat Communism; whether the rule of [men] who shoot their prisoners, enslave their citizens, and deride the dignity of man, shall displace the rule of those to whom the individual and his individual rights are sacred; whether we are to survive with God's hand to guide and lead us, or to perish in the dead existence of a Godless world.

7. If these be true, and to me they are, beyond any possibility of challenge, then this has long ceased to be a fight for freedom for our Korean Allies alone and for their national survival. It has become, and it continues to be, a fight for our own freedom, for our own survival, in an honorable, independent national existence.

8. The sacrifices we have made, and those which we shall yet support, are not offered vicariously for others, but in our own direct defense.

9. In the final analysis, the issue now joined right here in Korea is whether Communism or individual freedom shall prevail, and, make no mistake, whether the next flight of fear-driven people we have just witnessed across the HAN [River], and continue to witness in other areas, shall be checked and defeated overseas or permitted, step by step, to close in on our own homeland and at some future time, however distant, to engulf our own loved ones in all its misery and despair.

10. These are the things for which we fight. Never have members of any military command had a greater challenge than we, or a finer opportunity to show ourselves and our people at their best—and thus be an honor to the profession of arms, and a credit to those who bred us.

11. I would like each commander to whom this is addressed, in his own chosen ways of leadership, to convey the foregoing to every single member of his command at the earliest practicable moment.

> [Signed M. B. Ridgway]
> M. B. Ridgway
> Lieutenant General, United States Army, Commanding[15]

Ridgway dictated this message to help restore his beleaguered army's pluck. And while it was distributed not quite as closely to the beginning of an offensive as Eisenhower's D-Day order, Ridgway would initiate his own counterattack just four days later.[16] Still, this represents a significant departure from tradition—a shift in tenor from the emotional to the rational. True, battle exhortation is fundamentally rhetorical discourse, and rhetorical discourse is fundamentally reason-giving, but traditionally many of the reasons to fight were wrapped in pathos. Pipes and drums, for instance, stir something within one's breast. The desire to demonstrate one's worth as a brother-in-arms is just that, a desire. In Ridgway, here, we witness a sudden adaptation. Whereas a month ago he favored succinct, hard-hitting communiqués appealing more to the heart than to the head, he now opts for a self-professed "full and reasoned answer" to troop misgivings. Contributing to this rationality is Ridgway's departure from assumed premises and uncontested terms to detailed explanation. Previously he and Eisenhower could employ expressions such as "free men," "brave Allies," and "tyranny," trusting that such phrases were acceptable and affective. Now Ridgway pauses to delineate the bravery of the South Koreans. He turns to political philosophy to contrast rights-based government from Communism. And he discusses God rather than merely invoking his blessing or alluding to him metaphorically (as in Eisenhower's Great Crusade).[17]

To be sure, there are still traditional topics and tensions. Ridgway vilifies the enemy, men who "shoot their prisoners, enslave their citizens, and deride the dignity of man." He appeals to future and past reputation, relishing the "opportunity to show ourselves and our people at their best . . . a credit to those who bred us." He establishes distance, warning his audience against the "slightest questioning" of orders. But Ridgway's elaborate ideological discussion precludes immediate emotional involvement. Because "our own direct defense" is, admittedly, reserved for "some future time, however distant," the text mutes a bold response. In exhorting the way he does, Ridgway shifts from emotional fire-starter, where everyone must give their "utmost," to rational firefighter, where everyone need calm down and do "their best." Otherwise, graver circumstances await down the road.

Another manifestation of this more cerebral discourse is Ridgway's use of a previously unused (because unnecessary) topic, something we might call reference to proper authority. In Ridgway's mind the issue is of minor consequence. He raises it through the question "Why are we here?" so that he may summarily move beyond it. A constitutional answer is for him "simple and conclusive," making "further comment . . . unnecessary." But the need to address the question at all is something new. Previously troops might question whether accolades, the cause, or their leadership compensated for the hazards of combat, but now we see the start of legalistic concerns. Whether because this is the first large-scale commitment of American blood and treasure without a conventional declaration of war or because, for the troops, there seems insufficient commitment is difficult to answer. The point is that theater battle exhortation has become less belligerent.

Slide into Oblivion

If World War II proved a good forum for traditional battle exhortation, and Korea the forum for something newer, Vietnam was not a good place for it. There are several reasons for this, and the first rests with General William Westmoreland, theater commander from the start of U.S. escalation in 1964 to the trials of 1968 (Tet, Khe Sanh, My Lai). Westmoreland was a tall, square-jawed combat veteran, but he was no firebrand. One biographer refers to him as a "soft-spoken" commander, another as a consistently "closemouthed cautious person."[18] En route to Vietnam, Westmoreland told West Point cadets that a leader should be seen by his men precisely because "this tells them without saying so in words that you have a sincere interest in them."[19] For him, "presence"—literally being present and exuding confidence—made the difference between inspiring or uninspiring command.[20] A rhetorical exercise like Eisenhower's or Ridgway's was not necessary or natural for Westmoreland.

Westmoreland's commitment primarily to presence, however, had unintended consequences. His "habit of flitting about" South Vietnam, to get a firsthand perspective of things and "to remind his forces of his presence and his attitude,"[21] diminished his exhortative impact. Proper timing, something ancient Greek rhetoricians called *kairos,* plays an important role in rhetorical situations, and someone "hopping all over Vietnam" could not possibly time his visits for maximum impact.[22] A commander with more rhetorical ability might have *created* occasions through symbolic action, but this was not Westmoreland's style.

Several brief examples suggest that Westmoreland struggled in encouraging men. In a hometown newspaper article not intended to be critical, an Associated Press correspondent innocently reports two. In the first case, while striding to his helicopter after receiving a briefing in Long Binh, Westmoreland notices two junior enlisted men struggling to erect a radio antenna atop a Quonset hut. Rather than leaving them to their work, or directing an officer to get them some help, Westmoreland interrupts them. He tries "to put them at ease with questions about the frequency of mail and the quality of the food," but it does not work. The AP reporter observes, "They were uneasy and confused in his presence. The GI halfway up the pole didn't seem to know whether to come to some sort of attention, despite the precarious perch, or shimmy down and salute."[23]

Many helicopter hops later that day, further forward, Westmoreland interrupts again. While striding to his helicopter in the gathering dusk, he glimpses a heavily armed patrol heading for the jungle and intercepts it. The meeting reportedly proceeds this way:

> The general questioned them at length about the night's operation, kneeling with them around a field map and going over the plan in minute detail. "What will you do if any of your men smoke?" he asked the squad leader.
>
> "It won't happen," the sergeant answered with unflinching assurance. "These men have been up against old Charlie before. They know what the score is."
>
> Content with the answer, Westmoreland turned to a . . . trooper cradling a grenade launcher. "What do you think of the new M79 attachment?"
>
> "It's hanging in there," came the reply.
>
> The slang seemed to stun the commander. "What did you say?"
>
> "I said it's hanging in there—sir."
>
> The craggy face suddenly parted in a wide smile, followed by a huge booming laugh. "You men look lean and mean," he said. "I wish you the best tonight and every night."[24]

One can only wonder what the patrol members thought of this encounter as they continued beyond their lines. The commanding general had made a point of briefly visiting with them, but he had mismanaged distance, focusing first on their patrol route (identifying too closely with them), then failing to relate to the grenadier (too far). The general neither managed their capacity for making violence nor offered them reason to be impressed with (or love) him. By suddenly delaying their departure, in fact, he may have upset the timing of their mission. Westmoreland even undersells reputation, employing the unimaginative "lean and mean" compliment, then wishing the troops "the best," as if they were headed for a more lighthearted engagement.

A more capable battlefield orator might have suggested that the auspices were favorable, given the recent success of the patrol members' battalion. He might have established some magnitude for the occasion, connecting the patrol's success or failure to the larger U.S. effort. He might have promised the soldiers that the evening's hazards would some day make good storytelling. But Westmoreland seems unable to speak to men this way.

In fact, without self-awareness, Westmoreland tells the AP reporter as they return to Saigon, "Visitors are always a problem"—referring to a congressman who must be entertained that evening—"but I like to meet them as often as I can. It gives [them] a perspective about the war that you can't get from maps and conferences." In that moment Westmoreland reveals that his many field visits serve his purpose of gaining perspective but probably inconvenience his hosts a great deal. Whereas Eisenhower or Ridgway could make it up to the troops, providing some motivating words, Westmoreland does not or cannot, relying chiefly on presence instead.

A most explicit example may be found in the memoirs of Norman Schwarzkopf. Having just survived a running two-week battle early in the war, Major Schwarzkopf saw the sky fill with helicopters as Westmoreland, his staff, and reporters arrived on the scene. (Schwarzkopf carefully avoids mentioning Westmoreland by name, but Westmoreland's identity is unmistakable.) When the general emerged from a briefing, his South Vietnamese colonel host introduced Schwarzkopf as having been the senior U.S. adviser on the ground during the battle. Schwarzkopf then remembers:

> The general came over and recoiled a little because I hadn't had a change of clothes in a week and had been handling bodies and stank. Meanwhile, the cameramen had followed and several reporters came up with microphones. "No, no," the general said. "Please get the microphones out of here. I want to talk to this man."
>
> I'm not sure what I expected him to say. Maybe something like, "Are your men all right? How many people did you lose?" or "Good job—we're proud of you." Instead there was an awkward silence, and then he asked, "How's the chow been?"
>
> *The chow?* For chrissakes, I'd been eating rice and salt and raw jungle turnips that Sergeant Hung had risked his life to get! I was so stunned that all I could say was, "Uh, fine, sir."
>
> "Have you been getting your mail regularly?"
>
> All my mail had been going to my headquarters in Saigon and I assumed it was okay. So I said, "Oh, yes, sir."
>
> "Good, good. Fine job, lad." *Lad?* And with that he walked off. It was an obvious PR stunt. He'd waved off the microphones, but the cameras were still whirring away. At that moment I lost any respect I'd ever had for that general.[25]

Schwarzkopf may be mistaken about Westmoreland's motives. "Based on my previous command experience," Westmoreland recounts in his own memoirs, "I vowed that, whatever else, three things would be done well for the troops in Vietnam: food, mail, and medical care."[26] In two of our three examples we see him inquiring about just such things, and we must assume his interest is genuine. But Schwarzkopf's reaction to the general's presence and discourse is telling. Westmoreland's appreciation for some of the foundations of good morale is equaled by his lack of skill in the sort of words that contribute to it, especially shortly before and after combat.

It is also instructive to compare photographs of Eisenhower and Westmoreland in exhortative action. If one consults any of the famous photographs of Eisenhower interacting with members of the 101st Airborne Division shortly before their jump into Normandy with one of Westmoreland "in a favorite stance atop a jeep, talking to men" (his words), the difference is striking.[27] Eisenhower—himself a mild-mannered believer in "mingling"—is nevertheless speaking forcefully. His timing is reflected in the paratroopers' already camouflaged faces. And they are giving him their rapt attention. Westmoreland, by contrast, is speaking leisurely, even enjoyably. The relevance of his presence is difficult to determine because the troops are in all stages of dress: some wear blouses, some only T-shirts, at least one wears no shirt at all; none wear a helmet. And though all face the general, several of the soldiers photographed are not looking directly at him. The comparison of only two photographs does not prove anything, but it suggests theater commanders of very different rhetorical ability. The comparison may also reflect different types of war.

Strategic decisions during the Vietnam War and the tactical situation on the ground did not lend themselves to the deliberate combat seen so often during World War II and the Korean War. Deliberate combat, anticipated and prepared for, be it offensive or defensive, tends to occasion battle exhortation. Vietnam included planned offensives and engagements, but strategically U.S. involvement increased and decreased more gradually than in previous wars. Tactically, the actions it featured were patrolling, ambush, and counter-ambush. Such incremental and chance combat is less inviting to battle exhortation— at any level of command. As a company-commander recipient of the Medal of Honor remarked: "My biggest fight . . . began simply by walking down into a valley. It was spontaneous. There was no opportunity for exhortation."[28]

There were other challenges to battle exhortation in Vietnam. By the time Westmoreland was called home, the American effort had lost whatever initiative and confidence it originally enjoyed. Robert McFarlane, who in 1965 led the first Marine artillery unit into Vietnam, and who in 1967 returned to the fighting, describes it this way:

> In the early sixties, the pinnacle of American wealth and power, it was easy to go do things. The challenge in Kennedy's inaugural address resonated

in all of us, even the junior-enlisted high school drop out. We all wanted to do something of value.

Well, we get there, on the ground, and start looking around. And we start seeing discontinuities: We weren't trained for what we were being asked to do. Not all of the South Vietnamese wanted us there. Leadership in Saigon would say that we'd be home by Christmas but at the same time was asking Washington for more troops.

Especially in the officer corps, it became clear that our strength, firepower, would best be employed in the North, but we weren't permitted to go there. So within five months of landing at Da Nang—we're inappropriately trained but figuring it out—it becomes clear that we don't have the authority to do what ought to be done.[29]

The situation deteriorated from there. As described by William Hauser: "Cases of manipulation of 'body count' and other statistical indicators, embezzlement of club and post exchange funds, medal-grabbing and glory-hogging by senior officers, cover-ups of war crimes, and (perhaps worst) tactical incompetence by officers 'ticket-punching' their way through abbreviated command tenure—all these instances (however exceptional in the overall history of the war) had a cumulatively devastating impact."[30]

Meanwhile grounds on which to base exhortation were disappearing back home as well. Assassinations, racial tensions, a flourishing drug culture and biased draft, unprecedented television coverage of the horrors of war—these combined with an apparently mismanaged war to erode popular support for the troops. Emblematic of this crisis in confidence was the practice of some soldiers chalking "UUUU" on their helmets in the latter years of the war, abbreviation for "the unwilling, led by the unqualified, doing the unnecessary for the ungrateful."[31]

Of course even in more popular wars, battle exhortation is not always appropriate. E. B. Sledge remembers that during the stubborn fighting for Okinawa "I existed from moment to moment, sometimes thinking death would have been preferable. We were in the depths of the abyss, the ultimate horror of war. . . . Men struggled and fought and bled in an environment so degrading I believed we had been flung into hell's own cesspool."[32] Under such conditions, grim determination and routinized acts count for more than spirited words or gallantry. And in Vietnam there *were* expressions of combat spirit. A Marine rifle company defending one of the hills at Khe Sanh, for instance, insisted on holding a flag ceremony every morning and evening. Varying the time of execution, the company would carefully take twenty-nine seconds for each ceremony, then dive for cover, knowing it took thirty-one seconds for enemy mortar fire to arrive. Likewise, members of the Army Air Cavalry swaggered through Vietnam with "cav scarves" and Stetson "cav hats" in a cocky imitation of their horse-mounted forefathers.[33]

But once warriors begin to believe, as many did in Vietnam, that their trial will be unrecognized or unappreciated, a mainstay of even self-exhortation buckles. The sentiment that interested "eyes are upon you" becomes difficult. Idealism, often regarded as "bullshit" even during World War II, becomes still rarer. Similarly, when troops begin to regard one another as racial adversaries, and their officers as motivated by personal rather than collective interest, appeals to fraternal standing become obnoxious. Once the United States began its slow extrication from Vietnam in 1969, grounds for encouragement vanished altogether. "The officers and noncoms who were charged with making their troops continue fighting had a near-hopeless task," notes Hauser, "for their authority to compel risk of life and limb had lost the legitimacy which national purpose bestows."[34] In the minds of many U.S. troops, the pressing need before combat—when combat could be anticipated—became less "How can I proceed despite my dread?" and more "How can I avoid proceeding?"

As a radio operator for Army infantry company commanders in 1969 and 1970, Tim O'Brien observed the effects of this "patent absurdity," of asking troops to wander amid "Charlie" and mines when the United States was clearly leaving Vietnam: enlisted men disregarded officers; junior officers disregarded more senior ones; risky missions were feigned complete. What O'Brien did not see was an agreeable battle exhortation.

Consider, for example, the battalion commander's exhortation once he had drawn Alpha Company (O'Brien's company) into a semicircle and put the men at ease:

> You're going after the VC Forty-eighth Battalion. [It's] a helluva fighting unit. They're tough. Some of you have tangled with them before. They're smart. That's what makes them tough. They'll hit you when you're sleeping. You look down to tie your boot laces, and they'll hit you. You fall asleep on guard—they'll massacre you. You walk along the trails, where they plant the mines because Americans are lazy and don't like to walk in the rice paddies, and they'll blow you all back to the world. Dead.
>
> Okay. So you gotta be smart, too. You gotta be smarter. You're American soldiers. You're stronger than the dink. You're bigger. You're faster. You're better educated. You're better supplied, better trained, better supported. All you need is brains. Common sense will do it. If you're sleepy on

guard, wake up a buddy, have him take over. Be alert while you're on the march. Watch the bushes. Keep an eye out for freshly turned earth. If something seems out of place, stay clear of it and tell your buddy to stay clear. Okay? Pinkville [in other words, territory neither fully Red nor fully pacified] is a bad place, I know that. But if you're dumb, [you can] die in New York City.[35]

Considered in a vacuum, this is not bad battle exhortation. The battalion commander addresses the men personally and employs a handful of classic topics and tensions. But the larger situation made for an uncomplimentary reception. "Christ, what a pompous asshole," a junior officer remarked once the colonel had departed. "Sends us to Pinkville and says we'll be okay if we're smart. New York, my ass." O'Brien himself reflects that the colonel "seemed to think we were a bunch of morons. He thought he was teaching us, helping us to live. And he was sending us out there anyway."[36] This is indeed a reception by the unwilling, who are being asked to do the unnecessary.

If the colonel was not unqualified to lead, Alpha's next company commander *was*, and he was relieved of command after a single month. Even before this captain displayed incompetence, however, his exhortation was not well received: "He planted his legs and gave us a pep talk. He wanted a good, tough fighting unit. He wanted professionals, he said, just as the battalion motto called for in big gold letters. He tried to sound authoritative, but it did not work. No one trusts a green officer, and if he's short and fat and thinks he's a good soldier, he had better be Patton himself."[37]

To the only officer he remembers fondly, Captain Johansen, O'Brien does not attribute exhortation. Neither does O'Brien attribute to Johansen tactical or relationship genius. What makes Johansen "the best man around" is that he goes about his job bravely despite the political, strategic, and tactical difficulty surrounding him. His personal example helps to "mitigate and melt" the futility of Vietnam, "showing the grace and poise a man can have under the worst of circumstances, a wrong war."[38]

Ironically, then, it is Johansen's *presence* that gives those around him "some amount of reason to fight," the very leadership practice that Westmoreland prized but struggled to carry off. How can we account for the difference? It seems to be a matter of relevance. As an infantry company commander, Johansen belongs with his company, when it is in the field and even in base camp, and this is where we find him, sharing his example. As theater commander, Westmoreland might visit any unit, any time, anywhere, but he exercised the privilege too often; almost inevitably, his rank and timing lacked relevance. A better command of speech or drama might have compensated: something like the Ike grin or Ridgway grenade. A smaller, more familial army—or some desperate climactic moment—might have helped. Then again, after several years, probably nothing would have. Once a war's mission becomes "suspect," the presence of anyone other than those immediately necessary, like Johansen, becomes suspect as well.[39]

Return Transformed: Schwarzkopf and Franks

For all of their differences in rationale and consensus, for all of the contrast between the theater commanders who led them, the 1991 and 2003 U.S. blitzes against Iraq were attended by fundamentally similar battle exhortation. Together, that discourse is fundamentally different from Eisenhower's for D-Day. This suggests two things. First, the American battlefield has changed more dramatically since World War II (and across Korea and Vietnam) than we often recognize. Second, the change has been substantive enough to resist (essentially) the significant differences between the wars in Iraq. In order to identify how the exhortations of Operation Desert Storm and Operation Iraqi Freedom resemble one another and how they represent a distinct shift from Eisenhower's message, let us start by noting what is different about them. Below on the left is General Norman Schwarzkopf's exhortation, which he released to the troops shortly after midnight, January 17, 1991, and then read personally to the officers in his command center. On the right is the exhortation of General Tommy Franks, which he released to the troops on the evening of March 20, 2003, without further comment.

Schwarzkopf

Soldiers, sailors, airmen, and Marines of United States Central Command:

This morning at 0300 we launched Operation Desert Storm, an offensive campaign that will enforce United Nations resolutions that Iraq must cease its rape and pillage of its weaker neighbor and withdraw its forces from Kuwait. The President, the Congress, the American people, and indeed the world stand united in their support for

Franks

Men and women of Operation Iraqi Freedom:

The President of the United States—our Commander in Chief—in agreement with the leadership of our coalition partners has ordered the initiation of combat operations.

Our objectives are clear. We will disarm Iraq and remove the regime that has refused to disarm peacefully. We will liberate the Iraqi people from a dictator who uses torture, your actions. You are a member of the most powerful force our country, in coalition with our allies, has ever assembled in a single theater to face such an aggressor. You have trained hard for this battle and you are ready. During my visits with you, I have seen in your eyes a fire of determination to get this job done and done quickly so that we may return to the shores of our great nation. My confidence in you is total. Our cause is just! Now you must be the thunder and lightning of Desert Storm. May God be with you, your loved ones at home, and our country.

H. Norman Schwarzkopf,
Commander in Chief, U.S.
Central Command[40]

murder, hunger, and terror as tools of oppression. We will bring food, medicines, and other humanitarian assistance to Iraqis in need. We will take care to protect innocent civilians and the infrastructure that supports them, and we will help the Iraqi people start anew to build a future of their own with a government of their choice. You have my highest personal confidence and the confidence of your Commander in Chief.

You are now in harm's way. Our task will not be easy, but we are fighting for a just cause and the outcome is not in doubt. I am proud of you—all that you have done and all you will achieve in the days ahead.

We will all do our duty.

May God bless each of you, this coalition, and the United States of America.

Gen Franks[41]

One difference between these exhortations stems from the difference in rhetorical sense and ability of the generals. Stylistically, Schwarzkopf's text flows more smoothly and economically. It is more felicitous with its metaphors. It recognizes the importance of service identification in its audience ("Soldiers, sailors, airmen, and Marines"). As to its means of delivery, Schwarzkopf was not content to have the message distributed via the chain of command, first electronically, then by unit readings and flier. He verbalized it for those physically about him. Moreover, he had his command-center reading followed by a word of prayer by the command chaplain and a playing of Lee Greenwood's song "God Bless the U.S.A." Schwarzkopf's outsized physique and demeanor are even echoed in the matchless title that he applied to the bottom of his message. By contrast, Franks is less polished and less grand, offering an unembellished message without ceremony. His references to the "Commander in Chief" are to the president rather than himself. He even abbreviates his rank, closing simply "Gen Franks." When launching the war against Afghanistan a year and a half earlier, Franks had offered nothing at all. Accounting for this generally lower profile, Franks remembered in a news conference (shortly after the start of his war in Iraq) the first book he ever read: "It was a book about Julius Caesar. I remember parts of it. The book said Julius Caesar was a general. He made long speeches. They killed him."[42]

Another difference between the two exhortations is their description of the mission. Operation Desert Storm is described by Schwarzkopf in a single, simply stated sentence. By contrast, the objectives of Operation Iraqi Freedom require four sentences from Franks, more space than any other matter he addresses. This reflects the more complex nature of his campaign and, perhaps, his more limited ability to sum it up. It may also betray a degree of defensiveness. Lacking the international consensus enjoyed by Schwarzkopf in the earlier war, Franks makes much of disarming, liberating, protecting, and assisting, as if to clarify who is wearing the white hats in his venture.

There is still another reason Franks may devote so much of his message to the mission—and here we transition to what is fundamentally similar between him and Schwarzkopf and fundamentally different from Eisenhower. Both Franks's and Schwarzkopf's most formative years were spent in Vietnam and the post-Vietnam military. In waging the largest fight of their respective careers, and rhetorically framing those fights, these generals are righting old wrongs. In Franks's case, he still smarts from the "pessimism and negativism" that pervaded the military after Vietnam, its listless "Vietnam-era draftees," and the constraints of "a largely *static* war of attrition" on the "dynamics of combat." In response, he offers a busy, wholehearted, can-do operation for Iraq. Its objectives "are clear" and manifold. By stringing them together in rapid succession, Franks conveys action, even movement, and self-assurance. Five times, in this part of the message, he refers to his force in terms of "we will," leaving no room for the loitering "rotten apples" of the mid-1970s.[43] Later in the text he again leaves no room for idlers with an unmoored "We will all do our duty." For Schwarzkopf, his Vietnam-era demon, and his answer to it, are still clearer. In his memoirs, he remembers painfully of his first war: "It was a nightmare that the American public had withdrawn its support: our troops in World War I and World War II had *never* had to doubt for one minute that the people on the home front were fully behind them. We in the military hadn't chosen the enemy or written the orders—our elected leaders had. Nevertheless, we were taking much of the blame. We soldiers, sailors, airmen, and Marines were literally the sons and daughters of America, and to lose public support was akin to being rejected by our own parents."[44]

In his Desert Storm exhortation Schwarzkopf fully preempts this injustice: "The President, the Congress, the American people, and indeed the world stand united in their support for your actions." While Eisenhower accounted for earlier Allied setbacks, he did not have to deal with such a long-festering specter. Franks and Schwarzkopf do, and they address it plainly.

Reference to proper authority is another topic common to the Iraq war exhortations that is absent from Eisenhower's. Now there is a difference in pitch. Schwarzkopf, who enjoyed broad backing for his confrontation of Iraq's invasion of Kuwait, makes the reference in brief, in "United Nations resolutions." Franks, asked to forge into Iraq without international consensus, is more explicit. His opening words identify on whose authority the operation is being launched ("The President"), and if anyone doubts whether that authority is sufficient, Franks clarifies the chain of command. The general also makes reference to the leadership of coalition partners, but the dashes around "Commander in Chief" make clear who has ordered the invasion. Eisenhower, by contrast, had no interest in such legalism. That proper authority backed the Great Crusade is assumed by his text, and that assumption is well grounded: Two and a half years earlier the United States had declared war on Germany. Naked aggression by Germany had been protracted before then. It is in Ridgway, when a sudden war hung perilously in the balance and the fighting took place without a conventional declaration of war, that concern for proper authority first emerged. Confusion and loss in Vietnam only furthered that interest. By the time of Iraq, the growth of unparalleled American military might and the potential for its abuse require treatment of the topic.

Delayed timing of address is another difference between the Iraq war exhortations and Normandy's. Recall that the most conventional time for battle exhortation is immediately before combat. Military discourse far in advance or long afterward is inevitably addressing a situation other than bracing troops for a fight. Of course battle exhortation operates in the midst of combat, too, but then it is typically within the domain of more junior leaders, and its form is briefer and less politic. Classically, in keeping with Caesar's "military custom," battle exhortation takes the form of a general addressing his army immediately before combat. This is not, however, the practice of Schwarzkopf and Franks. Their battle exhortations come after the fact. Schwarzkopf speaks in the past tense, explaining, "This morning at 0300 we launched Operation Desert Storm." Franks speaks in the present and future tense but did not release his exhortation until the evening of D+1, roughly twenty-four hours after the commencement of hostilities. Moreover, receipt of Schwarzkopf's and Franks's discourse could not be immediate. Troops found the messages posted or heard them read as they broke from combat already underway.

The change in timing may be attributed to at least two factors on the contemporary American battlefield: instant, widely accessible news reporting and (also because of advances in communication technology) hair-trigger diplomacy. In the case of news reporting—or more specifically, the news media reporting troop movements, objectives, and timing to the enemy, however innocently—Schwarzkopf and Franks can only cloak such information until battle is joined. While it took days for Eisenhower's enemy to ascertain fully the nature of the attack that had commenced against them, Schwarzkopf's and Franks's enemies would only have to watch televised news for a short while as it raced among a multitude of intelligence-producing reporters and satellites. Preliminary battle exhortation would be known to the enemy as quickly as to its intended audience, compromising the element of surprise and the relative safety that surprise affords the attacker. Thus no responsible theater commander can exhort today when Eisenhower did.

As for diplomacy, instantaneous communications have created the opportunity for last-minute concessions by an adversary to stay or change the mission of U.S. forces, rendering preliminary battle exhortation moot. Iraqi leadership did not afford itself this opportunity in 1991 or 2003, but, as we shall see in the next section, a Haitian junta did in 1994, suddenly changing the temper of a U.S. invasion. In the past, communications were not swift or sure enough to make such an abrupt stay of combat possible. (The Battle of New Orleans is the classic example: the Treaty of Ghent was signed on December 24, 1814, but unwitting American and British forces clashed on January 14, 1815.) For Schwarzkopf and Franks an abrupt change of plans is a real potentiality, effectively delaying their battle exhortation.

Accounting for delay, for references to proper authority, and for rebuttals to Vietnam in Schwarzkopf and Franks is relatively straightforward. There are two more subtle features operating in their discourse, however: a pervading sense of restraint and an undoing of the tension of reputation. Let us identify each first, then speculate about their causes.

In the case of restraint, Schwarzkopf is again the more economical, checking his "offensive" and "battle" terminology with a paradoxical sentence that is, in the end, about moderation. "During my visits with you," he says, "I have seen in your eyes a fire of determination to get this job done and done quickly so that we may return to the shores of our great nation." Perhaps coaxing the troops, Schwarzkopf sees fire and determination, but it is not to slaughter or occupy; it is to complete the job efficiently and leave. Franks, for his part, pushes "combat operations" and "fighting" aside with his lengthy objectives statement. There, to "disarm" and "remove" the enemy is as close as he comes to advocating violence. The rest of the mission, as mentioned before, is about liberation, humanitarian assistance, self-government, and protecting people and infrastructure. Eisenhower was a warmonger in comparison, encouraging troops (through text and letterhead) to participate in a flaming-sword crusade. He called for "the destruction" of the enemy and "the elimination" of its tyranny. He boasted of the Allies having "inflicted" upon the enemy "great defeats, in open battle, man-to-man," and he pointed to vast Allied stores of "weapons and munitions" and "trained fighting men." Explicitly, evocatively, he articulated confidence in his audience's "skill in battle." Schwarzkopf and Franks both express confidence in their troops but are vague about what talent they are confident in.

Contrasting the restraint of Schwarzkopf and Franks with the belligerence of Eisenhower is not to suggest that Eisenhower did not employ other means to manage the violence in his men. There is an inherent need to manage violence in armies. The point here is that more recent theater exhortation is fundamentally more reserved.

Before identifying how Schwarzkopf and Franks undo the tension of reputation, we should remember how Eisenhower and others once built it. "The eyes of the world are upon you," Eisenhower cautioned. "Hopes and prayers" —not guarantees of appreciation—"march with you." Likewise, Washington warned, "The Eyes of all our Countrymen are now upon us, and we shall have their blessings, and praises, if happily we are the instruments of saving them from the Tyranny mediated against them." Conversely, he noted, "If we now shamefully fail, we shall become infamous to the whole world." Even the less stiff and demanding Morgan explained to his militiamen that future accolades required them to briefly stand their ground; "And then, when you return to your homes, how the old folks will bless you, and the girls will kiss you for your gallant conduct." Traditionally, future reputation is conditional. Warnings to perform before others' gaze and judgment make for a self-conscious prod.

Against this, and certainly in no small measure because of the trauma of Vietnam, approval of the troops is not explicitly dependent upon anything in Schwarzkopf and Franks. Schwarzkopf's confidence in his troops "is total." He catalogs authorities and observers "united in their support for your actions." Franks is already "proud of you—all that you have done and all you will achieve in the days ahead." Troops are not required to rise a great deal to the occasion but asked to remain present and execute well-rehearsed tasks.

Neither commander demands an *if* for his *then,* guaranteeing a favorable future reputation.

Psychologically this can only soothe the audience rather than spur it, and this is the cumulative effect of all of the changes we have identified. Schwarzkopf's and Franks's messages are not fiery addresses that precede battle but gentle explanations that follow the joining of it. The intent seems less to animate troops than to keep them informed and reassure them that their destructive acts are warranted. The shift is evident even in punctuation and delivery. Whereas Eisenhower's message is filled with exclamation marks, Schwarzkopf offers but one exclamation and Franks none at all. To stir his immediate audience, Schwarzkopf follows with prayer and music, but his choices fly in the face of tradition. Montecuccoli would have prayer precede battle exhortation, and significantly so, experience having taught him that "when one is engaged in combat, prayer is untimely, resembling the entreaties of armed rabbits." Montecuccoli would also advocate horns and drums, instruments "more suitable than others for arousing pugnacity."[45] But Schwarzkopf opts for Greenwood's "God Bless the U.S.A.," which tends toward the weepy. This is not to say that Schwarzkopf is making bad choices or that he fails in his intent. (After the playing of Greenwood, Schwarzkopf remembers with satisfaction, "Every member of the staff stood a little taller and I could see tears glisten in more than one eye.")[46] It is to say that Schwarzkopf is making *new* choices. Franks's simple release is, in his lower-key way, still consistent with his immediate predecessor's choices. When, in time, troops catch up with his message, they are more apt to take quiet satisfaction from it than jostle one another combatively.

To what can we attribute this change from Eisenhower, a change in battle exhortation manifest enough to eclipse the different personalities of Schwarzkopf and Franks and the different circumstances of their wars? It seems likely that it is a change in audience. Compared to Eisenhower, and most theater commanders in history, Schwarzkopf and Franks address forces that include no conscripts, plus unprecedented proportions of technology-driven combat roles, support roles, female troops, and news correspondents. While each of these changes could be studied at length, let us consider them here very briefly.

Volunteers join the armed forces for many reasons. Some pursue economic benefit, some violence, still others high-minded ideals. When it comes time for battle, however, concern for one's reputation comes to the fore in today's all-volunteer force like never before. For plunder is no longer fashionable, the boost of combat pay negligible, and violence checked by additional constraints. Moreover the volunteer cannot claim after battle, as can the conscript: "I had no choice. The government drafted, armed, and pointed me in that direction." In essence the volunteer has asked for it, freely joining up, and this can lead to a question the conscript never faces: "What have I gotten myself into?" The prospect of a wrong, ugly, or injurious war haunts a volunteer's conscience, and that doubt is not redressed through belligerent cadences. It requires assurances.

The rise in technology-driven combat roles (such as aviation and computerized fire direction) and the support roles behind them means an ever-smaller proportion of troops actually closes with the enemy and slashes it out in a melee, at least in the blitz phase of Western war. While heavily laden, blade-carrying warriors who jump from aircraft and landing craft benefit from a good "pumping up," troops who manage sophisticated consoles and maintain complicated equipment do not. Undue excitement can lead to error. Tech-warriors benefit from cooler, calming discourse.

The increasing presence of women on the battlefield is explicitly acknowledged in Franks's opening to the "men and women" of Operation Iraqi Freedom, but the company of women may also be inferred by untraditional silences. Schwarzkopf and Franks make nothing of fraternity, for instance, while Eisenhower (echoing Shakespeare's Henry V) spoke of "brothers-in-arms" and "fighting men." The unwinding of the tension of reputation may also stem in part from women typically not sharing men's insecurity about their gender. Put another way, the dramatic public challenge to prove oneself a man—especially through the test of combat—does not have an equivalent for women.[47] A taunt to masculinity by Schwarzkopf or Franks would not apply to their female troops, and a taunt to womanliness would not make sense. Audience, then, summons not merely gender-neutral language but a discourse that is less anxious.

Finally, there are the news media of the contemporary battlefield. While Eisenhower faced journalists as well ("There was, at one time, a total of 943 within the European theater"[48]), Schwarzkopf and Franks face a generally less sympathetic press corps that is far better equipped to record, editorialize, and speed news to market. The military's increased sense of "consequence management"[49] even influenced when the first war against Iraq ended. Chairman of the Joint Chiefs of Staff General Colin Powell recommended Desert Storm conclude once Iraqi troops' last major route of retreat started being dubbed the "Highway of Death" by reporters and its carnage widely televised.[50] The overall result of such attendance by the press has been a dramatic loss of privacy on the battlefield. Eisenhower addressed his troops not unlike a coach in the locker room: spiritedly, knowing the press would find out what was said but in time and as a secondary or tertiary audience. By contrast Schwarzkopf and Franks address their troops sounding like school officials at a commencement ceremony. Their discourse is directed at the troops but highly conscious of the rest of those immediately present, the parents and friends, so to speak. Exhortation in their case cannot be too bellicose.

There are commonalities between Eisenhower's, Schwarzkopf's, and Franks's discourse: the continued sense that the start of battle is an occasion for speech; the timeless need to counter warrior anxiety. But the audience is now male and female, more technically oriented, entirely volunteer, and—really—boundless in scope. Combine these changes with theater commanders who cut their teeth in Vietnam, and it is small wonder that battle exhortation has returned (from Vietnam) transformed. Theater-level encouragement, at least, has assumed the form of soothing assurances.

Differences by Combat Arm

We have observed the evolution of American battle exhortation toward a drier, calming, retroactive discourse. But we have based this observation on ecumenical texts addressed to all of the troops in a given theater, hundreds of thousands of troops fulfilling a variety of combat and combat support roles. Might battle exhortation sound different when directed to more specific audiences, such as only aviators, or only sailors or infantry? There are several reasons to think so. One is the rank of senior commanders at the military-specialty level. A field-grade rather than general-grade officer, the commander of an air squadron, ship, or infantry battalion is not expected to wax as strategically as the theater commander. Nor has the field-grade officer been subject to the promotion criterion of careful speech to quite the same degree. A second reason is that this level commander typically enjoys a more private forum when addressing his or her (smaller) unit. While an embedded reporter can change this dynamic, by and large field-grade exhortation is removed from the public eye. These elements of rank and privacy are apt to lead to discourse that is less sanitized than the theater variety—and more sensitive to the unique circumstances of a given military specialty. Varying specialties constitute a third reason to expect battle exhortation to differ among air, sea, and land forces.

William Hauser, when cautioning that the will to fight tends to vary across the services, notes important service differences, particularly between air and sea forces on the one hand and ground forces on the other. He starts by defining the basic fighting entity of each combat arm as the airbase, ship, and ground battalion. While aircraft temporarily leave the airbase and the ship moves, aviators and sailors nevertheless operate from fixed environments or platforms. (Naval aviators experience both varieties of movement, but their airbase ship still provides them a stable home.) Further, the airbase and ship project violence through "complex machines" that are manned by "officer-fighters," and when the immediate mission is over, the officer-fighters relinquish their weapon systems back to "the system" for maintenance. By contrast, the ground battalion does not enjoy a fixed physical environment; its fighters are primarily enlisted personnel rather than officers; it wages close rather than projected combat; and its fighters and weapons are "inseparable." Hauser argues that these are more than just physical and organizational differences. "Their most profound effects are psychological."[51] We may go further, finding effects that are rhetorical. Indeed a comparison of discourse across the naval expeditionary group that participated in Operation Uphold Democracy in Haiti reflects different rhetorical choices stemming from different psychological concerns.

First, let us briefly describe the composition of a naval expeditionary—or amphibious—group and the background of the operation. Simply put, such a group is amphibious because it consists of an amalgam of Navy vessels designed specifically for ship-to-shore operations, the sailors who operate them, and a complement of air- and ground-oriented Marines. The fliers help transfer the ground force between ship and shore and support the ground force while ashore. The ground force constitutes the "focus of effort," the forwardmost projection of American troops and assets during an operation.

Operation Uphold Democracy represented the culmination of tensions between the administration of President Bill Clinton and the Haitian junta of Lieutenant General Raoul Cedras. Already supporting the United Nations economic blockade of Haiti in support of deposed president Jean-Bertand Aristide, Clinton announced on television on September 15, 1994, "The message of the United States to the Haitian dictators is clear. Your time is up. Leave now or we will force you from power."[52] While a U.S. delegation headed by former President Jimmy Carter attempted to negotiate the junta's departure and terms that would introduce enforcing U.S. forces peaceably, Clinton established the timetable for a forcible landing. The Army's Eighty-second Airborne Division readied to seize Port-au-Prince, Haiti's largest city and capital, while the amphibious group centered around the USS *Wasp* readied to seize Cap Haitien, Haiti's second-largest city.

Command of all of the Marines involved (air and ground) rested with Colonel Thomas Jones. From the start it had been difficult for him to predict the mission. When the amphibious group had originally come within striking distance of Haiti, the Marines' most probable mission seemed to be the evacuation of American citizens and other foreign nationals from Port-au-Prince. As the prospect of full-scale invasion increased, shifting the Marines' objective to Cap Haitien, the type of mission remained contingent upon Carter's diplomacy. Preparing his Marines for the most violent scenario, Jones began articulating his hortatory intent through meetings with his officers and addresses to his enlisted men and by personally writing the "commander's intent" section of the operation order. Jones's "intent," consistent with his oral presentations, reads:

> We will attack and overwhelm the enemy with absolute force and resolution, while treating the populace with dignity, fairness, and compassion. We must win and maintain the "Hearts and Minds" of the Haitian people! We must immediately capture—to hold—the port and airfield, using surprise, shock, and simultaneity of execution. We must maintain security of the force always; all maneuver and movement of forces must be accomplished within the framework of absolute security! We must rapidly paralyze the [Haitian military]; consequently, the northern military district headquarters . . . is the Center of Gravity and must be controlled quickly. Secure all objectives using non-lethal force to the maximum extent possible. Once deadly force becomes necessary, it must be used decisively and unhesitantly. Prepare a reservoir of "audibles" for every planned/expected action. We will comport ourselves always as liberators not dominators. Mental and physical toughness must be our watchwords; be prepared to do what others couldn't, wouldn't, or shouldn't. UPHOLD ALWAYS the standards of our Corps and legacy of those who have gone before us.[53]

Although doctrinally Jones was addressing both air and ground Marines, and technically there was a battalion commander intermediating between him and the ground Marines, Jones was the de facto ground commander of the operation. He was an infantryman by trade and hands-on in nature. He faced far more ground than aviation Marines, and he soon established his command post ashore. Not surprisingly, then, this text predominantly addresses issues relevant to the infantry: capturing and holding physical objectives, interacting with the local populace, and protecting Marines on the ground. The discussion of lethal versus nonlethal force, for instance, is couched in the decision-making framework of the infantry, not aviation, where all force is assumed to be lethal.

More telling, Jones speaks in aggressive, close-with-the-enemy terms. His verbs are vivid ("overwhelm," "paralyze," "controlled"), his tense imperative (nine instances of *must*, two of *will*), and his tone superlative ("rapidly," "quickly," "absolute," "ALWAYS"). Besides conveying purpose to the infantrymen, Jones's language is clearly designed to stimulate them. This is particularly apparent from the last third of the text, which breaks into less mission-specific, more clichéd cadences. Young American males are apt to grow excited from admonitions to be ready for sudden, line-of-scrimmage changes in plan ("audibles") and to carry themselves like World War II "liberators." Having volunteered and trained for close combat, they would want to prove tough, daring, and equal to Marines elsewhere (Jones's challenges).

In addition to this grammar of belligerence, there was in Jones's delivery a belligerence. For the de facto ground commander did not merely share his intent by operation order, letting his subordinate commanders soak up the message and share it down the chain of command. Jones made a point of speaking personally to his men. He gathered his officers in the *Wasp's* wardroom. To address enlisted Marines he moved about the *Wasp* and flew to the other Marine-bearing ship in the amphibious group. In these large groups, two significant things happened: First, Marines were able to witness the personification of an aggressive message. Jones spoke with the intensity, abruptness, and resolve of a proven warrior. At the same time the Marines were able to feed emotionally off of the rising fervor of the group. Gathered together in tropical heat; sharing in the "lust" for contact with the enemy; eager to demonstrate fraternal standing—the riflemen absorbed not only Jones's passion but also each other's. Personal misgivings about the utility of the mission or the adequacy of the rules of engagement were eclipsed (at least partially) by a collective aggressive confidence.[54]

How does exhortation directed specifically toward aviators and sailors aboard the *Wasp* compare? Let us look at the rest of the Marines first. Doctrinally, the Marines of the helicopter squadron answered to Jones like the infantry, but philosophically this was less the case. A dyed-in-the-wool infantryman, Jones was a "ground pounder," a "mud fighter," a "grunt." His single-minded sternness was fairly at odds with the high-spirited humor of the pilots. The customary risk and dash of their line of work led many of them (particularly the younger ones) to suffer through the colonel's admonishments for toughness, then return to their movies and pranks. Among the enlisted men of the squadron, Jones's sternness represented the high-strung unapproachability of officers on "the ground side of the house." (In the "air wing" enlisted maintenance crews and officers tend to interact less formally.) Thus the exhortation that the maintenance crews and pilots better identified with was that of their more immediate superior, squadron commander Lieutenant Colonel Anthony Zell.

As the hour for the landing drew nearer, Zell exhorted his men on two occasions. At the conclusion of a squadron formation within the massive hangar deck of the *Wasp,* when both day and night air crews were together, Zell called for the troops to gather round and addressed his enlisted Marines with officers still present. Then, during a ready briefing, he addressed his officers exclusively.

Zell's two exhortations vary on tangential points. For the enlisted Marines, most of whom would remain aboard ship, Zell underscored the importance of their support role. For the officers, most of whom had not flown in the face of ground fire before, he explained what they could expect during their first time in combat. In both forums, however, Zell devoted the majority of his exhortation to safety. "From the beginning, the importance of the mission is drummed into us Marines," Zell acknowledged, but "Marine aviation must guard against getting caught up in the mission. Shortcuts on maintaining aircraft jeopardize everything—shortchanging most of all the Marines on the ground. Suddenly going to the rescue may not be the best thing to do, either. In the Marines, aviation's close relationship with ground-pounders can lead to *wrong* decisions."[55]

This was Zell's exhortation shortly before his squadron went into action, and yet it is clearly different from Jones's ground talk. Rather than being prepared, as Jones is, "to do what others couldn't, wouldn't or shouldn't," Zell urges caution. Rather than privileging "security of the force," Jones's variation on the martial stricture to leave no man behind, Zell raises the possibility of limited rescue. Rather than embracing "our Corps" as a brotherhood that supersedes military specialty, Zell recognizes a potential hazard in closeness. But a more careful reading reveals not a circumvention of Jones's intent but an assurance of its completion through levelheadedness. For properly maintaining and flying aircraft do not require "mental and physical toughness" so much as they require sticking to procedures that stem from decades of aviation mishaps and misadventures. Careless maintenance or cockpit bravado can down an aircraft as quickly as ground fire, needlessly endangering lives and derailing the mission.

Might Zell's call for prudence be more of a symptom of the limited threat that aircraft faced in Haiti rather than a reflection of aviation exhortation generally? Certainly a particularly desperate or suicidal air mission would engender discourse less focused on safety. But short of such a situation, the complexity and inherent risk of aviation involve different psychological pressures than those faced by the infantry. A quick look at Navy bomber pilots who participated in the first strikes of Operation Iraqi Freedom seems corroborative. Prior to launching from the USS *Constellation*—while sitting amid briefings on targets, routes, rules of engagement, and safety—the pilots "get into their bubble," a quiet, undemonstrative state that might be interpreted as frightened cocooning by ground warriors. But the pilots have technicalities on their mind and nothing, physically, on their back that requires more physical and emotional intensity. When a Navy commander concedes after his first sortie, "I wasn't actually scared of dying from the [anti-aircraft fire], but I'm always scared of landing on the carrier at night,"[56] he lays bare the aviator's nightmare. It is not being overrun by the enemy, which is the infantryman's nightmare. It is not even death by enemy fire. It is making a technical mistake in a particularly unforgiving line of work. In this light, Zell's exhortation is fitting.[57]

The exhortation that sailors aboard the *Wasp* received from their captain likewise reflects peculiarities of their service. Navy Captain Robert Chaplin exhorted his crew twice before the scheduled forcible landing. Some twelve hours prior, he announced over the ship's intercom: "*Wasp*, this is the ship's captain. We're heightening our state of readiness. . . . Everyone's job is important. From the [operations specialist] who's watching his screen, to the engineers in the engine room, to the messmen who keep the mess lines going so everybody gets fed. Nobody's job is more important than anybody else's." Six hours later, he added and amplified: "The leadership in Haiti has not heeded an ultimatum by the President. . . . We're currently steaming for Cap Haitien at twenty knots. We have received the execution order to put our Marines ashore a little after midnight. This is not practice. There is no room for mistakes. Everyone must do their job flawlessly. . . . God bless the United States." And on the heels of this second message he had recordings of the Navy's and the Marines' hymns played.[58]

Here, too, like the ground and air commander, the ship's captain exhorts his crew for battle. His stroking of personnel assigned less glamorous duty and the playing of the upbeat service hymns confirms that his intent is to inspire. Chaplin's invocation that God bless the United States suggests that he himself is moved. But a comparison with the discourse of Jones and Zell reveals differences. The *Wasp*'s captain speaks in terms of continuing action.

Watches, engineers, messmen, all are directed to carry on with their duties, albeit with extra care. It is "our Marines" who are going ashore to do something extraordinary. Chaplin's discourse keeps his sailors informed and on an even keel. This contrasts sharply with Jones's demands that his men be bold and tough enough to take charge of a squalid, unfamiliar city. It also contrasts, though less dramatically, with Zell's warning to be careful.

Not only does the ship's captain employ a different grammar than the ground and air commanders, but he also employs a different delivery. Jones and Zell, remember, address their troops in person. That is what Marine commanders do. It is also what they *can* do, because the Navy minds the ships while Marines gather for communication. Chaplin, on the other hand, must deliver his address over the ship's intercom, because his thousand sailors (and nearly two thousand embarked Marines) are spread throughout the ship. The Navy crew in particular is not easily assembled because of the ongoing tasks it must perform. But address by this means limits how fiery Chaplin's exhortation can be. At one end, he physically addresses a microphone in a small, quiet room. The impersonality of this probably checks his emotional involvement to some degree. At the other end, in the relative quiet and isolation of the ship's compartments, sailors are less likely to be roused to fever pitch than if they were assembled in large groups. Beyond this dispersion of the audience and separation between audience and speaker, the intercom is the ship's routine means for keeping the crew informed and working together. It is associated with efficient news sharing, while the Marines' habit of "passing the word" in person is as demonstrative as it is newsworthy.

The lesser emotional charge to ship's communication may also be observed in the fact that the Navy lacks a motivational catchword or phrase. In the Marines, it is "Oo-rah!" In the Army, "Hoo-ah!" "Airborne!" or "All the way!" The rugged, in-person circumstances of ground fighters engender this sort of spirited grunting back and forth. But a comparable grunt over the intercom, either by the captain or a junior in reply, would sound ridiculous.

Might a more perilous naval situation than Operation Uphold Democracy produce battle exhortation of more belligerent nature? Perhaps, but generally, systemically, no. Let us eavesdrop, for instance, aboard the submarine USS *Barb* during World War II. Part of a wolf pack in the South China Sea, having lost one sister submarine to enemy fire and the other having just fired the last of her torpedoes, the *Barb* bears in on the enemy. Commander Eugene Fluckey sounds battle stations, waits for the gonging over the intercom to stop, then announces to his crew: "Men, we have a nice fat convoy of five big tankers and six or seven escorts. *Queenfish* hit one that hasn't slowed, so they're alerted. We may have a bit of tangle, but oil for the lamps of Japan makes the *Barb* thumb her nose at anyone. On your toes! We're heading in!"[59]

Two patrols and four months later, Fluckey led the *Barb* on an unprecedented attack inside a Chinese harbor being used by Japanese shipping. This time offering words before the sounding of battle stations, he announced: "Men, we've successfully entered Namkwan Harbor undetected. We've got the biggest target of the war in front of us. Our approach is starting. Make ready all tubes. I figure the odds are 10 to 1 in our favor. MAN BATTLE STATIONS TORPEDOES!"[60]

In both cases, information for the crew constitutes the majority of the message. Yes, Fluckey adds color in the first address, thumbing the sub's collective nose at enemy warships. In the second, he addresses the odds, countering heightened anxiety among his crew. (He also declined to have his men don life jackets, lest the precaution unnerve them.) But the majority of these messages help the crew understand how their boat is situated in relation to the enemy and what they, technically, are likely to be asked to do. Given that the men are below decks, compartmentalized, and performing specialized tasks, this is the sort of discourse they need to wage combat effectively, not motivating cadences.

Having compared the battle exhortation of ground, air, and sea forces, we might characterize their discourse as the belligerent, cautious, and informative species of the genus, respectively. In each case the audience and its brand of combat seem to be the driving influences on the discourse rather than the personal style of individual commanders. Exhortation of ground troops is most pugnacious because pugnacity is a state of mind most appropriate to warriors who still carry bayonets. Exhortation of fliers and maintenance crews is most cautious because aircraft are best served by careful procedure. Exhortation of sailors is most informative because, compartmentalized, sailors are the least able to observe their leadership, the enemy, and one another.

How each combat arm aboard the *Wasp* responded to the abrupt cancellation of forcible invasion is also instructive. Four and a half hours before the Marines were scheduled to assault Cap Haitien, literally as they were drawing weapons from the *Wasp*'s armories, Captain Chaplin toggled the intercom and announced: "*Wasp*, this is the ship's captain. The operation has been delayed. We're on a twelve to twenty-four hour tether. We're not doing the landing tonight."[61] Certainly this information affected the duties of some of the *Wasp*'s sailors. By and large, however, their work continued whether

Marines went ashore or not. In the berthing and staging areas of the infantry, however, the news was greeted with disappointment and anger. Some Marines continued to camouflage their faces in denial.[62] By vocation, training, and exhortation, they were more than ready to do Jones's belligerent bidding. The squadron had a problem of its own. Zell had put his crews in a sleep cycle that enabled his most experienced pilots to participate in the midnight assault. Once the mission shifted to a daytime administrative landing, with reduced but continued risk of shooting, the squadron's least experienced pilots were suddenly slated to lead. Despite the request of many senior fliers, however, Zell would not upend the sleep cycle. In aviation, he made clear, for safety's sake, "Crew rest is paramount."[63]

Summary

In this chapter we have been reminded that individual commanders can make a difference in the quality of battle exhortation. Westmoreland struggled, for instance, underestimating the importance of relevance behind one's visits. Schwarzkopf was more polished than Franks.

But we have underscored that environment and audience can influence the discourse significantly. Ridgway held "rhetoric" in low regard but within a month of taking command in Korea felt the need to rally his demoralized army in almost Jeffersonian terms. At the other extreme, the war in Vietnam and its accompanying chaos at home rendered nearly all exhortation moot.

In the broadest sense, the American battlefield has changed so dramatically that exhortation at the theater level has evolved from bold challenge, as before the invasion of Normandy, to after-the-fact conscience soothing, as in operations Desert Storm and Iraqi Freedom. The commencement of hostilities still produces troop anxiety and is still regarded as an occasion for speech, but a host of factors—preeminent military power; a high-tech, coed, all-volunteer force; a loss of privacy—demand assurance more than exclamation.

When we have individuated by combat arm, we perceive that ground, air, and naval forces are each encouraged differently. Ground combatants benefit from battle cries, fliers from checklists, and sailors from shipboard newscasts.

These findings support Onasander's contention that the battlefield commander needs to be a ready speaker. They also help us understand why the ready speaker cannot afford to be insensitive to the many elements and demands of the rhetorical situation.

Conclusion

At the start I alluded to the pervasive use of battle exhortation, in civilian as well as military life, and chose to focus on theory and practice within martial settings. Even in its primary context, the battlefield, however, the genre has not been a popular object of study. Morally, it can be regarded as suspect, this advocacy of fighting, this *talk*. Practically, it is sometimes deemed affected or impossible. So as the vehicle for reviewing my conclusions, let us observe battle exhortation from a nonmilitary context. Doing so offers perspective on these questions of morality and probability. It also provides, by analogy, a measure of validation to our military-context conclusions.

Imagine being a fourteen-year-old Jewish boy in the spring of 1944 when, suddenly, you, your family, and your community are wrested from your homes, crowded into trains, and shipped to points unknown. Imagine, further, that upon your arrival at some prison facility you are deprived of your packed possessions, separated from your mother and young sister, stripped of your clothes, shorn of your hair, disinfected with gasoline and hot water, issued prison clothing, and marched from holding area to holding area. Sometime during those first hours you are informed, "Work or the crematory —the choice is in your hands," and you witness babies being dumped alive into a burning pit. Your own fate seems to hinge on which line you are instructed to stand in. At midnight, your second or third evening in this terrifying place, you find yourself and others standing before yet another prison block. The prisoner in charge explains:

> Comrades, you're in the concentration camp of Auschwitz. There's a long road of suffering ahead of you. But don't lose courage. You've already escaped the gravest danger: selection. So now, muster your strength, and don't lose heart. We shall all see the day of liberation. Have faith in life. Above all else, have faith. Drive out despair, and you will keep death away from yourselves. Hell is not for eternity. And now, a prayer—or rather, a piece of advice: let there be comradeship among you. We are all brothers, and we are all suffering the same fate. The same smoke floats over all our heads. Help one another. It is the only way to survive. Enough said. You're tired. Listen. You're in Block 17. I am responsible for keeping order here.

Anyone with a complaint against anyone else can come and see me. That's all. You can go to bed. Two people to a bunk. Good night.[1]

This is an Elie Wiesel recollection from the murderous Nazi death camps in which his mother, sister, father, and millions of others would perish. He himself would be reduced to a living corpse there. And yet the speech above he remembers as "the first human words" during his ordeal. How does this text exemplify the issues discussed in this book?

By this point the contours of battle exhortation are readily apparent. While the specific circumstances are different from military combat, the general situation is the same: a group of persons face grim circumstances; their plight is addressed by a formal or self-appointed leader, who addresses topics and manages tensions to counter group dissolution. Encouragement will flow in other directions (laterally, for instance, when Wiesel and his father urge one another on). Encouragement will be provided nonverbally (in the sharing of scarce soup or the sound of Allied bombs). But this text is symbolic action—the audible, verbal sort—intended to brace its audience for the psychological demands of significant challenge.

The mention of danger ("a long road of suffering," "selection"), a cause (seeing "the day of liberation"), and a commander ("responsible for keeping order") reminds us of common topics recorded in chapters 1 and 2. If, wafting up from chronicles, such topics seem rehearsed, how could they be in this tortured nonmilitary context, where a Pole exhorts Jews within the confines of a Nazi death camp? And yet here such topics are, remembered by a participant. The centerpiece call for fraternity is both familiar and a little different from the call by Shakespeare's Henry V or Plutarch's Spartan mother. Here it has nothing to do with reputation. It is purely a matter of commiseration ("we are all suffering the same fate") and survival ("the only way to survive"). In the military contexts there was, in addition to these imperatives, the concern for fraternal standing: the concern for how others would measure the solider in the face of combat. The absence of that dimension here dramatizes its importance among military personnel.

The speaker's alternating between drawing his audience near ("Comrades," "We are all brothers") and keeping it at arm's length ("I am responsible . . . come and see me"), his tender tips for survival balanced by plain protocol ("That's all. . . . Two people to a bunk"), remind us of the tensions surfaced in chapter 3. Rarely are all tensions managed in a single battlefield discourse, and here the speaker has little interest in baiting the prisoners over their reputations or advocating violence as their way out. But he inspires some affection from Wiesel, and that would seem to be response to the balancing of leadership responsibilities. The prisoner in charge caresses the new arrivals, at the same time leveling with them and establishing order. He positions himself in that rhetorical spot that is neither too close nor too distant—in relation to the prisoners. Probably it is for this reason that he is relieved of his responsibilities a few weeks later. The Nazis had no use for deft leadership among the prisoners. Opportunistic brutality was preferred.

In chapter 4 we traced how the larger situation, including audience, can shape battle exhortation, but here we must be careful how we apply our analogy. One nonmilitary instance does not enable us to trace evolutions over time or multiple audiences. It does speak volumes, however, about the versatility and general morality of our speech genre. For as long as we can remember, in the West at least, combatants have preceded or combined fighting with symbolic action. The speech of the prisoner in charge reminds us that this sort of discourse is applicable, and applied, in countless forums: not only on the battlefield but in the concentration camp, the locker room, the political convention hall, and the business teleconference. Nor is it reserved for the powerful and prepared. In fact, the less powerful and prepared have more need for it. Because humanity is, ultimately, a collection of frail bodies and independent wills, to accomplish anything really difficult we must appeal to others for disciplined, corporate behavior. Potential teams must privilege symbolicity over animality. Battle exhortation calls for this, to behave differently than instinct, to manage one's individual will, to get on the line and stay on the line—with others—for the decency or sheer necessity of doing so.

Yes, it is true, battle exhortation can be employed for evil ends. Not long after Wiesel received those "first human words" before Block 17, German troops manning the Siegfried Line were exhorted in the following terms: "*Volksgrenadier!* Traitors from our ranks have deserted to the enemy. Their names are. . . . Deceitful Jewish mud-slingers taunt you with their pamphlets and try to entice you into becoming bastards also. Let them spew their poison. . . . As for the contemptible traitors who have forgotten their honor, rest assured the division will see that they never see home and loved ones again. Their families will have to atone for their treason. . . . Long live Germany! Heil the Führer!"[2] It is the old conundrum, that rhetoric, like the soldier or even the kitchen knife, can be wielded for both good and bad. But the possibility of abuse does not lead us to ban free speech, abolish the armed forces, or dull cutlery. The risk leads us to scrutiny and accountability. Part of my intent through this work has been to show that battle exhortation does not equate to bloodlust or cheerleading but can aim for regulation and significance.

Providing symbolic context for physical action, it tells us whether we fight out of hatred or for something praiseworthy. Exhortation such as that directed to the *volksgrenadier* cannot long endure. It neither nourishes the spirit nor builds the team. But exhortation like that remembered by Wiesel epitomizes the rallying of desperate souls for combined, higher purpose. It addresses a common need. It pursues a common good.

Although I have referred to other cultures in this study, primarily Greco-Roman and English antecedents, my focus has been on battle exhortation from the United States. Now it is commonly said that opposing troops have more in common with one another than with their respective leadership, but that suggests that American troops and American exhortation are fairly representative of troops and exhortation elsewhere—when there is reason to suspect differences. Baron von Steuben, after working the Continental Army into shape, wrote a colleague back home: "The genius of this nation is not in the least to be compared with that of the Prussians, Austrians, or French. You say to your soldier, 'Do this' and he doeth it; but I am obliged to say 'This is the reason why you ought to do that,' and then he does it."[3] While some of the baron's frustration may be attributed to the lack of military tradition in the fledgling United States, certainly there are real and consequential differences between American troops today and their European, Middle Eastern, or Chinese counterparts. These soldiers are likely motivated by different priorities and, to some degree, by different means. International comparisons of battle exhortation could offer insight not only into speech communication but into comparative ethics and sociology. There would likely be practical benefits, as well. From a coalition perspective, if military leaders better understood what language Allied soldiers valued, then they would more likely address allies in fitting terms. From a know-your-enemy perspective, an understanding of rival exhortation might inform psychological warfare's interest in persuading enemies to lay down their arms.

In addition to an American focus, this study has concentrated on the most classic direction of battle exhortation, commanders addressing troops. The other directions identified in chapter 1 merit further investigation, as does perhaps another: an appropriate application of battle exhortation after combat. Onasander and Vegetius recognized the utility of postcombat exhortation but in relation to beaten armies.[4] What about winning armies that are nonetheless wracked with survivor's guilt, killer's guilt, physical mutilation, and post-traumatic stress? Might troops benefit not only from downward, lateral, and interactive battle exhortation but from a fitting echo as well? A reconciliation between traditional battle exhortation and the latest readjustment strategies might elicit new therapies.

In exploring the socialization of society at large into battle exhortation, we hardly scratched the surface, limiting our scope (until the very end) to military settings in history, literature, and cinema. One need only watch the latest children's movie involving a collection of friends and some challenge, however, and odds are that figurative battle exhortation will occur before the climactic scene. Setback and rally—complete with hortatory speech and rising background music—have become as conventional in children's cinema as the contest between good and evil. Indeed, it has become the common formula by which good trumps evil. Investigation into exhortative forums unrelated to the military would deepen our understanding into the need and expectation for such discourse.

Finally, we might ask whether the Department of Defense's pursuit of certain imperatives has inadvertently robbed troops of encouragement on the battlefield. Consider three lost opportunities, starting with the fatigue uniforms of U.S. ground forces. While gear is added for combat, the uniforms are nevertheless the same ones in which these troops run the most routine errands. In other words, they put on the same outfit whether they are about to wage war or get a haircut. Consider, further, the general proscription of "nose art," the hand-painted artwork that used to adorn and individualize military aircraft. Whether depicting sharks' teeth, pinups, or some other image of war or home, such art used to raise the spirits of flight and maintenance crews. Rather than continuing, updated by basic standards, the practice has essentially been stopped. Consider, last, for the sake of this point, music. Armies used to take heart from it on the march and in combat. It is still employed liberally in garrison. And yet when we send troops into combat today, we send them without music, unless they have rigged sound systems of their own. Admittedly, these current practices husband expenditures and lessen the risk of offense—but what is lost for the youngsters being asked to walk the last one hundred meters? Instead, what if, before combat, troops donned a variation of the fatigue uniform reserved for battle? What if, as they emerged from hangars and well decks, they found their aircraft and landing craft sporting decals reserved for battle? What if, as these craft swept toward their objectives (engines droning so loudly that they typically numb rather than animate those on board), motivating music pealed through the cargo hold or vibrated through seats? Without hearing an exhortative word, but still experiencing a lot of symbolic action, these troops would disembark better steeled against the clutches of fear and uncertainty.

Given the present-day challenge of finding time and space for battle exhortation, the symbolism described above might be all the encouragement some troops can get. But we should be slow to dismiss the most traditional form of the genre. The use of encouraging words before dramatic team effort is an entrenched, time-honored institution. Moreover, words may be particularly suited to the operation that grinds into its fifth day, fifth week, or fifth month. Is the struggle still worthy of hardship and danger? Troops might continue to receive answers haphazardly, or we can cultivate the situation through study and practice.

NOTES

Introduction

1. MacArthur's legacy does not include readily remembered battle exhortation like Farragut's or Patton's. The following rhetorical studies reflect MacArthur's non-battlefield rhetorical focus: Bernard K. Duffy and Ronald H. Carpenter, *Douglas MacArthur: Warrior as Wordsmith* (Westport, Conn.: Greenwood Press, 1997); and Ronald H. Carpenter, *Rhetoric in Martial Deliberations and Decision Making: Cases and Consequences* (Columbia: University of South Carolina Press, 2004). "Dugout Doug" was coined by U.S. soldiers on Bataan when MacArthur remained holed up in Corregidor rather than visit them. Although MacArthur routinely braved unsecured areas throughout his career, this derogatory label stuck, probably because he escaped the surrender of the Philippines and because of his generally aloof bearing. See William Manchester, *American Caesar: Douglas MacArthur, 1880–1964* (Boston: Little, Brown, 1978), 3, 236–38.

2. I. A. Richards, *The Philosophy of Rhetoric* (New York: Oxford University Press, 1936), 24, 3.

3. Marine Commandant C. E. Mundy Jr., foreword to MCWP 6-11, *Leading Marines* (Washington, D.C.: U.S. Marine Corps, 2002), ii; Pelopidas in 375 B.C.E. adapted from *Plutarch's Lives*, trans. Bernadotte Perrin, vol. 5, Loeb Classical Library (London: Heinemann, 1917), 17.2 (literally, "Why any more than they into ours?"); Patton remembering a visit to Major General Willard Paul and his Twenty-sixth Division, George S. Patton Jr., *War as I Knew It*, annotated by Paul D. Harkins (Boston: Houghton Mifflin, 1947), 326.

4. Samuel A. Stouffer et al., *Studies in Social Psychology in World War II*, vol. 2, *The American Soldier: Combat and Its Aftermath* (Princeton: Princeton University Press, 1949), 108–11.

5. John Keegan, *The Mask of Command* (New York: Viking Penguin, 1987), 318–21.

6. Army Staff Sergeant Eugene Simpson Jr., home from Iraq, quoted in Bob Herbert, "Paralyzed, a Soldier Asks Why," *New York Times*, October 15, 2004, http://www.nytimes.com/2004/10/15/opinion/15herbert.html.

7. "The art of war will provide a parallel" from *The Institutio Oratoria of Quintilian*, trans. H. E. Butler, Loeb Classical Library (1921; London: Heinemann, 1933), 2.5.15; "the weapons of oratory," 2.16.10; other comparisons to combat, 2.8.3–4, 2.8.16, 3.2.2, 6.4.8, 7.10.13; "military custom" according to Julius Caesar, *The Civil War*, trans. J. M. Carter, Oxford World's Classics (Oxford: Oxford University Press, 1998), 3.90.

8. Lloyd Bitzer, "The Rhetorical Situation," *Philosophy and Rhetoric* 1 (1968): 1–14. It is worth noting for those not steeped in rhetorical theory that by "rhetorical situation" Bitzer means a situation in which real influence is possible. This has little to do with the more popularly encountered "rhetorical question," where no answer is expected.

9. "Essential . . . correspondences" from Richard M. Weaver, *The Ethics of Rhetoric* (1953; Davis, Cal.: Hermagoras, 1985), 56–57.

Chapter 1: Bracing for Combat

1. Xenophon attributes these words to Cyrus the Great, king of Persia, in *The Education of Cyrus* [*Cyropaedia*], trans. Wayne Ambler (Ithaca, N.Y.: Cornell University Press, 2001), 3.3.50; still, Xenophon's Cyrus exhorts his troops shortly thereafter, 3.3.62; S. L. A. Marshall, *Men against Fire: The Problem of Battle Command in Future War* (1947; Gloucester, Mass.: Peter Smith, 1978), 142.

2. Deuteronomy 20:2–4, *NIV/KJV Parallel Bible* (Grand Rapids, Mich.: Zondervan, 1985). Moses, God, the people, Joshua, David, and Hezekiah subsequently use one hortatory expression—"Be strong and courageous"—eleven times: Deuteronomy 31:6, 31:7, 31:23; Joshua 1:6, 1:7, 1:9, 1:18, 10:25; 1 Chronicles 22:13, 28:20; 2 Chronicles 32:7 (NIV).

3. Homer, *The Iliad of Homer,* trans. Richmond Lattimore (Chicago: University of Chicago Press, 1951), 5.529–32.

4. Julius Caesar, *Seven Commentaries on the Gallic War,* trans. Carolyn Hammond, Oxford World's Classics (Oxford: Oxford University Press, 1998), 2.20–21.

5. Bernal Díaz del Castillo, *The Discovery and Conquest of Mexico, 1517–1521,* trans. A. P. Maudslay (1956; New York: Da Capo Press, 1996), 110.

6. Elizabeth quoted in Anne Somerset, *Elizabeth I* (1991; London: Phoenix, 1997), 591.

7. Young Hawk quoted in Herman J. Viola, with Jan Shelton Danis, *It Is a Good Day to Die: Indian Eyewitnesses Tell the Story of the Battle of the Little Bighorn* (1998; Lincoln: University of Nebraska Press, 2001), 32.

8. Exhortation prior to Operation Iraqi Freedom on flyer embossed with division colors, Major General J. N. Mattis to First Marine Division (REIN), "Commanding General's Message to All Hands," March 2003, in *Operation Iraqi Freedom: The Inside Story / NBC News* (Kansas City, Mo.: Andrews McMeel, 2003), 103; undated exhortation prior to the First Marine Division's return to Iraq, Mattis, "First Marine Division Returns to Iraq: Letter to All Hands," published as "A Marine's Letter to His Troops," *Dallas Morning News,* March 21, 2004; embossed letter to families, Mattis, "A Letter from the Commanding General to the Families of Our Sailors and Marines Deploying to the Middle East," February 2004, posted on the Web site of the Key Volunteer Network of Eleventh Marines, http://www.11thmarineskvn.org/2newsletters.htm (accessed April 10, 2004). In all three cases I have removed paragraphing for brevity and consistency.

9. Morale defined as that which "holds the team together and keeps it going" per Field Manual no. 6-22 (FM 6-22), *Army Leadership* (Washington, D.C.: Department of the Army, 2006), 7–8; Dwight D. Eisenhower, *Crusade in Europe* (Garden City, N.Y.: Doubleday, 1948), 210; King and Napoleon under "Morale," in Peter G. Tsouras, *Warriors' Words: A Dictionary of Military Quotations* (London: Arms & Armour, 1992), 269–74; Xenophon, *The Persian Expedition*, trans. Rex Warner, Penguin Classics (1949; Harmondsworth, U.K.: Penguin, 1961), 3.1.

10. Ardant Du Picq, *Battle Studies: Ancient and Modern Battle*, trans. John N. Greely and Robert C. Cotton (1880; Harrisburg, Penn.: Military Service Publishing, 1958), 109, 50, 53–54, 168, 98–100, 102.

11. Lord [Charles] Moran, *Anatomy of Courage* (1945; London: Keynes, 1984); John Baynes, *Morale: A Study of Men and Courage* (New York: Praeger, 1967); F. M. Richardson, *Fighting Spirit: A Study of Psychological Factors in War* (London: Leo Cooper, 1978); Anthony Kellett, *Combat Motivation: The Behavior of Soldiers in Battle* (Boston: Kluwer-Nijhoff, 1982); Edward L. Munson, *The Management of Men: A Handbook on the Systematic Development of Morale and the Control of Human Behavior* (New York: Holt, 1921), 305, 419–21; Stouffer et al., *American Soldier*, chaps. 3 and 4.

12. Stouffer et al., *American Soldier*, 125.

13. Du Picq, *Battle Studies*, 95–96, 170, 175, 102, 99; Du Picq's mortal wounding per "Extract from the History of the 10th Infantry Regiment," in his *Battle Studies*, 35.

14. Quintilian, *The Institutio Oratoria of Quintilian*, 2.16.8. In 12.1.28–29 Quintilian recognized that the "supreme orator" he was trying to create may "in time of war . . . be called upon to inspire his soldiers with courage for the fray," but he offered no systematic analysis.

15. Onasander, "The General," in *Aeneas Tacticus, Asclepiodotus, Onasander*, trans. Illinois Greek Club, Loeb Classical Library (1923; London: Heinemann, 1948), 1.13–16. Onasander's popularity is addressed in the translators' introduction, 351–52.

16. Ibid., 13.1–3, 14.3.

17. Common Vegetius maxims quoted in Tsouras, *Warriors' Words*, 50, 331, 101; his discussion of battle exhortation, *Vegetius: Epitome of Military Science*, trans. N. P. Milner (Liverpool: Liverpool University Press, 1993), 3.12.

18. Paleologus translated and quoted in John R. E. Bliese, "Rhetoric Goes to War: The Doctrine of Ancient and Medieval Military Manuals," *Rhetoric Society Quarterly* 24 (1994): 116–17.

19. Niccolò Machiavelli, *The Art of War*, trans. Ellis Farneworth (1521; Indianapolis: Bobbs-Merrill, 1965), 128.

20. In his treatise on rhetoric, Aristotle's discussion of topics (or lines of argument) distinguishes between universal topics and special topics. The former are so general they may be applied to all subject matter (science, politics, and so on). The latter are particular to a given subject (such as combat motivation). Within a given subject, however, we may say its topics are common, or commonplaces. See Aristotle, "Rhetorica,"

in *The Basic Works of Aristotle,* ed. Richard McKeon (New York: Random House, 1941), books 1–2.

21. Machiavelli, *Art of War,* 75, 128.

22. Raimondo Montecuccoli, "Concerning Battle," trans. Thomas M. Barker, in Barker's *The Military Intellectual and Battle* (Albany: State University of New York Press, 1975), 83, 132. Montecuccoli wrote his treatise while a prisoner of war.

23. Ibid., 130.

24. Ibid., 130–36. Montecuccoli's discussion of topics is more rambling than my synopsis.

25. Ibid, 156–58, 133.

26. Ibid., 128.

27. Ibid., 138.

28. Ibid., 139.

29. For symbolic action see Kenneth Burke, *Language as Symbolic Action: Essays on Life, Literature, and Method* (Berkeley: University of California Press, 1966), 27–29; for more on the social construction of reality or nondiscursive presentational forms, see respectively: Peter L. Berger and Thomas Luckmann, *The Social Construction of Reality: A Treatise in the Sociology of Knowledge* (1966; New York: Anchor, 1990), 36–37, and Susanne Langer, *Philosophy in a New Key: A Study in the Symbolism of Reason, Rite, and Art* (New York: Mentor, 1942), 66–80; Montecuccoli, "Concerning Battle," 133–36.

30. Marshall, *Men against Fire,* 133, 135, 124–26, 133; for postcombat interview of Colonel George B. Crabill, 139–40; for Staff Sergeant Pete F. Deine, 142.

31. Hannah Arendt, *The Human Condition* (Chicago: University of Chicago Press, 1958), 175–81.

32. Marshall, *Men against Fire,* 50, 137, 124, 163–64.

33. W. Kendrick Pritchett, "The General's Exhortations," in *Essays in Greek History* (Amsterdam: J. C. Gieben, 1994); additional commentary may be found in Pritchett, "Ancient Greek Battle Speeches and a Palfrey," in *Ancient Greek Battle Speeches and a Palfrey* (Amsterdam: J. C. Gieben, 2002); John R. E. Bliese, "Rhetoric and Morale: A Study of Battle Orations from the Central Middle Ages," *Journal of Medieval History* 15 (1989): 201–26; "not verbatim reports" is discussed in Bliese's "Rhetoric and Morale," but I am quoting his more succinct statement in "Rhetoric Goes to War," 105.

34. Theodore C. Burgess, *Epideictic Literature* (1902; New York: Garland, 1987), 195, 215, 202, 209, 211–12.

35. Elizabeth Keitel, "Homeric Antecedents to the *Cohortatio* in the Ancient Historians," *Classical World* 80 (1987): 171–72; Mogens Herman Hansen, "The Battle Exhortation in Ancient Historiography: Fact or Fiction?" *Historia* 42 (1993): 180; more in Hansen, "The Little Grey Horse: Henry V's Speech at Agincourt and the Battle Exhortation in Ancient Historiography," *Classica et Mediaevalia* 52 (2001): 95–116.

36. Plutarch criticized the presentation of battle exhortation by historians Ephorus, Theopompus, and Anaximenes in *Plutarch's Moralia,* trans. Harold North Fowler, vol. 10, Loeb Classic Library (London: Heinemann, 1936), 803b; Polybius criticized

historian Timaeus in Polybius, *The Histories*, trans. W. R. Paton, vol. 4, Loeb Classical Library (London: Heinemann, 1925), 12.7.1.

37. Some of these allowances are found in Pritchett, "The General's Exhortations," 50–51, and Burgess, *Epideictic Literature*, 202.

38. Keitel, "Homeric Antecedents," 171.

39. Thucydides, *History of the Peloponnesian War*, trans. Rex Warner, Penguin Classics (1954; Harmondsworth, U.K.: Penguin, 1985), 5.69–70.

40. My characterizations of military discourse benefit from motivations identified by John A. Lynn, *Bayonets of the Republic: Motivation and Tactics in the Army of Revolutionary France, 1791–94* (Urbana: University of Illinois Press, 1984), 35–36, and from Carpenter, *Rhetoric in Martial Deliberations*.

41. Rhetoric has been studied and defined variously since the fifth century B.C.E. Aristotle, for instance, grounded rhetorical discourse in persuasion, Kenneth Burke in symbols, Karl Wallace in good reasons, and Lloyd Bitzer in situation. These definitions are complementary, and in this book I draw across this rich tradition. Here I am featuring elements of Karl R. Wallace, "The Substance of Rhetoric: Good Reasons," *Quarterly Journal of Speech* 49 (1963): 247–48,; and Bitzer, "Rhetorical Situation," 6–8.

42. Thucydides, *History of the Peloponnesian War*, 5.71–74.

43. Generally helpful in this reconstruction: Victor Davis Hanson, *The Western Way of War: Infantry Battle in Classical Greece* (New York: Oxford University Press, 1990); J. F. Lazenby, "Mantineia," chap. 7 in *The Spartan Army* (Warminster, U.K.: Aris & Phillips, 1985); W. Kendrick Pritchett, "The Marching Paian," chap. 7 in *The Greek State at War, Part I* (Berkeley: University of California Press, 1971); Pritchett, "The Pitched Battle," chap. 1 in *The Greek State at War, Part IV* (Berkeley: University of California Press, 1985); Nick Sekunda, *The Spartan Army* (1998; Oxford: Osprey, 2004); Xenophon, "Polity of the Lacedaemonians," in *The Works of Xenophon*, trans. H. G. Dakyns, vol. 2 (London: Macmillan, 1892).

44. Here I am using a fragment of a Spartan war song—although I have adjusted it for the Brasidan audience—quoted in Ian Rutherford, *Pindar's Paeans: A Reading of the Fragments with a Survey of the Genre* (Oxford: Oxford University Press, 2001), 44–45, 461. Unaltered, the fragment reads, "Come, O boys of Sparta, rich in men, of citizen fathers, thrust forward your shield with your left hand, shaking your spear with courage, and not sparing your life. For it is not the ancestral custom of Sparta." Rutherford believes these lines represent the part of a marching war song that the commander sung, and the lines were answered by a communal war cry sung by the army as a whole. In my adjustment I have also injected the phrase "savage valor," borrowing from "the savage valor of Tyrtaeus," Eric Voegelin, *Order and History*, vol. 2, *The World of the Polis* (Baton Rouge: Louisiana State University Press, 1957), 188–94.

45. The Spartan war cry appears to have been sometimes "ἐλελεῦ" and sometimes "ἀλαλαί", according to Rutherford, *Pindar's Paeans*, 20, 43, and to Xenophon, *Persian Expedition*, 1.8, 4.3. For the interactive, stamping nature of the war song, see Rutherford, 45, 65–66. A film that well conveys what war songs, dances, and cries can sound like is *Zulu*, directed by Cy Endfield (Diamond Films, 1964).

46. Tyrtaeus, "Tyrtaeus," in *Elegy and Iambus: Being the Remains of All the Greek Elegiac and Iambic Poets,* vol. 1, ed. and trans. J. M. Edmonds, Loeb Classical Library (London: Heinemann, 1931), poem 12.

47. Walter J. Ong, *Orality and Literacy: The Technologizing of the Word* (New York: Methuen, 1982), 72.

48. Erich Maria Remarque, *All Quiet on the Western Front,* trans. A. W. Wheen (1928; New York: Ballantine, 1982), 212, 132.

49. Norman Mailer, *The Naked and the Dead* (1948; New York: Holt, Rinehart & Winston, 1974), 511.

50. The "psychology of form" arouses and fulfills appetites, according to Kenneth Burke, *Counter-Statement* (Berkeley: University of California Press, 1968), 31, 37.

51. Xenophon, *Persian Expedition,* 6.5.

52. Plutarch, "Lycurgus," in *Greek Lives: A Selection of Nine Greek Lives,* trans. Robin Waterfield, Oxford World's Classics (Oxford: Oxford University Press, 1998), 21; Athenaeus quoted in Tyrtaeus, "Tyrtaeus," 57.

53. By way of example, three ditties popular today: the marching cadence "The Prettiest Girl," the double-time cadence "C-130," and the vulgar longtime favorite "Roll Me Over." Incessant choruses of the last made it the veritable "theme song" of the European theater during World War II, according to Stephen E. Ambrose, *Band of Brothers: E Company, 506th Regiment, 101st Airborne from Normandy to Hitler's Eagle's Nest* (1992; New York: Pocket Star Books, 2002), 354. Apparently it was popular in the Pacific as well, given Mailer, *Naked and the Dead,* 707–9. Ditties are sometimes called "Jodies" because Jody is a common character within the lyrics.

54. Plutarch, "Lycurgus," 22.

55. I discuss identification especially in chapter 2. The concept comes from Kenneth Burke, *A Rhetoric of Motives* (New York: Prentice-Hall, 1950), xiv, 19–29, 46, 55; and Burke, *Language as Symbolic Action,* 301.

56. William (Bill) H. Puntenney, "For the Duration: An Autobiography of the Years of Military Service of a Citizen Soldier during World War II: June 6, 1941–December 21, 1945" (bound manuscript, 1998), 2. Reprinted by permission of Peggy Puntenney Withers.

57. Quoted in Bruce Seton and John Grant, *The Pipes of War: A Record of the Achievements of Pipers of Scottish and Overseas Regiments during the War 1914–18* (Glasgow: MacLehose, Jackson, 1920), 84. For clarity, I have added a comma and replaced another comma with a period.

58. William H. McNeill, *Keeping Together in Time: Dance and Drill in Human History* (Cambridge, Mass.: Harvard University Press, 1995), 2–3.

59. Voegelin, *World of the Polis,* 190.

60. E. B. Sledge, *With the Old Breed at Peleliu and Okinawa* (1981; New York: Oxford University Press, 1990), 52.

61. Round with one's name on it, Puntenney, "For the Duration," 103–4; Xenophon, *Persian Expedition,* 3.1.

62. Díaz, *Discovery and Conquest of Mexico*, 286.

63. Daly quoted in Floyd Gibbons, *And They Thought We Wouldn't Fight* (New York: Doran, 1918), 304; essentially the same exhortation attributed to Frederick the Great when his troops hesitated at the Battle of Kolin, June 18, 1757, per *Oxford Dictionary of Quotations*, 2nd ed. (New York: Oxford University Press, 1953), 211. Cota quoted in the thirty-three-page publication of the U.S. Army, Forces in the European Theater, *29, Let's Go!* (Paris: Desfossés-néogravure, 1945), 5; the booklet presented at http://www.lonesentry.com/gi_stories_booklets/29infantry/ (accessed April 23, 2007); essentially the same D-Day exhortation attributed to one of the division's regimental commanders, Charles D. Canham, per Cornelius Ryan, *The Longest Day: June 6, 1944* (1959; New York: Touchstone, 1994), 264–65. Ranger squad leader quoted in Field Manual no. 22-100 (FM 22-100), *Army Leadership* (Washington, D.C.: Department of the Army, 1999), 3–6. Farragut quoted in Chester G. Hearn, *Admiral David Glasgow Farragut: The Civil War Years* (Annapolis: Naval Institute Press, 1998), 263; actually Farragut shouted to flagship captain Percival Drayton, "Damn the torpedoes! Full speed ahead, Drayton!"

64. Puntenney, "For the Duration," 82–83.

65. Ibid., 46.

66. Ambrose, *Band of Brothers*, 73–74; one of several U.S. Army photographs of Eisenhower speaking with members of the 101st Airborne Division before their jump, Stephen E. Ambrose, *Eisenhower: Soldier and President* (New York: Simon & Schuster, 1990), 224.

67. "Listening to spoken words forms hearers into a group, a true audience, just as reading written or printed texts turns individuals in on themselves." Ong, *Orality and Literacy*, 136. Marshall, *Men against Fire*, 136.

68. Díaz, *Discovery and Conquest of Mexico*, 110, 124, 129–30.

69. Ibid., 135, 230. The urging by Cortés's and Alvarado's men is reported by Hernan Cortés, *Letters from Mexico*, trans. Anthony Pagden (1971; New Haven, Conn.: Yale Nota Bene, 2001), 234.

70. Xenophon, *Persian Expedition*, 6.5.

71. Sledge, *With the Old Breed*, 217–18.

72. Ibid., 81. Puntenney, "For the Duration," 69.

73. Sledge, *With the Old Breed*, 79.

74. Cicero, *Cicero Philippics*, ed. D. R. Shackleton Bailey (Chapel Hill: University of North Carolina Press, 1986), 4.11.

75. Xenophon, *Persian Expedition*, 6.5, 4.3, 5.2; Díaz, *Discovery and Conquest of Mexico*, 400, 362, 378, 125, 362; Lakota war cry according to Black Elk as quoted in Viola, *It Is a Good Day to Die*, 39.

Chapter 2: Indoctrination

1. Mailer, *Naked and the Dead*, 175; Marshall, *Men against Fire*, 78; degeneracy and debauchery from Bernard Lewis, *The Crisis of Islam: Holy War and Unholy Terror*

(New York: Modern Library, 2003), 81, 162–63; Thomas E. Ricks, *Making the Corps* (New York: Scribner, 1997), 43, 45, 57, 30–31.

2. Burke, *Rhetoric of Motives,* 20–22, and Burke, *Language as Symbolic Action,* 301. I have removed italics.

3. J. Glenn Gray, *The Warriors: Reflections on Men in Battle* (New York: Harcourt, Brace, 1959), 40.

4. For militaristic sermons early in American history, see Marie L. Ahearn, *The Rhetoric of War: Training Day, the Militia, and the Military Sermon* (New York: Greenwood Press, 1989); Twain's charge against Scott in Gerald F. Linderman, *Embattled Courage: The Experience of Combat in the American Civil War* (New York: Free Press, 1987), 16; charge against Kipling in Richard Holmes, *Acts of War: The Behavior of Men in Battle* (New York: Free Press, 1989), 60; charge against Wayne quoted in Garry Wills, *John Wayne's America* (New York: Touchstone, 1998), 12, 316; Buckley at the battle for Hill 660, Cape Gloucester, New Britain, for which he received the Navy Cross, remembered by eyewitness George C. MacGillivray (section sergeant within one of Buckley's 37mm platoons), in discussion with the author, July 18, 1993.

5. Daniel Webster, "The Bunker Hill Monument," in *The Works of Daniel Webster,* 8th ed., vol. 1 (Boston: Little, Brown, 1854), 72; George H. Sage, *Power and Ideology in American Sport* (Champaign, Ill.: Human Kinetics, 1990), v.

6. Sociologist Harry Edwards quoted in Sage, *Power and Ideology,* 207.

7. *Knute Rockne, All American,* DVD, directed by Lloyd Bacon (1940; Burbank, Cal.: Warner Home Video, 2006).

8. MacArthur quoted in Manchester, *American Caesar,* 135.

9. Patton quoted in Carlo D'Este, *Patton: Genius for War* (New York: HarperPerennial, 1996), 602.

10. *Hearts and Minds,* DVD, directed by Peter Davis (1974; Irvington, N.Y.: Criterion Collection, 2002.).

11. Spartan dancing described by Philostratos the Athenian, "The Art of the Athletic Trainer" [Gymnasticus], trans. Don Jackson, the University of Iowa (unbound manuscript, 1991), 19; Francis Fukuyama, "A Reply to My Critics," *National Interest* 18 (Winter 1989/90): 28.

12. Deine quoted before from Marshall, *Men against Fire,* 142; Sledge, *With the Old Breed,* 56.

13. Bitzer, "The Rhetorical Situation," 13.

14. Exhortation from *Plutarch on Sparta,* trans., ed. Richard J. A. Talbert, Penguin Classics (London: Penguin, 1988), 161; this is saying number sixteen of "unnamed Spartan women," or 241 F 16 in older translations of Plutarch's *Moralia* (literally, "Another woman, as she was handing her son his shield and giving him some encouragement, said: 'Son, either with this or on this'").

15. Discussion of shield and casting it aside according to Hanson, *Western Way of War,* 27–28, 63–68, 119; Aristotle, "Rhetorica," 1383b 20. Incidentally, the hoplite shield has come to be known as the *hoplon,* but it was not always so. *Aspis* is the safer,

more literal term and the one used by Plutarch's Spartan mother and Aristotle. For scholarly debate about the shield's name, see J. F. Lazenby and David Whitehead, "The Myth of the Hoplite's *Hoplon*," *Classical Quarterly* 46 (1996): 27–33.

16. Plutarch, *Moralia*, 220a 2.

17. *Plutarch on Sparta*, 159–62; by "unnamed Spartan women" saying-number: "tainted by a bad reputation," 3; "creep back in here," 4; references to "battle line," 2, 13, 19–21; killing of sons, 1, 5, and that attributed to "Damatria"; interrupting mother, 6.

18. Talbert, *Plutarch on Sparta*, 108.

19. Lou Holtz with John Heisler, *The Fighting Spirit: A Championship Season at Notre Dame* (New York: Pocket, 1989), 7.

20. Air Force Instruction (AFI) 34–242, *Mortuary Affairs Program*, as discussed by the director of the port mortuary at Dover Air Force Base, Karen Giles, in E-mail and telephone conversation with the author, March 14, 2007; used by permission of Giles.

21. For eyewitness documentation of Agincourt and the battle generally, see Matthew Bennett, *Agincourt 1415* (Oxford: Osprey, 1991), 61; for Shakespeare's sources for *Henry V*, see John Russell Brown, "The Sources of Henry V," in *The Life of Henry V*, by William Shakespeare, rev. ed., Signet Classic (New York: New American Library, 1988), 170–71.

22. Use of *Henry V* shortly before H-Hour, Operation Desert Storm, according to Thomas V. Draude (Brigadier General, USMC, Ret.), in discussions with the author, January 3, 2005; December 22, 2004; and December 19, 1991; used by permission of Draude.

23. In the Signet Classic *Henry V*, one may consult Holinshed in the same volume as Shakespeare, as it includes fair representations of each, notes from the editor, John Russell Brown (University of Michigan), and commentaries. Holinshed's report of Henry's speech, 193–94.

24. Shakespeare, *Henry V*, 3.1.

25. Ibid., 4.3.18–67.

26. Translation of the refrain "Deo gratias Anglia redde pro victoria" recorded in Bennett, *Agincourt*, 86.

27. Maurice Keen, *Chivalry* (New Haven, Conn.: Yale University Press, 1984), 239–44, 248–50.

28. John Russell Brown, introduction to Shakespeare, *Henry V*, xxxiii.

29. J. Huizinga, *The Waning of the Middle Ages: A Study of the Forms of Life, Thought and Art in France and the Netherlands in the XIVth and XVth Centuries* (1924; London: Arnold, 1970), 58.

30. Comments by two Marine officers help portray the explicit and implicit dimensions of fraternity—love and standing. The month before he recited Shakespeare in the Saudi desert, General Draude visited groups of officers and noncommissioned officers, asking, "What will cause a Marine to jump on a hand grenade, killing himself in order to save his fellow Marines?" Drawing from his own experience and

shaping theirs, he answered himself: "Love. I have to tell you that they don't fight for their country, they don't fight for the Marine Corps, they don't fight for apple pie, motherhood, Sally Lou, or Lost Overshoe, Iowa. They fight for their buddies." For Draude, in his own words and in Shakespeare's, successful combat performance stemmed from heartfelt affection for one's comrades. But an older, less polished warrior helps finger the nuance of reputation in that. "Men join the Corps for Mom, etc., but once in combat they fight because of their buddies," agreed Colonel Wesley Fox. "They want to look good in their buddies' eyes." Not yet picking up on the subtlety of looking good, I asked the colonel whether that meant fraternal love was the primary driver of men in combat. Hard-bitten Fox (then in uniform forty-one years, wounded as a junior enlisted man in Korea, recipient of the Medal of Honor in Vietnam) made plain, "Love—and respect, too." Draude as shown in videotape, *This Week with David Brinkley,* January 27, 1991; Wesley L. Fox (Colonel, USMC), in discussion with the author, December 23, 1991; used by permission of Fox.

31. Historical Patton's exhortation termed "his famous speech to the troops" by Blumenson in *The Patton Papers: 1940–1945,* ed. Martin Blumenson (Boston: Houghton Mifflin, 1974), 456; termed simply "The Speech" by Carlo D'Este, *Patton,* 601.

32. Similar but not identical versions of Patton's historical speech reside within Blumenson, *Patton Papers,* 456–58; *Speech of General George S. Patton, Jr. to His Third Army on the Eve of the Normandy Invasion* (Cornwallville, NY: Hope Farm Press, 1963); Charles M. Province, *The Unknown Patton* (New York: Hippocrene, 1983), 26–37; and D'Este, *Patton,* 601–5. D'Este cites two additional primary sources in his endnotes, 909.

33. Regimental commander Paul Robinett commenting on a "fantastic" speech by Patton to officers in 1942, quoted in D'Este, *Patton,* 463.

34. Aristotle, "Rhetorica," 1377b 22–24.

35. Wayne Booth, "The Rhetorical Stance," *College Communication and Composition* 14 (October 1963): 139–45.

36. Enlisted witness quoted in Martin Blumenson, *Patton: The Man behind the Legend, 1885–1945* (New York: Morrow, 1985), 220; officer witness quoted in H. Essame, *Patton: A Study in Command* (New York: Scribners, 1974), 143.

37. "Stars and Stripes," *Patton,* DVD, directed by Franklin J. Schaffner (1970; Beverly Hills, Cal.: Twentieth Century–Fox Home Entertainment, 2006). Video clip and a transcript also available at http://www.americanrhetoric.com/MovieSpeeches/moviespeechpatton3rdarmyaddress.html (accessed September 9, 2007).

38. "Generals should adhere to one type of dress so that soldiers will recognize them." Patton, *War as I Knew It,* 354.

39. Bradley wondered "if this macho profanity was unconscious overcompensation for [Patton's] most serious personal flaw: a voice that was almost comically squeaky and high-pitched, altogether lacking in command authority." Omar N. Bradley and Clay Blair, *A General's Life* (New York: Simon & Schuster, 1983), 98. Another eyewitness recounted "a high and somewhat unpleasant voice," quoted in Essame, *Patton,* 143.

40. Quoted in Blumenson, *Patton*, 220–21.

41. Chaplain's role per historical Patton quoted in D'Este, *Patton*, 603, and *Speech of General George S. Patton, Jr.*, 4; it is not mentioned in Blumenson, *Patton Papers*, 457–58, where there is, nonetheless, a roll call of contributors.

42. While not the case here, cinematic representations of battle exhortation routinely include background music, which invariably rises in volume over the course of the speech to increase impact. So characteristic is this (signature) music that it helps signal to audiences that battle exhortation is under way. See, for example, the exhortation in *Braveheart*, DVD, directed by Mel Gibson (1995; Hollywood, Cal.: Paramount, 2000); *Crimson Tide*, DVD, directed by Tony Scott (1995; Burbank, Cal.: Walt Disney Video, 1998); *Gladiator*, DVD, directed by Ridley Scott (2000; Universal City, Cal.: Dreamworks Home Entertainment, 2000); or *Independence Day*, DVD, directed by Roland Emmerich (1996; Beverly Hills, Cal.: Twentieth Century-Fox Home Entertainment, 2003). Video clips with transcripts are also available at http://www.americanrhetoric.com/moviespeeches.htm (accessed September 9, 2007).

43. Patton's athletic feats in D'Este, *Patton*, 92, 131–34, 145, and Bradley, *General's Life*, 98; aristocratic upbringing, smothering Aunt Nannie, dyslexia, and loner per D'Este, *Patton*, 33–47, 73. Perhaps the best evidence we have of Patton's preference for the teamwork of sports over the fellowship of brothers comes from a childhood memory of Ruth Ellen, Patton's daughter. She recalled observing her father while he practiced his war face and recited verse before a mirror. So memorable or frequent was this act that Ruth Ellen and her older sister memorized the verse, learning only later that it was Shakespeare—Henry V's first battle exhortation. Recall that this exhortation is about fighting, while Henry V's second is about honor and brotherhood. Patton apparently preferred the former address. Moreover, the lines that Ruth Ellen remembered, and therefore probably heard most often, were the ones that can easily be applied to an athlete: stiffening the sinews, summoning up the blood, setting the teeth, stretching the nostril wide. This 1974 memory quoted in George Forty, *Patton's Third Army at War* (New York: Scribners, 1978), 54.

44. Sir Walter Scott, *Ivanhoe*, in *Waverley Novels: Abridged*, ed. William Hardcastle Browne (New York: P. F. Collier & Son, 1902), 168–70.

45. "Looking them over" quoted in Essame, *Patton*, 142; "grimly" from *Speech of General George S. Patton, Jr.*, 1; "make the German die" quoted in Blumenson, *Patton*, 220.

46. Stouffer et al., *American Soldier*, 108.

47. Mailer, *Naked and the Dead*, 455–56; Belushi/Matheson exhortation in "When the Going Gets Tough," *National Lampoon's Animal House*, DVD, directed by John Landis (1978; Universal City, Cal.: Universal Studios, 2003). Eric Burdon and the Animals' 1968 song "Sky Pilot" (*The Best of Eric Burdon and the Animals, 1966–1968*, Polydor B000001G1N) mocks military chaplains.

48. "Three-Hour Cram," *Stripes*, DVD, directed by Ivan Reitman (1981; Culver City, Cal.: Sony Pictures, 2005). The screenwriters are Len Blum, Dan Goldberg, and Harold Ramis.

49. Murray's general delivery style according to Janet Maslin, "At Ease," in *The New York Times Film Reviews: 1981–1982* (New York: Times Books and Garland, 1984), 78; Thucydides, *History of the Peloponnesian War,* 7.69.

50. I have removed a comma from Hunt's sentence as he is quoted in Richard Tregaskis, *Guadalcanal Diary* (New York: Random House, 1943), 26–27. Maximus' exhortation is part of the opening scene in *Gladiator.*

51. Montecuccoli, "Concerning Battle," 130.

52. Patton, *War as I Knew It,* 336.

Chapter 3: Tensions

1. Du Picq, *Battle Studies,* 154.

2. Francis Fukuyama, *Trust: The Social Virtues and the Creation of Prosperity* (New York: Free Press, 1995), 6.

3. Don Higginbotham, *War and Society in Revolutionary America: The Wider Dimensions of Conflict* (Columbia: University of South Carolina Press, 1988), 99.

4. Charles Royster, *A Revolutionary People at War: The Continental Army and American Character, 1775–1783* (Chapel Hill: University of North Carolina Press, 1979), 90, 92; also 88, 199, 205–11.

5. General Orders, Headquarters, New York, July 2, 1776, George Washington, *The Writings of George Washington from the Original Manuscript Sources: 1745–1799,* vol. 5, ed. John C. Fitzpatrick (Washington. D.C.: U.S. Government Printing Office, 1932), 210–13. Although there is a strong probability that these orders were first drafted by an aide, the point is not of major consequence here. Ghostwriters assisted Washington in the composition of nearly all of his public discourse, but he took a close interest in it. For more on Washington's rhetoric, see Stephen E. Lucas, "George Washington," in *American Orators before 1900: Critical Studies and Sources,* ed. Bernard K. Duffy and Halford R. Ryan (New York: Greenwood Press, 1987), 411.

6. Joseph J. Ellis, *His Excellency: George Washington* (New York: Knopf, 2004), 84. Another recent discussion of Washington's code of honor may be found in David Hackett Fischer, *Washington's Crossing* (New York: Oxford University Press, 2004), 13.

7. "Gordian knots" from James Thomas Flexner, *George Washington in the American Revolution (1775–1783)* (Boston: Little, Brown, 1968), 96; instances of Washington failing to rally troops per Douglas Southall Freeman, *George Washington: A Biography,* vol. 4, *Leader of the Revolution* (New York: Scribners, 1951), 166, 193–94; Washington's letter to Hancock, September 8, 1776, *Writings of George Washington,* vol. 6, 28–29; "one worry" of Greek veterans per Victor Davis Hanson, *Carnage and Culture: Landmark Battles in the Rise of Western Power* (New York: Doubleday, 2001), 73–74.

8. Clearest battlefield victory per Russell F. Weigley, *The American Way of War: A History of United States Military Strategy and Policy* (Bloomington: Indiana University Press, 1977), 30; "striking results" of oratory at Cowpens per Don Higginbotham, *War and Society,* 147. The most detailed account of this battle is Hugh F. Rankin, "Cowpens:

Prelude to Yorktown," *North Carolina Historical Review* 31 (1954): 336–69. Also helpful is Don Higginbotham, *Daniel Morgan: Revolutionary Rifleman* (Chapel Hill: University of North Carolina Press, 1961), 122–41; and the National Park Service's battlefield flyer *Cowpens National Battlefield, South Carolina* (Washington, D.C.: U.S. Government Printing Office, 1992).

9. Like his superiors Greene and Washington, Morgan had a low opinion of militiamen. Only two days before Cowpens he complained to Greene about "their fatal mode of going to war"; quoted in James Graham, *The Life of General Daniel Morgan, of the Virginia Line of the Army of the United States, with Portions of His Correspondence; Compiled from Authentic Sources* (New York: Derby, 1858), 286.

10. "Just hold up your heads, boys," according to Thomas Young, a sixteen-year-old cavalryman at the scene, quoted in Joseph Johnson, *Traditions and Reminiscences Chiefly of the American Revolution in the South: Including Biographical Sketches, Incidents and Anecdotes, Few of Which Have Been Published, Particularly of Residents in the Upper Country* (Charleston, S.C.: Walker & James, 1851), 450. Militia major Samuel Hammond confirms that Morgan revealed his fire-and-fall-back plan the night before; also in Johnson, 527. "Boys, get up," per South Carolina Militia captain (later major) Joseph McJunkin, quoted in Lyman Copeland Draper, series VV, vol. 23, Draper Manuscripts, State Historical Society of Wisconsin, Madison, 189.

11. Quoted in Graham, *Life of General Daniel Morgan*, 297.

12. Henry Lee, *Memoirs of the War in the Southern Department of the United States* (1812; New York: University Publishing Company, 1869), 227. Light-Horse Harry Lee—father of Robert E. Lee and famous eulogist of George Washington ("First in war, first in peace, and first in the hearts of his countrymen")—was with Major General Greene, not Morgan, at the time of Cowpens. But Morgan and Greene combined forces just two weeks after the battle, and Lee was "in habits of intimacy with Morgan" (ibid., 233, 237). Thus it is likely that Morgan recounted the battle and his contributions to Lee shortly afterward. The discrepancy between Lee's testimony and Young's (quoted earlier) over how many volleys Morgan asked of his second line (two or three) only confirms the gist of his instructions.

13. Ibid., 227–28.

14. "They give us the British halloo," remembered by Thomas Young as quoted in Johnson, *Traditions and Reminiscences*, 450; "Form, form," quoted in Higginbotham, *Daniel Morgan*, 139.

15. Lieutenant Joseph Hughes, remembered by Christopher Braudon, a member of Morgan's cavalry, Draper Manuscripts, series VV, vol. 13, 189.

16. "Shot down as an example," Washington's general orders, August 23, 1776, *Writings of George Washington*, vol. 5, 480; Morgan inspired exceptional battlefield performances according to Weigley, *American Way of War*, 30.

17. David D. Gilmore, *Manhood in the Making: Cultural Concepts of Masculinity* (New Haven, Conn.: Yale University Press, 1990), 17. This is not to say that women cannot be motivated by traditionally masculine appeals. Nor is it to say that women

have not already participated or will not participate increasingly on the battlefield. It is to acknowledge that rarely is women's "right to a gender identity questioned in the same public, dramatic way that it is for men" (ibid., 11).

18. Washington's demand to "acquit yourself like men" is found in a very similar set of general orders (again the middle section), August 23, 1776, *Writings of George Washington,* vol. 5, 478–80; Vegetius' dictum, one of his general rules of war, *Vegetius: Epitome of Military Science,* 3.12 and 3.26.

19. David I. Kertzer, *Ritual, Politics, and Power* (New Haven, Conn.: Yale University Press, 1988), 5.

20. A sergeant quoted in Sledge, *With the Old Breed,* 66.

21. Signed John Pope, Major General, Commanding, Headquarters Army of Virginia, Washington, DC, July 14, 1862; *War of the Rebellion: A Compilation of the Official Records of the Union and Confederate Armies,* series 1, vol. 12, pt. 3 (Washington, D.C.: U.S. Government Printing Office, 1885), 473–74.

22. Deemed "snide" and "singularly inept" by James M. McPherson, *Battle Cry of Freedom: The Civil War Era* (New York: Ballantine, 1989), 524; "patronizing" and "unfortunate," John J. Hennessy, *Return to Bull Run: The Campaign and Battle of Second Manassas* (New York: Simon & Schuster, 1998), 12.

23. McClellan to his wife quoted in Hennessy, *Return to Bull Run,* 20; emphasis is McClellan's.

24. Hennessy, *Return to Bull Run,* 6.

25. Jackson's bearing reported by Campbell Brown (a staff officer of Major General Richard Ewell, a division commander of Jackson's corps), quoted ibid., 182. Bracketed words supplied by Hennessy.

26. Joking and swearing per Theodore Roosevelt, *The Works of Theodore Roosevelt,* vol. 11, *The Rough Riders and Men of Action,* ed. Hermann Hagedorn (New York: Scribners, 1926), 84.

27. Observers regarded the attack a mistake according to Virgil Carrington Jones, *Roosevelt's Rough Riders* (Garden City, N.Y.: Doubleday, 1971), 182–83; "no one who saw Roosevelt . . . expected him to finish" quoted in 183n.

28. Composition of the ranks according to Roosevelt's executive officer, Alexander Brodie, quoted in Edward Marshall, *The Story of the Rough Riders* (New York: G. W. Dillingham, 1899), x; "Come on!" quoted in Jones, *Roosevelt's Rough Riders,* 183n.

29. Roosevelt's words at the barbed-wire fence and after being wounded in the hand, quoted in Marshall, *Story of the Rough Riders,* 191–96. Marshall, a war correspondent, had been embedded with the Rough Riders until Spanish fire wounded him in an earlier engagement; he interviewed Rough Riders for his account of this battle. Roosevelt's own account mentions the fence but not the colonel's discourse there (Roosevelt, *Rough Riders,* 85).

30. Roosevelt, *Rough Riders,* 88. Roosevelt used the term *troopers* rather than *troops* because *troopers* was commonly applied to cavalrymen. For want of sufficient naval shipping, the Rough Riders and the majority of U.S. cavalry deployed to Cuba without horses.

31. Carl von Clausewitz, *On War,* trans. J. J. Graham (1832; London: Penguin, 1982), 1.1.2–3.

32. In his memoir of service in Vietnam, Phil Caputo recounts "the sudden disintegration of my platoon from a group of disciplined soldiers into an incendiary mob. . . . unrestrained savages," Philip Caputo, *A Rumor of War* (New York: Holt, Rinehart & Winston, 1977), 304–5; Plutarch, "Lycurgus," in *Greek Lives: A Selection of Nine Greek Lives,* trans. Robin Waterfield, Oxford World's Classics (Oxford: Oxford University Press, 1998), 22.

33. Garry Wills, *Certain Trumpets: The Call of Leaders* (New York: Simon & Schuster, 1994), 85–86.

34. Shaw quoted in the official regimental history: Luis F. Emilio, *A Brave Black Regiment: History of the Fifty-Fourth Regiment of Massachusetts Volunteer Infantry, 1863–1865,* 2nd ed. (Boston: Boston Book, 1894), 78. Emilio, one of the regiment's company commanders, participated in the battle, actually taking command of the regiment later that night.

35. Ibid., 1, 6.

36. Private letter from Abraham Lincoln to Andrew Johnson, March 26, 1863, in *The Collected Works of Abraham Lincoln,* vol. 6, *1862–1863,* ed. Roy P. Basler (New Brunswick, N.J.: Rutgers University Press, 1953), 149–50 (emphasis and commas are Lincoln's); *Virginian* quoted in Robert F. Durden, *The Gray and the Black: The Confederate Debate on Emancipation* (Baton Rouge: Louisiana State University Press, 1972), 75.

37. Lincoln, *1862–1863,* 28–31.

38. Shaw's delicate appearance and strict discipline per Lawrence Lader, *The Bold Brahmins: New England's War against Slavery, 1831–1863* (New York: Dutton, 1961), 282–83; "beautiful and awful" according to Whittier, quoted in Peter Burchard, *One Gallant Rush: Robert Gould Shaw and His Brave Black Regiment* (New York: St. Martin's Press, 1965), 94; Montgomery's actions and Shaw's correspondence per Burchard, *One Gallant Rush,* 101–18, and Emilio, *Brave Black Regiment,* 39–50.

39. Governor Andrew quoted in Emilio, *Brave Black Regiment,* 25–30. Reflecting the age's interest in classical antecedents, the Latin slogan originated from the first Christian Roman emperor, Constantine.

40. Shaw quoted ibid., 30–31.

41. The captain quoted ibid., 73.

42. The regiment's activities before final exhortation and advance, ibid., 74–77.

43. Strong quoted ibid., 77.

44. Shaw quoted ibid., 77–78.

45. Shaw quoted ibid., 79. I have taken liberty with the spelling of the commands to make them more reflective of military pronunciation.

46. Description of combat and casualties per Emilio, *Brave Black Regiment,* 79–88; also per official Army report within (by the hand of the regiment's wounded executive officer), 88–91.

47. Press, administration, and popular reaction according to Lader, *Bold Brahmins,* 290.

48. Sergeant Carney's comment that the American flag never touched the ground found on frontispiece, Emilio, *Brave Black Regiment;* also per Burchard, *One Gallant Rush,* 141; fate of state flag and staff, Emilio, *Brave Black Regiment,* 89.

49. Christian Meier, *Caesar: A Biography,* trans. David McLintock (New York: BasicBooks, 1982), 244–45.

50. Sledge, *With the Old Breed,* 40, 140–41.

51. Ibid., 140–41.

52. Julius Caesar, *Gallic War,* 1.39–40.

53. Ibid., 1.41; Caesar assessed as an orator by Cicero, *Brutus,* trans. G. L. Hendrickson, Loeb Classical Library (London: Heinemann, 1942), 261–62; assessed by Suetonius, "The Deified Julius Caesar," in *Lives of the Caesars,* trans. Catharine Edwards, Oxford World's Classics (Oxford: Oxford University Press, 2000), 55, referring in part to Cicero's *Brutus.*

54. Suetonius, "Deified Julius," 65, 67–68.

55. Caesar, *Gallic War,* 2.19.

56. Ibid., 2.25.

57. Ibid., 2.26–27.

58. "As if transformed" from Meier, *Caesar,* 244; report from Suetonius, "Deified Julius," 70. Emphasis added to the one-word titles of *citizens* and *soldiers.* Although Suetonius is often judged a scandalous historian, he is in fact a "neutral, non-committal" biographer scholar according to Andrew Wallace-Hadrill, *Suetonius: The Scholar and His Caesars* (New Haven, Conn.: Yale University Press, 1984), 25. Additionally, while the quality of Suetonius' work is uneven, Wallace-Hadrill maintains, "The *Julius* and *Augustus* are in a class apart for length, minuteness of focus, abundance of documentation and liberal citation of authorities" (ibid., 61). In any event, this story is also documented in Appian, *The Civil Wars,* trans. John Carter, Penguin Classics (London: Penguin, 1996), 2.92–94. Appian's account, written a generation after Suetonius', offers more detail but still hinges on Caesar's word choice of *citizens* rather than *soldiers.*

59. Not just soldiers but comrades according to Suetonius, "Deified Julius," 67; "grabbing them by the throat," 62.

Chapter 4: Evolutions

1. Eisenhower, *Crusade in Europe,* 210, 238; more on personal visits, 313–15. Several well-known Army photographs show Eisenhower mingling with members of the 101st Airborne Division late on June 5, 1944. One appeared on the front page of the *New York Times* on June 7, 1944.

2. Major General R. W. Barker, assistant chief of staff, presented Eisenhower a draft of this exhortation on May 1, 1944, with a cover letter beginning, "Sometime ago you indicated that you were interested in preparing a letter, or message, for delivery to troops of the Allied Expeditionary Force at an appropriate date prior to D-Day." Eisenhower returned the draft the next day, writing, "I've changed this a bit. Look it

over and show it to [chief of staff, Lieutenant General Walter B. Smith], before sub-
mitting to me again." Barker to Eisenhower, and Eisenhower's handwritten reply, per
"Message to Troops of Allied Expeditionary Force," May 1, 1944, SGS-SHAEF file
number 335.18, Record Group 331, National Archives. The final text cited here may
be found in *The Papers of Dwight David Eisenhower: The War Years,* ed. Alfred D.
Chandler Jr. et al. (Baltimore: Johns Hopkins University Press, 1970), 1913. For a
readable photograph of one of the circulars, see C. L. Sulzberger et al., *The American
Heritage Picture History of World War II* (New York: American Heritage, 1966), 496. I
have deferred matters of punctuation to the photographed copy.

3. Barker, "Message to Troops of Allied Expeditionary Force," May 1, 1944. Spac-
ing is Barker's.

4. Stouffer et al., *American Soldier,* 150, 131, 135.

5. Barker, "Message to Troops of Allied Expeditionary Force," May 1, 1944.

6. Eisenhower, *Crusade in Europe,* 157.

7. For picture, description, and historical origins of the SHAEF insignia, with its
Flaming Sword of Freedom, see "History, Chief of Staff to Supreme Allied Command," http://www.army.mil/cmh-pg/documents/cossac/Cossac.htm (accessed September 9, 2007); design so "the soldier will be able to retain his message in good
condition" discussed in Barker, "Message to Troops of Allied Expeditionary Force,"
May 1, 1944.

8. Hanson, *Western Way of War,* 139.

9. Meade's circular quoted in U.S. War Department, *The War of the Rebellion: A
Compilation of the Official Records of the Union and Confederate Armies,* series 1, vol.
27, pt. 3 (Washington, D.C.: U.S. Government Printing Office, 1889), 415. Portable
printing press at Meade's headquarters confirmed by Anthony Waskie (Temple University), in E-mail discussion with the author, May 19, 2005; confirmation by permission of Waskie.

10. During his flight to Tokyo Ridgway realized that the tactical problem for which
all military officers practice was "real now, not a theory but a fact. The Army Commander *was* dead. The tactical situation *was* bad. I was in command, and on my
answer to the question 'What do you do?' depended something far more important
than a grade in an instructor's book. On it hinged victory or defeat." *Soldier: The
Memoirs of Matthew B. Ridgway* (New York: Harper, 1956), 199.

11. Dismissal of "rhetoric" quoted in Roy E. Appleman, *Ridgway Duels for Korea*
(College Station: Texas A&M University Press, 1990), 7; separate identity for eulogy,
Ridgway, *Soldier,* 202; aim of second message, Ridgway, *Soldier,* 199–200; distribution
and text of second message, Matthew B. Ridgway, *The Korean War* (Garden City, N.Y.:
Doubleday, 1967), 262.

12. Ridgway, *Soldier,* 199–200.

13. Foreboding, ibid., 204; bewildered, etc., Ridgway, *Korean War,* 86.

14. Retirement to defensible positions (constructed by thousands of South Korean
laborers), Ridgway, *Soldier,* 207, 215; tactical requirements, Ridgway, *Korean War,*

88–90, and *Solider*, 205–6; "ubiquitous" according to Weigley, *American Way of War*, 390; chow, stationery, and gloves, Ridgway, *Korean War*, 87; Ridgway's belief that "glib" commentary "had made a deep impression on the men of the Eighth Army," *Soldier*, 207.

15. M. B. Ridgway, "Why We Are Here," January 21, 1951, tab 15, correspondence file 1951, Office of the Chief of Staff, Eighth U.S. Army, Records of U.S. Army Operational, Tactical and Support Organizations, Record Group 338, National Archives. A less complete, more refined version is included in both Ridgway, *Soldier*, 207–8, and Ridgway, *Korean War*, 264–65.

16. Dictated according to Ridgway, who is quoted in Appleman, *Ridgway Duels for Korea*, 158; timing of counterattack, Ridgway, *Korean War*, 106, 255.

17. Ridgway's departure from assumed premises and uncontested terms is consistent with observations (unrelated to Ridgway) by Richard Weaver, "The Spaciousness of Old Rhetoric," in *Ethics of Rhetoric*, 164–85.

18. "Soft-spoken" according to Ernest B. Furgurson, *Westmoreland: The Inevitable General* (Boston: Little, Brown, 1968), 315; "closemouthed" per Samuel Zaffiri, *Westmoreland: A Biography of General William C. Westmoreland* (New York: Morrow, 1994), 73.

19. Furgurson, *Westmoreland*, 291.

20. In his autobiography Westmoreland admires two former seniors for their "presence." William C. Westmoreland, *A Soldier Reports* (Garden City, N.Y.: Doubleday, 1976), 25.

21. Furgurson, *Westmoreland*, 314. To be fair to context, I should note that Furgurson's observation of this "habit of flitting about the country" is not made as a criticism.

22. "Hopping all over Vietnam" from Hugh A. Mulligan, "A Day with Westmoreland Keeps You Running," *State and the Columbia Record*, April 23, 1967. Like Furgurson, Mulligan does not mean the observation as a criticism.

23. Ibid.

24. Ibid. I have modified some of the newspaper article's paragraphing and corrected the spelling of one word.

25. H. Norman Schwarzkopf with Peter Petre, *General H. Norman Schwarzkopf: The Autobiography; It Doesn't Take a Hero* (New York: Bantam, 1992), 120–21.

26. Westmoreland, *A Soldier Reports*, 326.

27. A photograph from the Eisenhower series may be found in Ambrose, *Eisenhower: Soldier and President*, 224; also http://www.eisenhowerbirthplace.org/troops .htm (accessed September 9, 2007). Westmoreland is "in a favorite stance atop a jeep, talking to men of the 4th Infantry Division in March 1967," Westmoreland, *A Soldier Reports*, 326.

28. Fox, discussion, December 23, 1991; used by permission of Fox.

29. Robert C. McFarlane (Lieutenant Colonel, USMC, Ret.), in telephone discussion with the author, May 6, 2005; used by permission of McFarlane. See also

Robert C. McFarlane with Zofia Smardz, *Special Trust* (New York: Cadell & Davies, 1994), 141–42.

30. William L. Hauser, "The Will to Fight," in *Combat Effectiveness: Cohesion, Stress, and the Volunteer Military,* ed. Sam C. Sarkesian (Beverly Hills, Cal.: Sage, 1980), 189.

31. Cincinnatus [Cecil B. Currey], *Self-Destruction: The Disintegration and Decay of the United States Army during the Vietnam Era* (New York: Norton, 1981), 44.

32. Sledge, *With the Old Breed,* 253.

33. John Prados and Ray W. Stubbe, *Valley of Decision: The Siege of Khe Sanh* (Boston: Houghton Mifflin, 1991), 387; Lawrence H. Johnson III, *Winged Sabers: The Air Cavalry in Vietnam, 1965–1973* (Harrisburg, Penn.: Stackpole, 1990), 101, 106–7.

34. Hauser, "The Will to Fight," 189.

35. Absurdity per Tim O'Brien, *If I Die in a Combat Zone: Box Me Up and Ship Me Home* (1969; New York: Laurel, 1983), 129; battalion commander's exhortation, 109–10.

36. Ibid., 110, 109.

37. Ibid., 148.

38. Ibid., 105, 145.

39. "Reason to fight," ibid., 145; mission during the later phases of Vietnam termed "suspect" by Thomas S. Jones (Major General, USMC, Ret.), in discussion with the author, March 27, 1995; used by permission of Jones.

40. Schwarzkopf, *It Doesn't Take a Hero,* 413.

41. Tommy Franks with Malcolm McConnell, *American Soldier: General Tommy Franks* (New York: Regan, 2004), 469. Paragraphing and "Gen Franks" closing influenced by copies of the message in circulation on the Internet, which appear to stem from the original electronic release; for instance, within U.S. Army Corps of Engineers, "Part 1," http://www.nab.usace.army.mil/SBA_March05/presentations.htm (accessed May 24, 2005) or U.S. Navy Office of Information, http://www.chinfo.navy.mil/navpalib/people/secdef/franks030321.txt (accessed May 28, 2005).

42. Franks quoted in "Profile: General Tommy Franks," *BBC News,* May 22, 2003, http://news.bbc.co.uk/2/hi/americas/1647358.stm.

43. Pessimism, Franks, *American Soldier,* 124; static and dynamic, 118; rotten apples, 199, 121.

44. Schwarzkopf, *It Doesn't Take a Hero,* 181.

45. Montecuccoli, "Concerning Battle," 128, 138.

46. Schwarzkopf, *General,* 414.

47. Gilmore, *Manhood in the Making,* 11.

48. Eisenhower, *Crusade in Europe,* 299.

49. Consequence management discussed in the context of the second war with Iraq and training, Lieutenant General William S. Wallace, USA, interview with *Military Training Technology,* March 15, 2005, http://www.military-training-technology.com/article.cfm?DocID=837.

50. Colin L. Powell with Joseph E. Persico, *My American Journey* (New York: Random House, 1995), 520.

51. Hauser, "The Will to Fight," 195–96.

52. Clinton quoted in "Haiti's Military Junta Agrees to Step Down; U.S. Recalls Invasion Force; Aristide's Return Set," *Facts on File: World News Digest with Index* 54, no. 2808 (September 22, 1994), 673.

53. Thomas S. Jones, "Commander's Intent," Special Purpose Marine Air-Ground Task Force Caribbean (SPMAGTF CARIB) operation order for Operation Uphold Democracy (September 1994), page declassified by Second Marines, July 12, 1995. Reprinted by permission. Underlining is Jones's. An abbreviated version, with discussion of preparation and delivery, may be found in Thomas C. Greenwood, "Commander's Intent: The Seed of Haitian Success," *Marine Corps Gazette* 79 (February 1995): 43–44.

54. I was able to observe Jones. My interview of others present corroborated my impressions. The apt expression to "lust" for contact is from Caputo, *Rumor of War,* 71.

55. This discourse stems from Anthony J. Zell (Colonel, USMC, Ret.) recounting his exhortation to the author, May 13, 2005; used by permission of Zell.

56. Navy Commander John Geragotblis quoted in Cesar G. Soriano, "First-Strike Pilots Found Awe in Their Mission," *USA Today,* March 21, 2003, http://www.usatoday.com/news/world/iraq/2003-03-21-first-strike_x.htm. Soriano also describes the "Zen-like state they call 'getting into your bubble.'"

57. Former A-6 bombardier-navigator Scott McFarlane, USN, said his squadron did not receive traditional battle exhortation before or during Operation Desert Storm, either. Pre-sortie briefings focused on safety and keeping abreast of changing rules of engagement. Scott P. McFarlane, in telephone discussion with the author, January 18, 1996; used by permission of McFarlane.

58. Within twenty-four hours of delivery, I reconstructed these portions of Chaplin's exhortations with considerable confidence about their accuracy. He spoke for about three minutes at both noon and 6:30 P.M. (ship's time), September 18, 1994. The *Wasp*'s media system was not used to record the captain's messages.

59. Eugene B. Fluckey, *Thunder Below! The USS* Barb *Revolutionizes Submarine Warfare in World War II* (Urbana: University of Illinois Press, 1992), 127. The *Barb* sank one of the tankers and an escort carrier in this attack, September 16, 1944.

60. Ibid., 266. The *Barb* sank four vessels and damaged three in this attack, January 23, 1945. By the end of the war, the *Barb* had sunk more tonnage than any other U.S. submarine; Fluckey had received the Medal of Honor and four Navy Crosses; and his crew, in addition to individual awards, had received a number of unit commendations.

61. Chaplin, 8:00 P.M., September 18, 1994, according to my notes.

62. I personally observed this.

63. Zell, recounting, May 13, 2005; used by permission of Zell.

Conclusion

1. Elie Wiesel, *Night* (1958; New York: Bantam, 1982), 38–39.

2. Colonel Günther Hoffmann-Schönborn's proclamation to the Eighteenth Volksgrenadier Division, November 1944, quoted in Milton Shulman, *Defeat in the West* (1948; Westport, Conn.: Greenwood Press, 1971), 219.

3. Quoted in Royster, *A Revolutionary People at War*, 219.

4. Onasander, "The General," 1.13–16; Vegetius, *Epitome of Military Science*, 3.25.

BIBLIOGRAPHY

Ahearn, Marie L. *The Rhetoric of War: Training Day, the Militia, and the Military Sermon.* New York: Greenwood Press, 1989.

Ambrose, Stephen E. *Band of Brothers: E Company, 506th Regiment, 101st Airborne from Normandy to Hitler's Eagle's Nest.* New York: Pocket Star, 2002.

———. *Eisenhower: Soldier and President.* New York: Simon & Schuster, 1990.

Appian. *The Civil Wars.* Translated by John Carter. Penguin Classics. London: Penguin, 1996.

Appleman, Roy E. *Ridgway Duels for Korea.* College Station: Texas A&M University Press, 1990.

Arendt, Hannah. *The Human Condition.* Chicago: University of Chicago Press, 1958.

Aristotle. "Rhetorica." Translated by W. Rhys Roberts. In *The Basic Works of Aristotle,* edited by Richard McKeon, 1317–1451. New York: Random House, 1941.

Barker, R. W. "Message to Troops of Allied Expeditionary Force." May 1, 1944. SGS-SHAEF file number 335.18. Record Group 331. National Archives.

Baynes, John. *Morale: A Study of Men and Courage.* New York: Praeger, 1967.

Bennett, Matthew. *Agincourt 1415.* Oxford: Osprey, 1991.

Berger, Peter L., and Thomas Luckmann. *The Social Construction of Reality: A Treatise in the Sociology of Knowledge.* 1966. New York: Anchor, 1990.

Bitzer, Lloyd. "The Rhetorical Situation." *Philosophy and Rhetoric* 1 (1968): 1–14.

Bliese, John R. E. "Rhetoric and Morale: A Study of Battle Orations from the Central Middle Ages." *Journal of Medieval History* 15 (1989): 201–26.

———. "Rhetoric Goes to War: The Doctrine of Ancient and Medieval Military Manuals." *Rhetoric Society Quarterly* 24 (1994): 105–30.

Blumenson, Martin. *Patton: The Man behind the Legend, 1885–1945.* New York: Morrow, 1985.

———. *The Patton Papers.* Vol. 2, *1940–1945.* Boston: Houghton Mifflin, 1974.

Booth, Wayne. "The Rhetorical Stance." *College Communication and Composition* 14 (October 1963): 139–45.

Bradley, Omar N., and Clay Blair. *A General's Life.* New York: Simon & Schuster, 1983.

Burchard, Peter. *One Gallant Rush: Robert Gould Shaw and His Brave Black Regiment.* New York: St. Martin's Press, 1965.

Burgess, Theodore C. *Epideictic Literature.* 1902. New York: Garland, 1987.

Burke, Kenneth. *Counter-Statement.* Berkeley: University of California Press, 1968.

———. *Language as Symbolic Action: Essays on Life, Literature, and Method.* Berkeley: University of California Press, 1966.

———. *A Rhetoric of Motives.* New York: Prentice-Hall, 1950.

Caesar, Julius. *The Civil War.* Translated by J. M. Carter. Oxford World's Classics. Oxford: Oxford University Press, 1998.

———. *Seven Commentaries on the Gallic War.* Translated by Carolyn Hammond. Oxford World's Classics. Oxford: Oxford University Press, 1998.

Cannon, Roderick D. *The Highland Bagpipe and Its Music.* 1998. Edinburgh: John Donald, 2002.

Caputo, Philip. *A Rumor of War.* New York: Holt, Rinehart & Winston, 1977.

Carpenter, Ronald H. *Rhetoric in Martial Deliberations and Decision Making: Cases and Consequences.* Columbia: University of South Carolina Press, 2004.

Cicero. *Brutus.* Translated by G. L. Hendrickson. Loeb Classical Library. 1939. London: Heinemann, 1942.

———. *Cicero Philippics.* Edited by D. R. Shackleton Bailey. Chapel Hill: University of North Carolina Press, 1986.

Cincinnatus [Cecil B. Currey]. *Self-Destruction: The Disintegration and Decay of the United States Army during the Vietnam Era.* New York: Norton, 1981.

Clausewitz, Carl von. *On War.* Translated by J. J. Graham. 1832. London: Penguin, 1982.

Cortés, Hernan. *Letters from Mexico.* Translated by Anthony Pagden. 1971. New Haven, Conn.: Yale Nota Bene, 2001.

D'Este, Carlo. *Patton: Genius for War.* New York: HarperPerennial, 1996.

Díaz del Castillo, Bernal. *The Discovery and Conquest of Mexico, 1517–1521.* Translated by A. P. Maudslay. 1956. New York: Da Capo Press, 1996.

Draper, Lyman Copeland. Draper Manuscripts. Series VV, vol. 23. State Historical Society of Wisconsin, Madison.

Draude, Thomas V. Video footage aired on *This Week with David Brinkley,* ABC, January 27, 1991.

Du Picq, Ardant. *Battle Studies: Ancient and Modern Battle.* 1880. Translated by John N. Greely and Robert C. Cotton. Harrisburg, Penn.: Military Service Publishing, 1958.

Duffy, Bernard K., and Ronald H. Carpenter. *Douglas MacArthur: Warrior as Wordsmith.* Westport, Conn.: Greenwood Press, 1997.

Durden, Robert F. *The Gray and the Black: The Confederate Debate on Emancipation.* Baton Rouge: Louisiana State University Press, 1972.

Eisenhower, Dwight D. *Crusade in Europe.* Garden City, N.Y.: Doubleday, 1948.

———. *The Papers of Dwight David Eisenhower.* Vol. 3, *The War Years.* Edited by Alfred D. Chandler Jr., Stephen E. Ambrose, Joseph P. Hobbs, and Edwin Alan Thompson. Baltimore: Johns Hopkins University Press, 1970.

Ellis, Joseph J. *His Excellency: George Washington.* New York: Knopf, 2004.

Emilio, Luis F. *A Brave Black Regiment: History of the Fifty-Fourth Regiment of Massachusetts Volunteer Infantry, 1863–1865.* Boston: Boston Book, 1894.

Essame, H. *Patton: A Study in Command.* New York: Scribners, 1974.

Field Manual no. 6-22 (FM 6-22). *Army Leadership.* Washington, D.C.: Department of the Army, 2006.

Field Manual no. 22-100 (FM 22-100). *Army Leadership.* Washington, D.C.: Department of the Army, 1999.

Fischer, David Hackett. *Washington's Crossing.* New York: Oxford University Press, 2004.

Flexner, James Thomas. *George Washington in the American Revolution (1775–1783).* Boston: Little, Brown, 1968.

Fluckey, Eugene B. *Thunder Below! The USS* Barb *Revolutionizes Submarine Warfare in World War II.* Urbana: University of Illinois Press, 1992.

Forty, George. *Patton's Third Army at War.* New York: Scribners, 1978.

Franks, Tommy, with Malcolm McConnell. *American Soldier: General Tommy Franks.* New York: Regan, 2004.

Freeman, Douglas Southall. *George Washington: A Biography.* Vol. 4, *Leader of the Revolution.* New York: Scribners, 1951.

Fukuyama, Francis. "A Reply to My Critics." *National Interest* 18 (Winter 1989/90): 21–28.

———. *Trust: The Social Virtues and the Creation of Prosperity.* New York: Free Press, 1995.

Furgurson, Ernest B. *Westmoreland: The Inevitable General.* Boston: Little, Brown, 1968.

Gibbons, Floyd. *And They Thought We Wouldn't Fight.* New York: Doran, 1918.

Gilmore, David D. *Manhood in the Making: Cultural Concepts of Masculinity.* New Haven, Conn.: Yale University Press, 1990.

Graham, James. *The Life of General Daniel Morgan, of the Virginia Line of the Army of the United States, with Portions of His Correspondence; Compiled from Authentic Sources.* New York: Derby, 1858.

Gray, J. Glenn. *The Warriors: Reflections on Men in Battle.* New York: Harcourt, Brace, 1959.

Greenwood, Thomas C. "Commander's Intent: The Seed of Haitian Success." *Marine Corps Gazette* 79 (February 1995): 43–44.

"Haiti's Military Junta Agrees to Step Down; U.S. Recalls Invasion Force; Aristide's Return Set." *Facts on File: World News Digest with Index* 54 (September 22, 1994): 673–75.

Hansen, Mogens Herman. "The Battle Exhortation in Ancient Historiography: Fact or Fiction?" *Historia* 42 (1993): 161–80.

———. "The Little Grey Horse: Henry V's Speech at Agincourt and the Battle Exhortation in Ancient Historiography." *Classica et Mediaevalia* 52 (2001): 95–116.

Hanson, Victor Davis. *Carnage and Culture: Landmark Battles in the Rise of Western Power.* New York: Doubleday, 2001.

———. *The Western Way of War: Infantry Battle in Classical Greece.* New York: Oxford University Press, 1990.

Hauser, William L. "The Will to Fight." Chap. 6 in *Combat Effectiveness: Cohesion, Stress, and the Volunteer Military.* Edited by Sam C. Sarkesian. Beverly Hills, Cal.: Sage, 1980.

Hearn, Chester G. *Admiral David Glasgow Farragut: The Civil War Years.* Annapolis, Md.: Naval Institute Press, 1998.

Hearts and Minds. DVD. Directed by Peter Davis. 1974. Irvington, N.Y.: Criterion Collection, 2002.

Hennessy, John J. *Return to Bull Run: The Campaign and Battle of Second Manassas.* New York: Simon & Schuster, 1998.

Herbert, Bob. "Paralyzed, A Soldier Asks Why." *New York Times,* October 15, 2004. http://www.nytimes.com/2004/10/15/opinion/15herbert.html (accessed March 19, 2008).

Higginbotham, Don. *Daniel Morgan: Revolutionary Rifleman.* Chapel Hill: University of North Carolina Press, 1961.

————. *War and Society in Revolutionary America: The Wider Dimensions of Conflict.* Columbia: University of South Carolina Press, 1988.

Holmes, Richard. *Acts of War: The Behavior of Men in Battle.* New York: Free Press, 1989.

Holtz, Lou, with John Heisler. *The Fighting Spirit: A Championship Season at Notre Dame.* New York: Pocket, 1989.

Homer. *The Iliad of Homer.* Translated by Richmond Lattimore. Chicago: University of Chicago Press, 1951.

Huizinga, J. *The Waning of the Middle Ages: A Study of the Forms of Life, Thought and Art in France and the Netherlands in the XIVth and XVth Centuries.* 1924. London: Arnold, 1970.

Johnson, Lawrence H., III. *Winged Sabers: The Air Cavalry in Vietnam, 1965–1973.* Harrisburg, Penn.: Stackpole, 1990.

Johnson, Joseph. *Traditions and Reminiscences Chiefly of the American Revolution in the South: Including Biographical Sketches, Incidents and Anecdotes, Few of Which Have Been Published, Particularly of Residents in the Upper Country.* Charleston, S.C.: Walker & James, 1851.

Jones, Thomas S. "Commander's Intent." Special Purpose Marine Air-Ground Task Force Caribbean (SPMAGTF CARIB) operation order for Operation Uphold Democracy, September 1994. Page declassified by Second Marines, July 12, 1995. Reprinted by permission.

Jones, Virgil Carrington. *Roosevelt's Rough Riders.* Garden City, N.Y.: Doubleday, 1971.

Keegan, John. *The Mask of Command.* New York: Viking Penguin, 1987.

Keen, Maurice. *Chivalry.* New Haven, Conn.: Yale University Press, 1984.

Keitel, Elizabeth. "Homeric Antecedents to the *Cohortatio* in the Ancient Historians." *Classical World* 80 (1987): 153–72.

Kellett, Anthony. *Combat Motivation: The Behavior of Soldiers in Battle.* Boston: Kluwer-Nijhoff, 1982.

Kertzer, David I. *Ritual, Politics, and Power.* New Haven, Conn.: Yale University Press, 1988.

Knute Rockne, All American. DVD. Directed by Lloyd Bacon. 1940. Burbank, Cal.: Warner Home Video, 2006.

Lader, Lawrence. *The Bold Brahmins: New England's War against Slavery, 1831–1863.* New York: Dutton, 1961.

Langer, Susanne. *Philosophy in a New Key: A Study in the Symbolism of Reason, Rite, and Art.* New York: Mentor, 1942.

Lazenby, J. F. *The Spartan Army.* Warminster, U.K.: Aris & Phillips, 1985.

Lazenby, J. F., and David Whitehead. "The Myth of the Hoplite's *Hoplon.*" *Classical Quarterly* 46 (1996): 27–33.

Lee, Henry. *Memoirs of the War in the Southern Department of the United States.* 1812. New York: University Publishing, 1869.

Lewis, Bernard. *The Crisis of Islam: Holy War and Unholy Terror.* New York: Modern Library, 2003.

Lincoln, Abraham. *The Collected Works of Abraham Lincoln.* Vol. 6, *1862–1863.* Edited by Roy P. Basler. New Brunswick, N.J.: Rutgers University Press, 1953.

Linderman, Gerald F. *Embattled Courage: The Experience of Combat in the American Civil War.* New York: Free Press, 1987.

Lucas, Stephen E. "George Washington." In *American Orators before 1900: Critical Studies and Sources,* edited by Bernard K. Duffy and Halford R. Ryan, 406–15. New York: Greenwood Press, 1987.

Lynn, John A. *Bayonets of the Republic: Motivation and Tactics in the Army of Revolutionary France, 1791–94.* Urbana: University of Illinois Press, 1984.

Machiavelli, Niccolò. *The Art of War.* 1521. Translated by Ellis Farneworth. Indianapolis: Bobbs-Merrill, 1965.

Mailer, Norman. *The Naked and the Dead.* 1948. New York: Holt, Rinehart & Winston, 1974.

Malcolm, C. A. *The Piper in Peace and War.* 1927. London: Hardwicke, 1993.

Manchester, William. *American Caesar: Douglas MacArthur, 1880–1964.* Boston: Little, Brown, 1978.

Marshall, Edward. *The Story of the Rough Riders.* New York: G. W. Dillingham, 1899.

Marshall, S. L. A. *Men against Fire: The Problem of Battle Command in Future War.* 1947. Gloucester, Mass.: Peter Smith, 1978.

Maslin, Janet. "At Ease." Review of *Stripes,* directed by Ivan Reitman. In *The New York Times Film Reviews: 1981–1982,* 78. New York: Times Books & Garland, 1984.

Mattis, J. N. "Commanding General's Message to All Hands," March 2003. In *Operation Iraqi Freedom: The Inside Story / NBC News.* Kansas City, Mo.: Andrews NcMeel, 2003.

———. "A Letter from the Commanding General to the Families of Our Sailors and Marines Deploying to the Middle East," February 2004. Key Volunteer Network, Eleventh Marines. http://www.11thmarineskvn.org/2newsletter.htm (accessed April 10, 2004).

———. "A Marine's Letter to His Troops." *Dallas Morning News,* March 21, 2004.

McFarlane, Robert C., with Zofia Smardz. *Special Trust.* New York: Cadell & Davies, 1994.

McNeill, William H. *Keeping Together in Time: Dance and Drill in Human History.* Cambridge, Mass.: Harvard University Press, 1995.

McPherson, James M. *Battle Cry of Freedom: The Civil War Era.* New York: Ballantine, 1989.

Meier, Christian. *Caesar: A Biography.* Translated by David McLintock. New York: BasicBooks, 1982.

Montecuccoli, Raimondo. "Concerning Battle." Translated by Thomas M. Barker. Part 3 in *The Military Intellectual and Battle,* by Thomas M. Barker. Albany: State University of New York Press, 1975.

Moran, Lord [Charles]. *Anatomy of Courage.* 1945. London: Keynes, 1984.

Mulligan, Hugh A. "A Day with Westmoreland Keeps You Running." *State and the Columbia Record,* April, 23, 1967.

Mundy, Jr., C. E. Foreword to MCWP 6-11. *Leading Marines.* Washington, D.C.: U.S. Marine Corps, 2002.

Munson, Edward L. *The Management of Men: A Handbook on the Systematic Development of Morale and the Control of Human Behavior.* New York: Holt, 1921.

National Lampoon's Animal House. DVD. Directed by John Landis. 1978. Universal City, Cal.: Universal Studios, 2003.

National Park Service. *Cowpens National Battlefield, South Carolina.* Washington, D.C.: U.S. Government Printing Office, 1992.

NIV/KJV Parallel Bible. Grand Rapids, Mich.: Zondervan, 1985.

O'Brien, Tim. *If I Die in a Combat Zone: Box Me Up and Ship Me Home.* 1969. New York: Laurel, 1983.

Onasander. "The General." In *Aeneas Tacticus, Asclepiodotus, Onasander,* translated by the Illinois Greek Club, 341–527. Loeb Classical Library. 1923. London: Heinemann, 1948.

Ong, Walter J. *Orality and Literacy: The Technologizing of the Word.* New York: Methuen, 1983.

The Oxford Dictionary of Quotations, 2nd ed. New York: Oxford University Press, 1953.

Patton. DVD. Directed by Franklin J. Schaffner. 1970. Beverly Hills, Cal.: Twentieth Century–Fox Home Entertainment, 2006.

Patton, George S., Jr. *Speech of General George S. Patton, Jr. to His Third Army on the Eve of the Normandy Invasion.* Cornwallville, N.Y.: Hope Farm Press, 1963.

————. "Success in War." *Infantry Journal* 38, no. 1 (January 1931): 20–24.

————. *War as I Knew It.* Annotated by Paul D. Harkins. Boston: Houghton Mifflin, 1947.

Philostratos the Athenian. "The Art of the Athletic Trainer" [*Gymnasticus*]. Translated by Don Jackson (University of Iowa). Unbound manuscript, 1991.

Plutarch. "Lycurgus." In *Greek Lives: A Selection of Nine Greek Lives,* translated by Robin Waterfield, 3–41. Oxford World's Classics. Oxford: Oxford University Press, 1998.

Bibliography

179

———. "Pelopidas." In *Plutarch's Lives,* translated by Bernadotte Perrin, 5:339–433. Loeb Classical Library. London: Heinemann, 1917.

———. *Plutarch on Sparta.* Translated by Richard J. A. Talbert. Penguin Classics. London: Penguin, 1988.

———. *Plutarch's Moralia.* Vol. 1–10. Loeb Classical Library. London: Heinemann, 1914–1936.

Polybius. *The Histories.* Translated by W. R. Paton. Vol. 4. Loeb Classical Library. London: Heinemann, 1925.

Powell, Colin L., with Joseph E. Persico. *My American Journey.* New York: Random House, 1995.

Prados, John, and Ray W. Stubbe. *Valley of Decision: The Siege of Khe Sanh.* Boston: Houghton Mifflin, 1991.

Pritchett, W. Kendrick. "Ancient Greek Battle Speeches and a Palfrey." Chap. 1 in *Ancient Greek Battle Speeches and a Palfrey.* Amsterdam: J. C. Gieben, 2002.

———. "The General's Exhortations in Greek Warfare." Chap. 2 in *Essays in Greek History.* Amsterdam: J. C. Gieben, 1994.

———. "The Marching Paian." Chap. 7 in *The Greek State at War, Part I.* Berkeley: University of California Press, 1971.

———. "The Pitched Battle." Chap. 1 in *The Greek State at War, Part IV.* Berkeley: University of California Press, 1985.

"Profile: General Tommy Franks." *BBC News,* May 22, 2003. http://news.bbc.co.uk/2/hi/americas/1647358.stm (accessed March 19, 2008).

Province, Charles M. *The Unknown Patton.* New York: Hippocrene, 1983.

Puntenney, William (Bill) H. "For the Duration: An Autobiography of the Years of Military Service of a Citizen Soldier during World War II: June 6, 1941–December 21, 1945." Bound manuscript, 1998. Reprinted by permission.

Quintilian. *Institutio Oratoria of Quintilian.* Translated by H. E. Butler. Loeb Classical Library. 1921. London: Heinemann, 1933.

Rankin, Hugh F. "Cowpens: Prelude to Yorktown." *North Carolina Historical Review* 31 (1954): 336–69.

Remarque, Erich Maria. *All Quiet on the Western Front.* Translated by A. W. Wheen. 1928. New York: Ballantine, 1982.

Richards, I. A. *The Philosophy of Rhetoric.* New York: Oxford University Press, 1936.

Richardson, F. M. *Fighting Spirit: A Study of Psychological Factors in War.* London: Leo Cooper, 1978.

Ricks, Thomas E. *Making the Corps.* New York: Scribner, 1997.

Ridgway, Matthew B. *The Korean War.* Garden City, N.Y.: Doubleday, 1967.

———. *Soldier: The Memoirs of Matthew B. Ridgway.* New York: Harper, 1956.

———. "Why We Are Here," January 21, 1951, tab 15, correspondence file 1951, Office of the Chief of Staff, Eighth U.S. Army, Records of U.S. Army Operational, Tactical and Support Organizations, Record Group 338, National Archives.

Roosevelt, Theodore. *The Works of Theodore Roosevelt.* Vol. 11, *The Rough Riders and Men of Action.* Edited by Hermann Hagedorn. New York: Scribners, 1926.

Royster, Charles. *A Revolutionary People at War: The Continental Army and American Character, 1775–1783.* Chapel Hill: University of North Carolina Press, 1979.

Rutherford, Ian. *Pindar's Paeans: A Reading of the Fragments with a Survey of the Genre.* Oxford: Oxford University Press, 2001.

Ryan, Cornelius. *The Longest Day: June 6, 1944.* 1959. New York: Touchstone, 1994.

Sage, George H. *Power and Ideology in American Sport.* Champaign, Ill.: Human Kinetics, 1990.

Schwarzkopf, H. Norman, with Peter Petre. *General H. Norman Schwarzkopf: The Autobiography; It Doesn't Take a Hero.* New York: Bantam, 1992.

Scott, Sir Walter. *Ivanhoe.* In *Waverley Novels: Abridged,* edited by William Hardcastle Browne, 25–261. New York: P. F. Collier & Son, 1902.

Sekunda, Nick. *The Spartan Army.* 1998. Oxford: Osprey, 2004.

Seton, Bruce, and John Grant. *The Pipes of War: A Record of the Achievements of Pipers of Scottish and Overseas Regiments during the War 1914–18.* Glasgow: MacLehose, Jackson, 1920.

Shakespeare, William. *The Life of Henry V.* Edited by John Russell Brown. Rev. ed. Signet Classic. New York: New American Library, 1988.

Shulman, Milton. *Defeat in the West.* 1948. Westport, Conn.: Greenwood Press, 1971.

Sledge, E. B. *With the Old Breed at Peleliu and Okinawa.* 1981. New York: Oxford University Press, 1990.

Somerset, Anne. *Elizabeth I.* 1991. London: Phoenix, 1997.

Soriano, Cesar G. "First-Strike Pilots Found Awe in Their Mission." *USA Today,* March 21, 2003. http://www.usatoday.com/news/world/iraq/2003–03–21–first-strike_x.htm (accessed March 19, 2008).

Stouffer, Samuel A., Arthur A. Lumsdaine, Marion Harper Lumsdaine, Robin M. Williams Jr., M. Brewster Smith, Irving L. Janis, Shirley A. Star, and Leonard S. Cottrell Jr. *Studies in Social Psychology in World War II.* Vol. 2, *The American Soldier: Combat and Its Aftermath.* Princeton: Princeton University Press, 1949.

Stripes. DVD. Directed by Ivan Reitman. 1981. Culver City, Cal.: Sony Pictures, 2005.

Suetonius. "The Deified Julius Caesar." In *Lives of the Caesars,* translated by Catharine Edwards, 3–42. Oxford World's Classics. Oxford: Oxford University Press, 2000.

Sulzberger, C. L. *The American Heritage Picture History of World War II.* Edited by David G. McCullough. New York: American Heritage, 1966.

Thucydides. *History of the Peloponnesian War.* Translated by Rex Warner. Penguin Classics. 1954. Harmondsworth, U.K.: Penguin, 1985.

Tolstoy, Leo. *War and Peace.* 1869. Translated by Constance Garnett. New York: Modern Library, 1994.

Tregaskis, Richard. *Guadalcanal Diary.* New York: Random House, 1943.

Tsouras, Peter G. *Warriors' Words: A Dictionary of Military Quotations.* London: Arms & Armour, 1992.

Tyrtaeus. "Tyrtaeus." In *Elegy and Iambus: Being the Remains of All the Greek Elegiac and Iambic Poets,* edited and translated by J. M. Edmonds, 1:50–79. Loeb Classical Library. London: Heinemann, 1931.

U.S. Army Center of Military History. "History, Chief of Staff to Supreme Allied Command." http://www.army.mil/cmh-pg/documents/cossac/Cossac.htm (accessed May 8, 2005).

U.S. Army, Forces in the European Theater. *29, Let's Go!* Paris: Desfossés-néogravure, 1945.

U.S. War Department. *The War of the Rebellion: A Compilation of the Official Records of the Union and Confederate Armies.* Series 1, vol. 27, pt. 3. Washington, D.C.: U.S. Government Printing Office, 1889.

Vegetius. *Vegetius: Epitome of Military Science.* Translated by N. P. Milner. Liverpool: Liverpool University Press, 1993.

Viola, Herman J., with Jan Shelton Danis. *It Is a Good Day to Die: Indian Eyewitnesses Tell the Story of the Battle of the Little Bighorn.* 1998. Lincoln: University of Nebraska Press, 2001.

Voegelin, Eric. *Order and History.* Vol. 2, *The World of the Polis.* Baton Rouge: Louisiana State University Press, 1957.

Wallace, Karl R. "The Substance of Rhetoric: Good Reasons." *Quarterly Journal of Speech* 49 (1963): 239–49.

Wallace, William S. Interview with *Military Training Technology.* March 15, 2005. http://www.military-training-technology.com/article.cfm?DocID837 (accessed March 19, 2008).

Wallace-Hadrill, Andrew. *Suetonius: The Scholar and His Caesars.* London: Yale University Press, 1984.

Washington, George. *The Writings of George Washington from the Original Manuscript Sources: 1745–1799.* Vols. 5 and 6. Edited by John C. Fitzpatrick. Washington, D.C.: U.S. Government Printing Office, 1932.

Weaver, Richard M. *The Ethics of Rhetoric.* 1953. Davis, Cal.: Hermagoras, 1985.

Webster, Daniel. "The Bunker Hill Monument." In *The Works of Daniel Webster.* 8th ed. 1:57–78. Boston: Little, Brown, 1854.

Weigley, Russell F. *The American Way of War: A History of United States Military Strategy and Policy.* Bloomington: Indiana University Press, 1977.

Westmoreland, William C. *A Soldier Reports.* Garden City, N.Y.: Doubleday, 1976.

Wiesel, Elie. *Night.* 1958. New York: Bantam, 1982.

Wills, Garry. *Certain Trumpets: The Call of Leaders.* New York: Simon & Schuster, 1994.

———. *John Wayne's America.* New York: Touchstone, 1998.

Xenophon. *The Education of Cyrus [Cyropaedia].* Translated and annotated by Wayne Ambler. Ithaca, N.Y.: Cornell University Press, 2001.

————. *The Persian Expedition.* Translated by Rex Warner. Penguin Classics. 1949. Harmondsworth, U.K.: Penguin, 1961.

————. "The Polity of the Lacedaemonians." In *The Works of Xenophon*, translated by H. G. Dakyns, 2:293–324. London: Macmillan, 1892.

Zaffiri, Samuel. *Westmoreland: A Biography of General William C. Westmoreland.* New York: Morrow, 1994.

INDEX

Made in the USA
Middletown, DE
25 June 2017